T0338541

Redefining
Traffic
How AI Leads the Change

Redefining Traffic

How AI Leads the Change

Guanghui Zhao

Guizhou University of Finance and Economics, China

World Scientific

NEW JERSEY · LONDON · SINGAPORE · BEIJING · SHANGHAI · HONG KONG · TAIPEI · CHENNAI · TOKYO

Published by

World Scientific Publishing Co. Pte. Ltd.

5 Toh Tuck Link, Singapore 596224

USA office: 27 Warren Street, Suite 401-402, Hackensack, NJ 07601

UK office: 57 Shelton Street, Covent Garden, London WC2H 9HE

Library of Congress Cataloging-in-Publication Data

Names: Zhao, Guanghui, 1976– author.

Title: Redefining traffic : how AI leads the change / Guanghui Zhao,
    Guizhou University of Finance and Economics, China.

Description: New Jersey : World Scientific, [2023] | Includes bibliographical references and index.

Identifiers: LCCN 2022062254 | ISBN 9789811249747 (hardcover) |
    ISBN 9789811249754 (ebook) | ISBN 9789811249761 (ebook other)

Subjects: LCSH: Traffic engineering--Data processing. |
    Traffic congestion--Management. | Artificial intelligence.

Classification: LCC HE336.A8 Z436 2023 | DDC 625.7/940285--dc23/eng/20230519

LC record available at https://lccn.loc.gov/2022062254

British Library Cataloguing-in-Publication Data

A catalogue record for this book is available from the British Library.

For any available supplementary material, please visit
https://www.worldscientific.com/worldscibooks/10.1142/12655#t=suppl

Desk Editors: Balasubramanian Shanmugam/Amanda Yun

Typeset by Stallion Press
Email: enquiries@stallionpress.com

Printed in Singapore

Preface

Artificial intelligence has been recognized as an independent discipline by the international academic community and has produced more and more profound impacts on human society and the economy. Machines now realize the in-depth interaction between humans, systems and the environment via AI technology, instead of just passive machines. As a result, how to improve the efficiency and quality of intelligent machines has gradually become the focus of study of industry practitioners. Under the strong impact of subversive technology, all industries need to make corresponding adjustments, and so does the transportation industry. Artificial intelligence technology can provide strong support for building intelligent transportation and smart cities — which are part of an important foundation for building modern cities.

On the basis of reference to relevant research achievements at home and abroad and combined with the author's own experience in the field of transportation for many years, this book explains the key problems of the intelligent transportation industry in detail. This book fully expounds the development status, application direction and future trends of artificial intelligence, unmanned driving intelligence and other new technologies in the field of intelligent transportation; analyzes the problems existing in the fields of artificial intelligence, unmanned driving intelligence and intelligent transportation in China; and puts forward systematized and three-dimensional actual combat paths and coping strategies for the corresponding problems. This book can be used as reference material for scientific research and engineering technicians engaged in the research of related industries, such as intelligent transportation, artificial intelligence, unmanned driving, big data and the Internet of things, as well as for teachers and students of artificial intelligence, vehicle engineering, automation, computer science and other related majors. At the same time, it can also serve as a popular reading book for readers interested in unmanned driving technology.

About the Author

Guanghui Zhao is a researcher, professor, and Ph.D. in management science and engineering, at the Wuhan University of Technology, China; senior visiting fellow at the School of Engineering, University of Michigan, USA; Professor at Guizhou University of Finance and Economics, China; Founding Director of the research center for modern transport development in the College of management cadres of China's Ministry of Transport; Director of the training office of the Chinese Ministry of Transport in support of the western region; chief researcher of Beijing Jiaogan Think-tank Information Technology Research Institute; researcher at the research center for industrial, academic research issues in Wuhan University, China' tutor for the Master of Public Administration (MPA) program at the University of Science and Technology of China. He has been recognised as the "Young science and technology talent in traffic", an excellent manager of science and technology, and expert of the famous teacher's group of the Chinese Ministry of Transport. Prof. Zhao is also a teacher of the training course of the nationwide head of the bureau of transportation; core expert of think tank in Guizhou province; core expert of the Guangxi Zhuang Autonomous Region; Deputy Director of the bureau of transportation in Qinzhou City, Guangxi province; and the distinguished expert of the strong division of traffic, Guangxi transportation department. He has taken charge of numerous projects such as the National Social Science Fund, Research Projects entrusted by the business department of the Ministry of Transport, the Postdoctoral Foundation Project of China, the Special Fund Project of China Postdoctoral Foundation, and over 30 National Educational Science

Planning Projects. He has published more than 100 academic papers in various core academic journals and more than 20 treatises. He received his Master of Administration degree from Central South University of Finance and Economics; Master of Economics from Central Agricultural University; PhD in Management Science and Engineering from Wuhan University of Technology and his post-doctorate fellowship at Wuhan University and Chinese Academy of Social Sciences.

Contents

Introduction

In recent years, the rapid development of artificial intelligence (AI) technology in transportation, education, logistics, retail, manufacturing, medical and other industries has demonstrated an amazing capacity for value creation. The integration of AI technology and new energy, big data, cloud computing, as well as automatic control technology in the field of transportation makes it possible to construct a safe, convenient, efficient and green intelligent transportation system, which will lead to an unprecedented industrial revolution in the transportation industry and provide strong support for the construction unmanned vehicular traffic.

In January 2018, PricewaterhouseCoopers (PwC) reported that machine learning technology is expected to be widely used in transportation by 2040. With the emergence of fully automated transportation systems that do not require human participation in most of the world's major cities, providing vehicles with travel services such as road navigation combined with sophisticated infrastructure is of great value for controlling the total number of cars in major cities, and improving traffic safety and air quality.

A self-driving car with unmanned driving technology as its core will realize self-organizing and co-driving based on the real-time dynamic information of each vehicle. It takes human safety as the first priority. and scientifically and rationally solves the problem of road rights allocation. Through the integration of vehicle, road and intelligent traffic information networks, route planning and coordination are carried out in a unified way, freeing people from monotonous, high-intensity and high-concentration driving operations and realizing automatic driving and intelligent inter-connection. It will create great economic and social benefits.

Manual driving is highly dependent on the driver's independent capacity, and multi-subject driving scenes, such as those which involve pedestrians, private cars, bicycles, electric cars, as well as buses, increase the challenge to the driver's driving skills, contingency ability and psychological quality. Many factors can cause traffic accidents, such as equipment failure, human factors, environmental factors, as well as man-agement factors—though human factors (including intentional and unin-tentional behavior) undoubtedly occupy a higher proportion; for example, blind areas in a driver's visual sphere, driving while fatigued, drunk driv-ing, delayed brain response, forced overtaking and doubling, jumping the queue at an intersection, traffic blocking and parking, to name a few, in manual driving can easily lead to traffic accidents.

Unmanned vehicles can be equipped with cameras, LiDAR, millimeter-wave radar, ultrasonic radar and other sensors to act as their "eyes", help-ing them perceive the full range of information in real time. A vehicle-mounted intelligent system acts as the "brain," and optimizes the information based on the data captured by the unmanned driving vehicle's "eyes", as well as route and travel plans designed by data issued by the third parties such as vehicle networking platforms, transportation inte-grated information service platforms and combined real-time road conditions.

The control and operating system is the "driver" of unmanned driving vehicles. It makes use of features such as vehicle control technology and the automatic steering control system to ensure that the vehicle is always in a safe, stable and efficient operation state. Automotive autonomous driving systems. The autonomous driving decision-making system is responsible for route planning and real-time navigation. Planning and real-time navigation not only require high-precision digital maps, but also V2X communication network technology support, autonomous driving decision-making system to uniformly coordinate the arrangement of autonomous vehicle hardware, various radar, camera, sonar and other sen-sor hardware, organized into an overall system. Dynamic optimization of driving speed and distance makes the vehicles independently complete driving behaviors such as obstacle avoidance, overtaking, lane change, acceleration and deceleration, and parking. Of course, this requires the strong support of a series of subsystems such as the satellite navigation system, emergency braking system, lane deviation detection system, automatic parking system, as well as adaptive cruise control system.

The construction of a "traffic cloud" is an important foundation for the large-scale application of unmanned driving vehicles and the development of unmanned traffic. From a technical point of view, the vehicle-mounted intelligent system using artificial intelligence technology can indeed have thinking and decision-making abilities similar to that of the human brain. However, if the intelligent vehicle system is completely responsible for the decision-making of the vehicle, it will significantly increase its workload, thus posing a high challenge to the vehicle's hardware and software facilities.

Through the "traffic cloud" platform, all vehicles, roads and people in the target area can be integrated into an intelligent transportation network system, and vehicles can be coordinated and dispatched so that they can understand each other's current and next movement intentions, thus predicting potential risks and taking countermeasures, significantly reducing the probability of accidents such as tailgating and bumping, and also helping to control the development and production costs of driverless vehicles.

The transportation industry is an important service industry. Its level of development has a very important impact on the sustained and stable growth of the national economies, people's standards-of-living, and a nation's comprehensive national power and international competitiveness. Digital, intelligent and smart transportation is the mainstream trend in the transportation industry and an inevitable choice to further improve the level of transportation and achieve the strategic goal of a strong transportation country. Achieving this requires the participation of the government, enterprises, research institutions, capitalists and entrepreneurs.

In particular, government departments should determine and provide quality top-level design, guide the application of artificial intelligence in the field of transportation, and provide scientific guidance and assistance to speed up the improvement of relevant laws and regulations to clear policy obstacles for driverless vehicles on the road and traffic data sharing, and mining their value. Enterprises need to be guided to set up industry associations, build a convenient, fast and low-cost communication platform for the public, and form a "government supervision + industry self-regulation + enterprise autonomy + public supervision" unmanned traffic management mechanism.

As a veteran industry observer in the field of transport, the author has made an in-depth summary of his thoughts and analyses over the years. Based on a large number of actual cases, this book provides a detailed analysis of the macro background, current situation, strategic planning and industrial solutions for the development of the unmanned transportation industry. Through the book the author hopes to provide effective guidance and assistance to policymakers, entrepreneurs, enterprises, research institutions and other parties in the exploration and layout of the unmanned transportation field.

This book is divided into eight chapters to address the following aspects necessary to building a robust system for unmanned transportation. The topics covered include unmanned driving, setting off a transportation revolution, arrival of unmanned transportation opportunities, unmanned transportation development paths based on artificial intelligence, urban unmanned rail transportation system construction, unmanned aircraft, unmanned ships, unmanned ports, unmanned terminals, industrial development strategy. While providing theoretical guidance, this book combines the unmanned transportation exploration cases of Japan, the United States, Germany, France and other transportation powerhouses to develop an unmanned transportation development plan that meets China's national conditions.

This book highlights that there are many modes of transportation, such as road, rail, waterway, and air. However, there are some differences in the difficulty and current state of application of AI in different modes of transportation. For example, railway and air transport routes are relatively fixed and have less complex road conditions, which brings a lot of convenience to the implementation of AI application projects, and initial results have been achieved in some subsectors. The diversity of road transport routes and the complexity of road conditions present some obstacles to the application of AI technology. However, we have reasons to believe that with the joint efforts of the government, enterprises, entrepreneurs and other parties, the unmanned transport industry will see a series of new technologies, modes and business models that are expected to drive the unmanned transport industry to become increasingly mature and create new economic growth points.

Chapter 1

Artificial Intelligence: A New Way to Lead Future Traffic

Intelligent transportation system based on artificial intelligence

Concept, connotation and working principle of artificial intelligence

In recent years, traffic optimization has gradually become the focus of urban construction and there is huge potential for the development of intelligent transportation. According to Grand View Research, a leading research institute in San Francisco, the market share of intelligent transportation is predicted to rise to US$38.68 billion by 2020. Today, with rapid urbanization and rapid expansion of the car fleet, many cities are facing serious traffic congestion problems. Moreover, frequent automobile accidents and serious environmental pollution are adding to the burden of urban construction and development, and in this context, more and more regions are beginning to build intelligent transportation systems.

The artificial intelligence industry has grown rapidly over the past two years. With the help of neural networks and deep learning, artificial intelligence has improved its ability to learn and understand. Artificial intelligence will gradually penetrate into 'people's daily lives, improve their work efficiency and have an impact on the way people think as the field continues to develop. The application of artificial intelligence can accelerate the development of social economy, promote overall transformation and upgrading and play an increasingly important role in the field of road traffic management.

Conceptual connotation

The concept of "artificial intelligence" can be traced back to the United States in the mid-20th century. McCarthy,[1] who attended the academic conference at Dartmouth University with computer scientists, informatics scientists, neurophysiologists and information scientists, was among those who developed the concept. Today, artificial intelligence has been in development for more than 60 years and covers a wide range of fields. Generally speaking, AI is based on the exploration of human intelligent activity and the use of intelligent technology to create an artificial system with the aim of giving human intelligence to a computer system to replace traditional manual labor. Tasks that can only be performed by human intelligence in the traditional model can also be efficiently handled by computer hardware and software in the era of AI.

Artificial intelligence technology has been one of the three frontier technologies in the world after the 1970s and is an important part of the three frontier technologies in the world in the 21st century. After 40 years of exploration, the development of artificial intelligence has made a series of outstanding achievements, and its applications have been expanding. Nowadays, AI (as an independent discipline) has been recognized by the international academic community and has gradually formed a sound theoretical and practical system, which endows computers with intelligent behaviors such as human thinking, learning, planning and speculation, giving them some of the functions of the human brain and better reflecting the value of computers in the process of information processing. Essentially, artificial intelligence is a process of reproducing human thinking and transferring human intelligence to computers.

---

[1] John McCarthy, John McCarthy (1927–2011), who won the Turing Award in 1971 for his contributions in the field of artificial intelligence, is known as the "father of artificial intelligence". On the evening of October 24, 2011, John McCarthy passed away at the age of 84. Marvin Minsky (expert in artificial intelligence and cognition), Claude Shannon (founder of information theory), Allen Newell (computer scientist), and Herbert Simon (Nobel laureate in economics) attended the conference.

Intelligent principle

Intelligent perception, precision calculation and intelligent feedback are the core components of artificial intelligence, which in turn show the characteristics of artificial intelligence in the dimensions of perception, thinking and action.

To achieve artificial intelligence, it is necessary to first obtain large and rich structured data that objectively describe specific scenarios, enabling the computer to complete the task of information collection; secondly, it is necessary to calculate accurately, analyze the data resources obtained and refer to the thinking process of the human brain, enabling the computer to learn autonomously, make scientific judgments and make rational decisions. In this process, the human–computer interaction interface can represent the development of artificial intelligence, which can express the results of the previous decision-making step through media information and physical movements and can also communicate information to the user through external devices, thus facilitating the interaction of information between the user and the device and between the devices.

In the process of artificial intelligence, knowledge engineering, expert systems, human brain bionic technology and machine learning algorithms are used to simulate human control behavior through intelligent control technology. So far, Baidu, International Business Machines and Google have made extensive practical applications of computer deep learning technology developed on the basis of artificial neural networks, which can improve computer recognition of images and speech, optimize the performance of computer graphics processors and gradually form perfect large-scale artificial neural network systems. At the same time, the growing Internet business means that deep learning has a large number of data samples, and the application of this technology for data mining and analysis can effectively improve the accuracy of image recognition technology.

Artificial intelligence redefines intelligent traffic pattern

Although artificial intelligence is not a new concept, for quite a long time, the general public's knowledge of it has only been confined to films and dramas, with many believing it to be something unreal. However, in recent years, the application of artificial intelligence in many industries has led to a wide range of topics for discussion around the world, especially the World Go Champion and the AI AlphaGo battle, which once continued to fill the screens of WeChat moments, and people have higher expectations for the application of artificial intelligence in production and in everyday life.

From a technical point of view, artificial intelligence has been very active in the last two years, largely due to the development of deep learning technology. Because of deep learning technology, the intelligence level of machines has improved significantly, and intelligent machines applying deep learning algorithms can accomplish things that humans could not before.

It is now widely accepted by industry that artificial intelligence has a strong capacity to disrupt human economies and societies. Machines are no longer just cold tools. Empowered with artificial intelligence, they can interact with people, systems and environments and have a far-reaching impact on various industries. Improving work efficiency and quality through intelligent machines is the primary research focus of relevant practitioners. Under the strong impact of subversive technology, all industries need to adapt accordingly, and the transport sector is no exception. Artificial intelligence technology can provide strong support for building intelligent transportation and smart cities, which form an important foundation for modern cities.

Automatic driving, intelligent signal control system, best route recommendation and so on are the positive effects of artificial intelligence on intelligent transportation. Of course, in order to give full play to the role of artificial intelligence in the field of intelligent transportation, it should be combined with application scenarios ranging from shallow technology-driven to deep scene-driven. Combined with application scenarios, artificial intelligence will effectively promote industrial model innovation and provide broad cash flow space for entrepreneurs and enterprises.

In fact, artificial intelligence is not just a technology. Just like the Internet, it will bring us a brand-new mode of thinking, which is of great value to the optimization of industrial structure and the innovation of economic management concepts.

Building a powerful transportation country was emphasized upon at the 19th National Congress of the Communist Party of China. From the perspective of transportation infrastructure, transportation service providers and consumer scale, China is a well-deserved contender to the number one spot in the world, but large scale and volume do not mean high level strength. The application of artificial intelligence in the transportation industry provides a new way of thinking for China to complete its transformation from a big transportation country to a powerful transportation country.

At the same time, intelligent transport cannot be achieved without the support of big data. Assisted driving, driverless driving and route planning are all based on the collection and analysis of large-scale traffic data. Through data analysis, knowledge and patterns can be discovered, from which intelligence can then be extracted. The industry's level of development will be substantially enhanced. In both developed and developing countries, the level of development of industries with a high degree of information technology and digitalization is clearly in the lead.

Efficient and low-cost interaction between people, vehicles and roads through real-time data exchange is an important basis for the implementation of intelligent transportation. In the AI industry, many companies use terms related to the "brain," such as 'Wikipedia's brain, 'Baidu's brain and the city's brain. However, these "brains" are still in the shallow skull stage, with the internal "neuron" construction and linking work not yet completed, not to mention the formation of a perfect ecological coordination system.

Consideration index of intelligent transportation based on AI technology

After realizing the great development potential of artificial intelligence, many countries have invested more funds and resources to support the development in this field. Taking the United States as an example, the funds for the development of its artificial intelligence industry mainly come from public investment. In order to maintain its dominant position in the field of advanced manufacturing technology in the world, the United States invested $2 billion in the advanced manufacturing industry in the fiscal year 2017, providing support to the national network of 45 manufacturing innovation research institutes to vigorously promote innovation and growth in manufacturing. In addition, the US International Business Machines Corporation is working on the development of new bionic chips that will provide computer systems with the computing capabilities of the human brain. If the project proceeds well, the new product could be developed successfully in 2019.

The European Union issued the Horizon 2020 R&D and Innovation Plan to provide public investment support for the development of the artificial intelligence industry. On March 15, 2021, the European Commission approved the first strategic plan of the European Union's R&D and Innovation Framework Program "Horizon" with a budget of 95.5 billion euros, proposing strategic directions for research and innovation investment from 2021 to 2024, with the aim of ensuring effective connection between

EU policy priority areas and related programs, especially research and innovation projects funded by "Horizon Europe". By transforming transportation, energy, construction, and production systems, Europe has become the first economy to achieve circular, climate neutral, and sustainable development through digital means. The impact areas are: mitigation and adaptation to climate change, affordable clean energy, intelligent sustainable transportation, circular and clean economy. On December 6, 2022, the European Commission adopted the "Horizon Europe Work Plan 2023-2024", which stated that 13.5 billion euros would be invested to support scientific research and innovation in Europe. The aim is to strengthen the construction of high-tech research centers, provide support for the development and application of artificial intelligence technology in small and medium-sized enterprises, and accelerate the development of artificial intelligence testing and testing.

In order to accelerate the development of the artificial intelligence industry, China issued the Robot Industry Development Plan (2016–2020) in April 2016. Since 2017, the special research and development plan of the Public Safety Risk Prevention and Emergency Technology Equipment has also made development plans in the field of artificial intelligence and begun to pay attention to the research and development and application of related technologies, including road traffic safety active prevention and control technology, active prevention and control police robot key technologies.

In the future, artificial intelligence will become an infrastructure. The transportation industry itself is a field in which the public participates widely, and the two have a high fit. Intelligent transportation, which serves the daily travel of the general public and the efficient circulation of social resources, must prioritize safety, convenience, sustainability and high efficiency.

The application of artificial intelligence in the intelligent transportation industry can be regarded as a process from IT to OT and then to ET. At first, the transportation industry has to invest many resources to realize informatization and digitalization. In order to tap the value of data and output products and services, OT is needed to form a standardized operation process and mode, and finally, ET is carried out, that is, intelligence.

Automatic sensing is the basic work of intelligent transportation. The real-time collection of big traffic data should be achieved without disturbing the traveler. After automatic perception is realized, the value creation space of enterprises will be greatly expanded. Specifically, intelligent traffic considerations mainly include the following points:

(1) **Safety:** With regard to safety, under the coordinated control of the artificial intelligence system, people, cars and roads will interact in

real time and the probability of traffic accidents will be significantly reduced. With the advent of the driverless era, drunk driving, road rage, running red lights, fatigue driving and other problems will be fundamentally solved.

(2) **Convenience:** In terms of convenience, the current transportation system lacks systematicity and coordination, and various modes of transportation fail to serve as linkages. Taking interchange as an example, the setting of subway stations and bus stations is inefficient, resulting in a high time cost for people to interchange. Through the integration and analysis of various traffic data, artificial intelligence technology can predict changes in urban traffic flow and help transport operators to better set up bus and subway stations and reasonably arrange routes, etc., bringing great convenience to people.

(3) **Efficiency:** The intelligent transportation system can implement the whole optimization, coordinate all the resources through the "intelligent traffic brain" and "intelligent transportation brain," help people make more scientific and reasonable travel plans, and improve the carrying capacity of the traffic network and the efficiency of traffic operation.

(4) **People-oriented:** Serving people is the fundamental way to create value for intelligent transportation. Satisfying people's ever-increasing needs for a better life is an inevitable choice when it comes to building socialism with Chinese characteristics, and transportation, as a high-frequency demand, will have a direct impact on people's living standards and quality of life. In the intelligent transportation system, people's needs will be fully respected and the system will allocate resources from the perspective of the city's overall traffic ecology, to achieve a high degree of harmony between people and vehicles with a people-oriented concept.

Application of artificial intelligence in intelligent transportation

The intelligent transportation industry has developed rapidly in recent years, and major issues have arisen frequently. In order to ensure the healthy development of the industry, relevant state departments have carried out a series of research activities and plan to introduce some favorable policies. For example, the Basic Department of the National Development and Reform Commission conducted research in areas such as non-stop toll collection systems, container rail and water transportation information technology and the application of the BeiDou system in the transportation industry, followed by a visit to Hangzhou by Deputy Director Zheng Jian to conduct special research on the construction of comprehensive transportation hubs and the development of intelligent transportation. These studies show that intelligent transportation is highly valued by government departments.

In recent years, an increasing number of traffic checkpoints have been networked and more and more information on vehicle traffic records has been collected. With artificial intelligence technology, it is possible to analyze urban traffic flow in real time, effectively adjust the interval between traffic lights and shorten vehicle waiting time, thus effectively improving the efficiency of urban road traffic.

The application of artificial intelligence in transportation is equivalent to installing an artificial intelligence brain in the transportation system of the entire city, with real-time control functions for vehicle traffic information on city roads, parking information in residential areas and vehicle information in car parks. It can effectively predict changes in traffic flow and the number of parking spaces in advance, allocate resources rationally, divert traffic effectively, realize large-scale traffic linkage scheduling, improve the traffic operation efficiency of the whole city, alleviate traffic congestion and ensure smooth travel for residents.

License plate recognition is the most ideal application field of artificial intelligence

At present, the license plate recognition algorithm is the ideal application of artificial intelligence in the field of intelligent transportation. According to many manufacturers, car recognition rates of 99% can be achieved under the video conditions of a standard bayonet and some additional preset conditions. Under the conditions of a simple bayonet and bayonet picture, the car recognition rate is less than 90%. However, in the future, with the continuous development of artificial intelligence and deep learning algorithms, this situation can be significantly changed.

Many features of traditional image processing and machine learning algorithms are artificially formulated, including the Histogram of Oriented Gradients (HOG), and Scale-Invariant Feature Transform (SIFT), for example. These features occupy a very important position in target detection and feature matching, and the features used by many algorithms in the security field originate from these two features. According to past experience, because theoretical analysis is difficult and training methods require many skills, it takes five to ten years for human design features and machine learning algorithms to achieve a major breakthrough, and the requirements for algorithm engineers are increasing steadily.

Deep learning is different. Using deep learning for image detection and recognition does not require artificially set features, but rather requires preparing enough images for training and continuously iterating to achieve better results. From the current situation, as long as new data are constantly added and enough time and resources are available, the recognition rate can keep improving as long as the network level of deep learning keeps improving. Compared with traditional methods, this method is much better.

In addition, technologies in the fields of vehicle color recognition, unlicensed vehicle detection, vehicle retrieval, face recognition, non-motor vehicle detection and classification are also maturing.

(1) **License plate color recognition:** In the past, different lighting conditions and camera hardware errors led to perceived differences or changes in vehicles; colors. Nowadays, the problem of recognition error caused by image color change can be solved effectively with the help of artificial intelligence technology. The recognition rate of the vehicle color in the card port has increased from 5% to 85%, and the recognition rate of the main color of the alarm vehicle has exceeded 80%. The illegal vehicles will be automatically displayed in the artificial intelligence technology system, similar to "alarms" in the system.

(2) **Vehicle manufacturer identification:** In the past, vehicle manufacturers used traditional features like HOG, Local Binary Patterns (LBP), SIFT, and Speeded-Up Robust Features (SURF) to identify the logos of car manufacturers, and with the help of Support Vector Machine (SVM) machine learning technology, a multi-cascaded classifier was developed. Now, with the introduction of big data and deep learning technology, the recognition rate of vehicle manufacturers' logos has risen from 89% to 93%, or even higher.

Vehicle retrieval

In terms of vehicle retrieval, vehicle images can be overexposed or underexposed in different scenarios and the size of the vehicle can change. In such cases, if the traditional method of extracting vehicle features continues to be used, errors will occur, adversely affecting the vehicle retrieval rate. With the introduction of deep learning, the system can obtain relatively stable vehicle features and search for similar targets more accurately, with a search rate of over 95% for TOP-5.

Top-5 accuracy: For example, there are 1000 categories on ImageNet, then your network outputs 10 results, the probability is sorted from largest to smallest, and one of the TOP-5 results is the prediction result is the same as the actual one, that is, the accuracy of TOP-5. (This accuracy should be the probability that the prediction is right). TOP-5 error rate: that is, none of the first five predictions were correct. (The sum of these five probabilities should be the top-5 error rate). TOP-1 accuracy: For example, there are 1000 categories on ImageNet, then your network outputs 10 results, sorted by probability from largest to smallest, the prediction result with the highest probability is the same as the actual one, that is, the accuracy of TOP-1. (This accuracy should be the probability that the prediction is right). TOP-1 error rate: that is, after the probability is sorted from largest to smallest, the one with the highest probability is not predicted accurately, which is the TOP-1 error rate (this probability should be the TOP-1 error rate).

In face recognition, faces can change somewhat due to lighting, expression, pose and other factors. At present, many applications require fixed scenes and postures. After the introduction of deep learning algorithms, the face recognition rate of fixed scenes can be increased to 99%, and the requirements for light, postures and other conditions have been reduced.

Traffic signal system

Traditional traffic light switching systems use a default time sequence. Although this timing is updated every few years, as traffic patterns continue to evolve, traditional systems are being applied for shorter and shorter periods of time. The intelligent traffic signal system with artificial intelligence uses radar sensors and cameras to monitor traffic, and it uses artificial intelligence algorithms to determine the conversion time and optimizes the traffic flow in the urban road network by combining artificial intelligence with traffic control theory.

Police robots

In the future, robot police will replace human traffic police to ensure all-weather and all-round road traffic safety.

Big data analysis

Artificial intelligence algorithms can effectively analyze the data of urban people flow, traffic flow migration, urban construction, public resources and other factors based on urban people's travel preferences, lifestyles, consumption habits and other factors. The analysis results are used to assist urban planning decision-making and guide the infrastructure construction of public transport facilities.

Driverless and vehicle-assisted driving

In the field of artificial intelligence, image recognition is a very important technology. This technology can accurately identify vehicles, pedestrians, obstacles, roads, traffic signs, signal lights and other objects ahead, enhancing people's new experiences, reshaping the transportation system and ushering in the era of intelligent transportation.

Highway traffic safety prevention and control system involves many core technologies such as traffic behavior monitoring, traffic safety judgment, early warning of traffic risks, as well as traffic violation law enforcement. At present, these technologies have been organically integrated with artificial intelligence. We can clearly see the running state of highway traffic, find the track of vehicles, seize key illegal acts, eliminate potential safety hazards, quickly respond to road cooperation and linkage, and improve the service level of traffic information application. The realization of these goals necessitates the use of artificial intelligence technology.

Application of artificial intelligence in intelligent traffic control

Research on artificial intelligence in the field of traffic control

What is "traffic signal control"? It means that the traffic signals are initially set and managed according to the traffic flow information of the road network, and the timing scheme is constantly adjusted with reference to the current traffic flow situation to improve overall traffic control efficiency. From a systematic point of view, traffic control can provide scientific and effective timing schemes for traffic management departments.

Generally speaking, in order to improve the traffic efficiency of the whole intersection, the following measures should be taken:

(1) Employ the mathematical model to accurately predict vehicular density and speed in different directions at the intersection, and adjust traffic light conversion times according to the optimization theory and operational research knowledge.
(2) Apply intelligent control technology to manage traffic operation at intersections.

In consideration of the strong variability of urban transportation systems, it is hard to establish a mathematical model. With the widespread application of network technology and computer technology, artificial intelligence has developed rapidly. After realizing the value of AI applications in the field of transportation, professionals began to study the development of the combination of AI and traffic management and achieved initial results.

Basic research methods

There are many basic research methods of artificial intelligence in the field of traffic control, including, but not limited to, fuzzy control, genetic algorithm, neural network algorithm, and particle swarm optimization algorithm.

The fuzzy control method should be used to solve nonlinear problems and problems with a high degree of variability. Compared with other logic methods, the fuzzy system can show fuzzy knowledge more clearly, has commonality with human thinking and can be used in conjunction with reasoning techniques. In dealing with fuzzy information, fuzzy control has natural advantages, but its disadvantage lies in its lack of self-learning ability to produce refined rules.

With the help of the bionic principle, genetic algorithms can quickly search information in a short time and can achieve the purpose of batch combinatorial optimization. The algorithm is suitable for solving calculation problems related to traffic control. It can realize an all-round information search, select appropriate public periods, coordinate the signal control and management of different intersections, optimize the whole surface control system and avoid adverse consequences caused by conflicts of different traffic schemes.

Nonlinear mathematical models can be handled by neural network algorithms, which are more adaptable and capable of learning, play an important role in data mining and analysis, as well as pattern recognition, and are good at self-learning.

Regional coordination of urban transportation network

What is "regional coordination"? It means that the traffic center undertakes the task of macro-regulation, taking into account the traffic flow in each region, to achieve coordination and complementarity between different junctions, to share the pressure for junctions with high traffic flow and to speed up the entire road. Cooperation between different urban roads and between urban roads and expressways must be realized in this link,, but it is inevitable that different intersections will affect each other and conflicts between intersections will inevitably arise. This is a key issue to be solved in the future development of traffic control. Using artificial intelligence technology, road network coordination control can play an important role in this respect, and the application of agent technology based on distributed artificial intelligence in the field of traffic control is a typical representative in this respect. A multi-agent is a collection of many agents. These agents coordinate and serve each other to complete a task together. The intelligent decision-making system of urban transportation networks relies on the multi-agent, which integrates the theory of transportation network system, computer application and the knowledge and experience of authoritative experts. There are different knowledge systems in different agents, which makes it easier for users to search and apply information as well as for subsequent expansion and extension.

In the process of establishing the mathematical model of an agent-based intelligent traffic control system, agents firstly replace the functional modules of the traffic control system, and the corresponding functional structures are established according to the functions undertaken by different agents, so as to promote the collaborative operation between each agent and work together to accomplish the overall task.

The intelligent traffic control system consists of three levels of control structure, and different levels have different functions:

The decision agent of an intelligent traffic control system is located at the highest level of the organization-level control system. Holding the macro decision-making power, it can scientifically judge the overall traffic operation situation, analyze the data resources of all parties in a three-dimensional way, make plans and decisions on this basis and promote cooperation between different regional control systems, with the aim of achieving the best control effect and optimizing traffic control.

Regional coordination agents (RCAs) are located in the middle of the coordination layer of the control system and are primarily responsible for traffic supervision and maintenance of intersections in the region. When necessary, the regional coordination agent will enforce strong management of the intersections in its area and respond to emergencies in a timely manner. It can also cooperate with other agents for information sharing. Intersection agents, roadway agents, vehicle agents and traffic light agents are located at the bottom of the control level control system and are responsible for traffic control and management.

Among them, the intersection agent can obtain the data of the current intersection and nearby road sections. The fact that traffic flows in different directions gather at intersections, coupled with traffic diversions and long periods of traffic congestion, makes the intersection agent particularly valuable. Using this control system, traffic information of the intersection can be provided to nearby intersections, while relevant tasks can be completed in accordance with instructions of the regional control center and a cooperative relationship can be formed with other regional control centers. The road agent can quickly obtain traffic data from different road sections and use sensing technology to control the number and operation of vehicles and control the overall traffic order on that road. In a specific operation, the transport system and the various agents interact and influence each other. The requirements of the transport system vary, the function and composition of the agents differ and the way in which the whole system and each agent interact with each other differs. It should be set according to the actual situation.

Application of simulation tools in a traffic control field

Using simulation software, the benefits of artificial intelligence can be scientifically evaluated. At this stage, users can use the following methods: C language and Matlab to design simulation programs, and professional traffic simulation software to evaluate. Traffic simulation tools can vividly restore the traffic scene, making them efficient and convenient. This book focuses on the analysis of the microscopic traffic simulation software Paronics, which is used by the Intelligent Transportation Center of Beijing University of Technology and has a variety of useful functions.

Paramics is a kind of parallel microscopic simulation software, developed by the European Community, Edinburgh Parallel Computing Center and the British Department of Transport, and it is used in special research and development projects. Based on the exploration of the first three developers, Quadstone, in conjunction with the UK Ministry of Commerce and Industry, further developed and eventually commercialized Paramics. With the help of Paramics, researchers in the field of transportation can better understand and master the current road traffic situation and conduct in-depth data mining and analysis. The software can present traffic road conditions in a three-dimensional form, open its functions to multiple users and connect to application programs. In addition, Paramics is highly adaptable to different road networks, covering 32,000 areas, controlling 4 million road sections and managing 1 million nodes.

Paramics is supported by five tools: Modeller, Processor, Analyzer, Programmer, and Monitor. Modeller occupies a key position. Here, the five components are analyzed one by one.

(1) The main functions of Modeller include statistical data output, traffic network creation and 3D traffic simulation. All three functions can be displayed to users graphically. Each node of the actual traffic network is accommodated in Modeller's functions, such as intelligent traffic signal control, public transportation, roundabout, urban road network construction and improvement, as well as various types of lane management. With Modeller, the management department can not only understand the operation of individual vehicles in the actual traffic environment but also systematically grasp the current traffic situation.

(2) Processor can realize batch processing of data information and give statistical results quickly. The software also shows the analysis process to users graphically, and the output data, simulation parameters, etc., can be selected during the specific setup. In the batch processing mode, the position data of road networks and simulated vehicles are ignored, which effectively improves the efficiency of simulation calculation.

(3) After the analysis results are obtained by simulation calculation with Modeller or Processor, the results need to be output through Analyzer. This tool displays a variety of data results in the form of a graphical user interface, including road traffic flow, traffic density, vehicle route, vehicle queue length, management service and so on. While

outputting the results graphically, the tool can also output the statistical results in digital form, which is convenient for subsequent queries and applications.

(4) The Programmer tool opens the application program interface of C++, which can further expand the functions of Paramics. For example, Paramics was originally developed based on UK road traffic management methods and vehicle characteristics. If it is to be applied outside the UK, the corresponding application interface must be designed to comply with local driving rules. Through the use of an API interface, Paramics will have more functions and will be formulate traffic control and management measures according to the specific conditions of different regions.

(5) Some professionals have developed the API module Monitor based on Programmer. This module can accurately count and calculate the emission of vehicle exhaust in the traffic network and embody it in an intuitive way.

The application of Paramics in intelligent transportation systems can give full play to the role of microscopic traffic simulation technology, flexibly select variable information boards, traffic signals, variable speed control signs, and more, and implement intelligent scheduling of simulated vehicles on this basis. In addition, API functions can be used to develop more control modes for specific areas and road sections, thus introducing more targeted traffic control and management strategies.

Application of artificial intelligence in road management

What is an intelligent transportation system (ITS)? It means that, during the implementation of ground traffic management, advanced technical means such as electronic sensing technology, data communication technology, computer processing technology and other advanced technical means should be brought into play to gradually form a perfect traffic management system, maintain smooth traffic in all links and improve the work efficiency and management level of traffic control management departments.

How does ITS work? The road traffic and related information obtained is handed over to the traffic management department for deep mining and analysis, and then the analysis results are provided to residents, car owners, car parks, logistics companies and other users to provide them with effective reference data for making travel plans. In the meantime, traffic management departments can use the traffic system to deal with emergencies and traffic accidents in a timely manner; the transportation department can quickly understand the running status of vehicles and optimize its own management and service system accordingly.

Automobile automatic driving system, highway electronic information system, satellite communication system and satellite ground station are the components of the ITS system. In recent years, more and more scholars and enterprises have focused on the research of vehicle positioning and traffic navigation system, automated highway system and information system. With the help of advanced technical means, the intelligent transportation system has promoted the rapid development of domestic transportation. Many ITS products are now being developed in China, and some of them are being applied in practice. In the future, more ITS products will be used in the field of transportation to promote the development of domestic society and the economy.

In the application of artificial intelligence, robots and Internet-connected vehicles are very representative. After decades of exploration, the application of artificial intelligence in the field of traffic management has made initial achievements.

The application of artificial intelligence can effectively alleviate the traffic congestion problem faced by cities. According to authoritative statistics, on the economic side, the economic loss caused by traffic congestion in the United States is as high as US$121 billion per year. On the environmental side, the carbon dioxide emissions caused by traffic congestion are as high as 25 billion kilograms per year. When vehicles are running in urban areas, about 40% of the engines are idling because the city is not equipped with an intelligent traffic signal system.

To solve this problem, Stephen Smith, a robot professor at Carnegie Mellon University, is committed to introducing an intelligent traffic signal system in order to optimize urban road traffic management. The test results show that the application of the system can improve the efficiency of urban traffic management and greatly reduce the idling time of the engine.

The application of intelligent traffic signal systems can also reduce emissions, improve the carrying capacity of urban traffic roads and avoid the constant widening and renovation of roads by the relevant departments, thus lowering cost consumption. Under the traditional mode, the traffic lights installed on urban roads will change color according to a fixed time. Although the authorities adjust this timing every few years, it still does not meet the needs of the rapidly developing urban traffic system.

By contrast, the intelligent traffic signal system can accurately monitor and sense the current road conditions, automatically adjust the light color conversion time according to advanced artificial intelligence algorithms and improve the efficiency of urban road traffic management through advanced technical means.

The intelligent traffic signal system uses the decentralized mode to accurately control the operation of traffic network, which is obviously different from a commercial adaptive traffic control system. Specifically, each intersection determines the timing of the light color changeover based on current vehicle flow and provides the data to neighboring junctions so that they can easily predict the future number of incoming vehicles.

The traffic signal system adopting this mode can better adapt to the actual traffic conditions, and cooperate with neighboring intersections to optimize the overall road traffic management. Shortly after its introduction, the system was initially applied in a high-traffic East Liberty block in Pittsburgh and has since been expanded to provide comprehensive coverage and efficient management and dispatch of passing traffic by regulating the traffic signal system.

With the widespread use of artificial intelligence in the field of road traffic management, police robots will take up the work of the traffic police. This machine system can patrol roads 24 hours a day and implement an all-round supervision, thus improving the work efficiency of public security traffic management departments.

By using the highway traffic safety prevention and control system, the relevant departments can keep track of the traffic conditions of each road section, supervise traffic violations, deal with them quickly, restore normal traffic order, improve their overall control ability, improve the efficiency of service management, and correct traffic violations, thereby keeping the entire urban road system unblocked, reducing the probability of major traffic accidents and improving the safety of urban traffic.

Traffic behavior monitoring technology, traffic safety judgment technology, traffic risk early warning technology and traffic violation law enforcement technology are the main components of highway traffic safety prevention and control systems. Artificial intelligence has now realized the combined development with these four core technologies. By applying artificial intelligence technology in the field of highway traffic, the management departments can better grasp the traffic operation conditions and vehicle trajectory, handle violations in a timely manner while avoiding hidden dangers, promote cooperation among relevant departments, and optimize traffic management services.

At a time when the national public security traffic management departments are focusing on the smooth flow of cities and highway safety, the application of artificial intelligence technology in road traffic management can improve the work efficiency of traffic management departments and promote the development of public security traffic management.

Application of artificial intelligence in vehicle infrastructure cooperation

Overview of intelligent vehicle infrastructure cooperation

A vehicle infrastructure cooperative system (VICS) is a kind of advanced technology based on wireless communication and mobile Internet, a road traffic system that realizes seamless connection between vehicles and roads, uses real-time traffic data collection and analysis to realize active safety control of vehicles and cooperative management of roads, gives full play to the cooperative linkage of people, vehicles and roads, and improves traffic efficiency and safety. In the construction of intelligent transportation, a vehicle infrastructure cooperative system is an important part.

Generation and development of an intelligent vehicle infrastructure cooperative system

Traffic safety, traffic efficiency and energy-saving and environmental protection are the three major industry pain points in the transportation field. With the accelerating urbanization process in China, its negative impact is becoming more and more serious. In this context, a cooperative system to realize energy-saving and environment-friendly smart vehicle infrastructure has emerged while meeting the overall strategic needs of transportation, ensuring traffic safety and improving traffic efficiency. As the intelligent vehicle infrastructure cooperative system continues to mature, the unfavorable situation of vehicle and road management being separated will be broken. Vehicles and roads will interact in real time, making full use of existing traffic resources, improving the supply capacity of the traffic network and effectively reducing traffic accidents.

The development of the intelligent vehicle infrastructure cooperative system in China can be traced back to October 2010, when the Ministry of Science and Technology in China launched the Research Development Program (known as the 863 Program): Research on Key Technologies of Intelligent Vehicle Infrastructure Cooperative. Soon after, China's Ministry of Industry and Information Technology initiated the project and carried out in-depth research. In September 2011, Tsinghua University, Ministry of Transport of China and Ministry of Science and Technology of China were entrusted with the mission of implementing the "Research on Key Technologies of Vehicle Infrastructure Cooperative" project. In February 2014, the project was successfully delivered after acceptance by the Ministry of Science and Technology.

During the early stages of the development of the intelligent vehicle infrastructure cooperative system, the related research in China mainly focused on the verification of typical scenes of vehicle infrastructure cooperative, safe passage at intersections, traffic environment detection, dangerous situation identification and other fields. In December 2015, China's vehicle infrastructure cooperative technology began to converge with international standards, and the vehicle infrastructure system technology and system application were expanded to a certain extent, such as intersection speed guidance, on-road dynamic guidance with the goal of energy saving and environmental protection, and signal coordination control with fleet guidance.

In 2016, initial progress was made in the construction of China's intelligent vehicle integrated system experimental zone, and several national intelligent vehicles integrated system experimental zones opened. For example, on November 15, I-VISTA (Intelligent Vehicle Integrated Systems Test Area), an intelligent vehicle integrated system experimental zone located in Liangjiang, New District of Chongqing, officially opened. With the support of the experimental area, the research on vehicle infrastructure cooperative system in China can be changed from theoretical research to field testing and experimentation, such as assisted driving, an automatic driving of vehicle infrastructure cooperative, signal coordination-based public transport, decision making and control of multi-traffic subject group based on intelligent driving, to name a few—all which provide strong support to promote the transformation of scientific and technological achievements in autonomous transportation. The vehicle infrastructure cooperative system is one of the hot research directions in the ITS field, and it is highly dependent on information security technology, state awareness technology, multi-mode communication technology, data fusion and cooperative processing technology and many other technologies. The convergence of these technologies has emerged as a critical technology in intelligent vehicle infrastructure cooperative systems, including intelligent communication, intelligent vehicle key technology, intelligent system cooperative control, intelligent road test system key technology, and more:

(1) **Intelligent communication:** In the field of intelligent transportation and vehicles, mobile communication technology is the basic technology, which is the core of real-time interaction among people, vehicles and roads. Intelligent communication technology is based on vehicle-to-vehicle communication technology and vehicle-to-road communication technology, which enables real-time and efficient information interaction between vehicles and between vehicle and road during high-speed driving.

(2) **Key technologies of intelligent vehicles:** The key technology of intelligent vehicles is the installation of sensing equipment, such as GPS, gyroscope, electronic compass and LiDAR vehicle-mounted unit, to collect all kinds of information such as vehicle position, running status and driving environment in real time. By installing an electro-hydraulic braking system, an industrial control computer and other control equipment on the vehicle, the on-board devices can be intelligently controlled to avoid traffic accidents such as rear-end collisions.

(3) **Cooperative control of intelligent systems:** Cooperative control of intelligent systems can be divided into two categories: efficiency and safety. Among them, the cooperative control of the intelligent system for the purpose of efficiency includes precise parking control technology, dynamic cooperative special lane technology, intersection intelligent control technology, cluster guidance technology, traffic control and traffic guidance cooperative optimization technology.

(4) **Key technologies of intelligent road test systems:** Intelligent road test systems use hardware and software to perform a variety of

functions such as multi-channel road state information collection, multi-mode wireless data transmission, multi-channel traffic information collection, information fusion and rapid identification and location of sudden abnormal events.

Application of artificial intelligence in unmanned logistics

Scene application and prospect of artificial intelligence logistics

In recent years, artificial intelligence has risen rapidly in the market driven by the development of science and technology. Many logistics companies have actively launched explorations in an attempt to accelerate the operation of urban distribution through artificial intelligence technology and achieve the optimal allocation of vehicle resources by means of advanced technology, thus improving the overall consumption experience of users.

So, what impact will artificial intelligence have on the logistics industry? What changes will take place in the field of logistics as a result of the application of artificial intelligence technology? The impact is summarized in three aspects here:

(1) In the storage link, applying artificial intelligence can help logistics enterprises select an ideal warehouse address, reduce the negative impact of human factors on address selection, improve the accuracy of site selection, help enterprises reduce cost consumption and increase the income of enterprises.

(2) In warehouse management, the application of artificial intelligence has the functions of accelerating the operation of each link, improving the efficiency of logistics operation and shortening the time for consumers to receive goods.

(3) In path planning, the application of artificial intelligence has the functions of reducing the interference of external factors, selecting the best path to complete the distribution task, and improving the efficiency of urban distribution.

Application scenarios for artificial intelligence technology

Artificial intelligence mainly has the following five logistics application scenarios:

(1) **Intelligent operation rule management:** A machine learning algorithm is applied to endow the operation rule engine with self-learning ability so that it can make decisions based on business identification. For example, with the help of artificial intelligence technology, merchants can intelligently process orders based on commodity categories during the Double Eleven period, decide the mode of production of orders, determine freight, and respond to emergencies in time.

(2) **Warehouse site selection:** Using artificial intelligence technology, enterprises can comprehensively consider various factors, including supplier location, tax system, labor availability, transportation cost, construction cost, consumer factors, etc., and formulate the best site selection scheme.

(3) **Decision-making assistance:** Through machine learning technology, logistics equipment, vehicles and personnel within a certain range are intelligently identified and learn from rich manual management and operation experience, collaborating with management personnel to make auxiliary decisions and improve decision-making autonomy.

(4) **Image recognition:** During the operation of the handwritten waybill machine, convolution neural networks and intelligent image recognition technology are brought into play to improve recognition accuracy and effectively reduce manual errors.

(5) **Intelligent dispatching:** According to data information such as commodity volume and commodity quantity, intelligent dispatching is realized in packaging, vehicle arrangement and other links to speed up the operation of these links. For example, the volume and packaging standards of various commodities are measured, and with the help of intelligent technical means, the packaging of commodities is reasonably arranged, the corresponding box types are matched and the placement of commodities is optimized.

At present, the development of the Internet of Things and big data has entered a relatively mature period, and its application in the field of e-commerce has also been fruitful. In contrast, artificial intelligence is still in an early stage of development and has broad market prospects, which will attract the attention of many enterprises. In the specific application process, the Internet of Things and big data technology collaborate. The Internet of Things provides massive data information for big data analysis, while big data analysis technology can efficiently process data resources. Moreover, the application of artificial intelligence can further realize the deep mining and application of data value. Enterprises should fully exploit the driving role of these three technologies in the process of developing intelligent logistics.

The future of artificial intelligence and logistics

How far can the combination of artificial intelligence and logistics take us? We explore three scenarios as follows:

(1) **Intelligent hardware innovates logistics production factors:** Intelligent hardware equipment is applied to logistics production to automate and replace traditional manual work in order to complete the sorting of goods. Intelligent hardware equipment such as robotic arms, unmanned aerial vehicles (UAVs), intelligent sensing technology and robots are used in logistics operations, and their application scope is gradually expanding.

(2) **Intelligent calculation optimizes the logistics operation process:** The intelligent logistics cloud platform built by enterprises plays a particularly prominent role in this respect. Using this platform, enterprises can improve the intelligence and modernization level of logistics management. During the process of logistics operation and management, it employs logistics technology and artificial intelligence technology to accelerate information transmission in the supply chain system, promoting cooperation among various links and reasonably arranging goods storage and distribution, so as to fully explore the value of the industrial chain.

(3) **Establishing a perfect logistics ecosystem:** The logistics industry will gradually transition to multimodal transport, relying on artificial intelligence to achieve efficient transportation. Comprehensive use of technologies such as big data, the Internet of Things, cloud computing and artificial intelligence will combine road, rail and air transport to form multimodal transportation. It is necessary to establish and expand a reliable highway network, railway network, water transport network, aviation network and logistics park. With the help of big data, the Internet of Things, cloud computing, as well as artificial intelligence technology, a sound logistics ecosystem should be established as soon as possible to meet the needs of enterprises in logistics transportation, goods storage, commodity distribution and other aspects, and launch systematic solutions to contribute to social and economic development.

Application of artificial intelligence in the logistics distribution field

The application of advanced technologies such as big data, artificial intelligence and intelligent positioning in the logistics industry has promoted the development of instant distribution. It is necessary to develop the instant distribution market in depth, accurately perceive the changes in the market and take effective countermeasures according to the needs of consumers, so as to achieve success in the whole field. At this stage, the development of the instant distribution market shows the following trend: the scale of users in the industry is gradually increasing, the growth rate of users is decreasing, the growth rate of orders is decreasing, the efficiency of platform distribution cannot meet the needs of consumers, and users tend to choose unmanned distribution services. Therefore, logistics enterprises need to understand their own development, actively respond to challenges and seize development opportunities in the market environment.

The competition in the instant distribution market has gradually intensified in the past two years. The introduction and implementation of relevant industry standards have improved the standardization of market development. However, the instant distribution market does not have StringNet requirements for entrants. This field has attracted many entrepreneurs to join in and carry out market development and value mining through the use of software with functional and cost advantages. Today, with the rapid development of distribution system technology, distribution platforms represented by Meituan and Ele.me have launched intelligent dispatching systems and realized the landing of relevant technologies. Many entrepreneurs have explored the field of instant distribution, gradually expanding their business scale and enriching their business forms. With efficient execution and a perfect management system, they have developed rapidly and grown into local life service enterprises, occupying market advantages with professional services.

Demand factors are driving more and more companies to the instant delivery sector, which makes companies face fierce market competition. In this case, consumers put forward new requirements for instant distribution, which promoted the development and upgrading of the industry. So, what are the subsequent trends of instant delivery?

(1) **Advanced technology promotes the development of the industry:** In the traditional model, the speed of instant delivery was the focus of

customers' attention. Using big data, artificial intelligence, mobile internet and other technical means, instant delivery platforms have been expanding their services to cover areas such as express delivery, home delivery and fresh food. While shortening delivery times, they are also placing more emphasis on improving their own service systems.

(2) **New retail increases the demand for instant distribution:** People's demand for instant distribution will continue to increase with the development of new retail. Based on the widespread application of mobile Internet and Internet of Things, short-distance logistics distribution will be extended to people's daily life, promoting the development of instant distribution and broadening its business scope. Meanwhile, consumers will place a higher value on the humanity of distribution services.

(3) **The instant distribution platform relies on stable order volume to make profits:** In the past, the instant distribution industry was built on large-scale investment, but this business philosophy has since changed. At this point, the distribution costs obtained by many platforms still cannot offset their cost consumption. Platforms must strengthen cost control and improve operating efficiency to achieve sustainable development. The profit model of the instant distribution platform is relatively single. To cope with the fierce market competition, it is necessary to obtain income through stable order volume and maintain long-term development.

(4) **In the medium-term development stage, human–computer interaction is the leading direction:** At present, enterprises such as Meituan and Ele.me intend to focus on unmanned distribution and artificial intelligence applications. Some enterprises have already explored the fields of robot distribution and unmanned aerial vehicle distribution, and it may be possible to replace manual distribution with unmanned distribution in the future. However, the actual scene should be considered in the specific implementation process, and human–computer interaction is still the leading direction in the medium-term development stage.

With the development of society, the market development space of instant distribution is gradually shrinking. Only by analyzing the future development trend of instant distribution can we grasp the market opportunity and have a stronger voice in the midst of fierce competition. Moreover, effective measures should be taken by enterprises to achieve cost control and expand their profit margins during the development process.

Unmanned technology leads the new smart logistics era

In recent years, the application of unmanned distribution, unmanned storage, intelligent sorting, trunk transportation and other technologies has gradually penetrated into people's daily life, facilitating logistics enterprises to strengthen cost control and improve overall operating efficiency. Logistics enterprises are required to take effective measures as the daily express delivery volume increases. In this regard, Alibaba launched the China Intelligent Logistics Backbone Network Project, Suning Logistics released the "Baichuan Plan," emphasizing the construction of a backbone warehouse network and community warehouse network, and Jingdong Logistics built an intelligent logistics center. By using advanced technical means, logistics enterprises are expected to reduce the cost of socialized logistics by 10%.

Opening the era of unmanned logistics 2.0

Many logistics unmanned technologies entered the stage of practice and application in 2018. Intelligent logistics has been effectively promoted to develop by practical application of unmanned aerial vehicles, unmanned warehouses, unmanned vehicles and other technologies. Suning Logistics, which took the lead in the field of intelligent logistics, has also actively explored unmanned technology and terminal logistics services, which lays a solid foundation for the subsequent development of the logistics industry.

Suning has realized the application of unmanned technology in storage, transportation, sorting, distribution and other links, and Suning can not only accelerate the overall operation of logistics but also effectively cope with the increasing express delivery volume by reducing labor cost consumption in this way. So far, Suning Logistics has explored automated guided vehicle (AGV) robots, unmanned aerial vehicles (UAVs), and unmanned vehicles, to name a few.

Suning Logistics has built and put into operation AGV robot unmanned warehouses in Shanghai and Jinan, using pallet handling and robot technology to complete large-scale goods handling in an intelligent way. Not only that, Suning Logistics, which has also carried out robot warehouse construction in Shenzhen, Chongqing, Hefei and other cities, is committed to building a perfect robot warehouse network.

Jingdong Logistics, with the aim of building Jingdong's intelligent logistics network system, actively launches its layout in the unmanned retail field by using intelligent technologies such as unmanned aerial vehicles, unmanned warehouses and unmanned vehicles, effectively promoting the intelligent development of the entire logistics industry. Jingdong unmanned distribution robots were officially put into operation during the promotion period of June 18, 2018. Moreover, Jingdong established its unmanned vehicle headquarters in Changsha and devoted itself to building an intelligent manufacturing industrial base responsible for producing intelligent robots, intelligent equipment and intelligent vehicles, thus forming a complete industrial system.

The terminal distribution link is divided into urban terminal and rural terminal, and unmanned vehicles and unmanned aerial vehicles undertake logistics distribution tasks, respectively. Among them, unmanned vehicles can be applied to various climatic environments to realize all-weather logistics distribution; unmanned vehicles are suitable for package delivery in remote areas and can meet the needs of rural consumers.

Unmanned technology has gradually penetrated into all aspects of logistics operation, such as trunk transportation and terminal distribution. Thus, we can see that the application of advanced technology accelerates the development of unmanned logistics.

Form a network with points to areas

When the average express delivery volume reaches hundreds of millions of pieces daily, the logistics industry will find it difficult to cope with the ever-increasing logistics demand if it continues to use the traditional manual operation mode. In response to this situation, Alibaba is committed to building a platform connecting different logistics enterprises and realizing the purpose of cost saving by building a perfect intelligent logistics network system.

On May 31, 2018, Cainiao Network hosted the 2018 Global Smart Logistics Summit (GSLS) in Hangzhou. In his speech at the conference, Jack Ma put forward for the first time a plan for an intelligent logistics backbone network, saying that Alibaba would provide 100 million yuan of investment support for the project, with a view to reducing logistics

costs by 10% and speeding up logistics operations nationwide and globally. At the beginning of June, Cainiao announced that it would implement
the eHub (Digital Trade Hub) project in Hong Kong. The project with an
investment of 12 billion Hong Kong dollars accommodates B2B and B2C
business models, including import logistics, export logistics and international trade transit logistics services.

After long-term construction and improvement, Jingdong Logistics
Network has achieved comprehensive coverage of cross-border logistics,
cold chain logistics, large-scale logistics, small- and medium-sized logistics and B2B logistics. More than 500 logistics centers have been built in
all parts of the country, 15 large-scale intelligent logistics centers have
been completed and put into operation, and a complete logistics network
system for large- and medium-sized parts has been constructed throughout
the country. At the same time, Jingdong has also established a cooperative relationship with Dada to actively develop intra-city distribution
services.

In 2017, SF Express began to develop "three-stage air transport"
logistics and carried out logistics network construction around national
trunk lines, urban trunk lines and terminal logistics distribution in remote
areas. Large manned transport aircraft, regional large unmanned aerial
vehicles and terminal small unmanned aerial vehicles were introduced
and adopted, which could deliver express mail to customers within
36 hours.

Cainiao, Jingdong Logistics and SF Express have played a leading
role in building an intelligent logistics network system, which shows that
logistics enterprises have actively built an intelligent logistics network
system in a point-to-area manner and have realized the integration and
optimal allocation of resources.

The results of cost reduction and efficiency improvement have appeared

According to the China Procurement Development Report (2014), the
total cost of social logistics in China reached more than 10 trillion yuan
in 2013, accounting for 18% of GDP. Logistics enterprises can further
reduce logistics costs on the original basis by applying new technologies
such as unmanned aerial vehicles, distribution robots, and unmanned
warehouses.

From the viewpoint of enterprise development, the application of driverless technology can effectively improve the attraction of this field to investors, increase the market value of logistics enterprises and reflect the advantages of driverless technology while strengthening cost control and improving efficiency. In the subsequent development process, the level of driverless technology will continue to improve, relevant policy thresholds will be gradually reduced, and many manual means of transport will be transformed into driverless and automated methods.

Currently, the application of driverless vehicles and unmanned aerial vehicles in the logistics industry is still in the exploratory phase. Driverless technology needs to overcome many obstacles in the development process; specifically, factors like cost restrictions, standard setting, talent restrictions, policy factors, and other new challenges that may arise along the way. Due to these factors in the actual application process, it is difficult to achieve real landing for unmanned aerial vehicles, unmanned vehicles and unmanned warehouses. In the course of becoming intelligent, logistics enterprises should start with the sorting of goods, gradually transition to unmanned operation of express transfer stations, strictly follow safety standards, and promote the upgrading of the entire logistics industry.

Application of unmanned technology in smart logistics

Besides the logistics companies, the logistics market has also developed in a rapid way in recent years, creating development opportunities for many other industries.

Storage robot

Unmanned driving occupies a dominant position in intelligent logistics, and its application promotes the rapid development of the robot industry. When it comes to robots, many people will think of humanoid robots, such as Pepper. But in fact, industrial robots have a wider range of applications. Industrial robots, which are used in traditional manufacturing industries, can realize simple anthropomorphic operations. By contrast, intelligent robots can complete more difficult automatic operation tasks with the help of visual recognition, mechanical control and other technologies.

Unmanned technology can be introduced into goods sorting, goods packaging, transportation and terminal distribution in the course of logistics operation. Among them, storage robots may be used earlier than other machines. Replacing manual operation with robots can not only reduce labor costs and speed up logistics operations, but also improve operation accuracy, help enterprises improve logistics service levels and increase overall operating efficiency.

The robots application of logistics storage is becoming more and more common nowadays. According to Tractica, the global storage and logistics robot market will reach US$22.4 billion by 2021, with the United States and China occupying most of the market share and showing a rapid growth trend. The domestic intelligent logistics market has developed vigorously in recent years. Under this market situation, the development of China's storage robot market may lead other countries.

Self-driving car

In essence, a moving four-wheeled robot is a self-driving car. Logistics enterprises apply self-driving cars to commodity transportation and distribution, reduce labor costs by replacing driver operations, and use cloud scheduling to speed up commodity transportation and improve safety. Unmanned express vehicles will be applied to the terminal logistics distribution link. In this regard, Skype's founder set up a professional company to formulate terminal distribution solutions and developed unmanned vehicles that can complete the commodity distribution task within 5 kilometers in only 20 minutes.

An analysis of the development of the self-driving car industry shows that it takes a long time for people to accept unmanned cars, and their application is also limited by traffic laws. Based on the industry level, the vertical field will take the lead in the application of self-driving cars. Currently, specific scenes and unmanned delivery are two vertical fields with broad application prospects of self-driving cars. Commuter cars in airports and parks are the applications of self-driving cars in specific scenes.

Unmanned aerial vehicle

Unmanned aerial vehicles (UAVs) are developed in a rapid way in the past two years. DJI has made remarkable achievements in the development of this field. However, the layout personnel represented by DJI focus on the development and application of aerial unmanned aerial vehicles and do not have much involvement in other fields. Although there have been many reports of unmanned aerial vehicle delivery, most of them have not really landed. UAVs are more suitable for commodity distribution in remote areas because the population distribution density in such areas is relatively low and obstacles are relatively few. Even if unmanned aerial vehicles fail and fall, they will not cause serious losses and can replace traditional delivery methods to reduce delivery costs.

At present, powerful logistics enterprises, including SF Express and Jingdong Logistics, are actively developing unmanned aerial vehicle distribution services. SF Express launched the "three-stage air transport network" mode, dividing air capacity into different levels. Specifically, it includes large manned transport aircraft, large unmanned aerial vehicles and small unmanned aerial vehicles and has invested a large amount of funds in project development. It is committed to building a perfect logistics and transportation network, including national trunk lines, urban trunk lines and rural areas, and strives to complete commodity distribution in all parts of the country within 36 hours. In order to promote unmanned aerial vehicle delivery, Jingdong has established a global unmanned system operation headquarters and passed unmanned aerial vehicle flight applications in many regions, gradually expanding the application scope of unmanned aerial vehicle technology in the distribution process.

Automated logistics equipment

In order to speed up the logistics operation, robot technology will be widely applied to the handling system, and large-scale automated logistics equipment will be introduced in transportation or other segments to identify the types of goods and transport them to the corresponding goods sorting area; related equipment can also be used in the merchandise area for loading commodities.

For example, Cainiao Warehouse invested 100 million yuan in the project of introducing the automation system of KNAPP, Austria, and placed logistics conveyor belt equipment in each area of the warehouse to transport goods to the commodity area and realize the transportation of goods between different areas. Besides Cainiao, many logistics enterprises have introduced such automatic equipment into warehouses. The domestic intelligent logistics service enterprises can make use of advanced technical means in the future to manufacture automatic logistics equipment more suitable for China's national conditions and further improve the intelligent operation level of the logistics industry in the warehousing link.

With the application of automation, unmanned and intelligent technologies in the logistics industry, all aspects of this field will change, which will drive the development of unmanned aerial vehicles, unmanned vehicles, robots and other related industries and give rise to powerful enterprises.

NTOCC: New logistics with cost reduction and efficiency increase

Concept, formation and current situation of non-truck operating common carriers

In September 2016, the Chinese Ministry of Transport published "Opinions on Promoting Reform Pilot and Accelerating the Innovation and Development of Truckless Carrier Logistics," which proposed that in order to adapt to the tide of supply-side reform and achieve "cost reduction and efficiency," the road freight non-truck operating common carrier (NTOCC) pilot program would be launched in October 2016. The development of this new logistics mode, however, has encountered many difficulties and setbacks, instead of being plain sailing. Next, we will analyze the logistics mode of NTOCC from various perspectives.

What is NTOCC?

The idea of NTOCC comes from a track broker in the United States and extends from the idea of non-vessel operating common carriers (NVOCCs). NTOCC refers to units and individuals that do not have vehicles but are engaged in cargo transportation. NTOCCs can have dual identities; they can simultaneously be both shippers and carriers. An NTOCC does not really undertake the transportation of goods under normal circumstances but is responsible for organizing the transportation and distribution of the goods, selecting the transportation mode and route, etc.—the typical liabilities and responsibilities of carriers. Its income mainly comes from the freight difference caused by large-scale wholesale transportation.

Formation and current situation of NTOCCs

There are three reasons for China to launch the NTOCC pilot:

(1) China's logistics cost is too high. The proportion of logistics cost in GDP has been hovering around 15%, while in developed countries such as Europe and the United States, the proportion of logistics cost in GDP is only about 8%. The main cause for this problem is that China's third-party logistics enterprises have not formed a scale of sizeable economic advantage.

(2) China's tax law stipulates that logistics businesses can only be carried out with vehicles, resulting in the delay in the maturity of the multi-modal transport system. In this case, the emergence of NTOCCs and NVOCCs makes it possible to realize the whole supply chain operation across industries.

(3) The integration of commercial channels by Internet enterprises provides many possibilities for the realization of "Internet+" efficient logistics.

After several years of development, the logistics mode of NTOCCs has gradually taken the dominant position in the field of logistics and transportation organization. It has played an important role in the integration of logistics transportation resources and the improvement of logistics operation efficiency. In the modern logistics system of developed countries, NTOCCs are the core and driving force behind the development of multimodal transport.

However, at present, the laws and regulations of China's logistics and transportation industry are still based on car ownership, which is in conflict with the car-free model. On the one hand, under such laws and regulations, it is difficult for NTOCCs to obtain business qualifications; on the other hand, NTOCCs also face many difficulties in taxation and setting up offices in different places.

In addition, the government has not yet established a sound means of market regulation in respect of the non-truck-operated common carriage, resulting in a confusing market operation. In practice, transport enterprises have to purchase a small number of vehicles or rent some of them in order to obtain transport qualifications, but more than 80% of their transport operations are outsourced, thus forming a special situation where the truck-operated common carriage and non-truck-operated common carriage operate in a mixed manner.

Analysis of four advantages of NTOCC mode

Case 1: C.H. Robinson

C.H. Robinson is the largest truck transportation company in the United States and the largest NTOCC in the world, with more than 218 branches in the world, covering the United States, Canada, Mexico and many countries in Asia and Europe. The company serves 50,000 shipper enterprises, integrates 1 million trucks, accepts 15 million orders every year, has a market value of nearly US$15 billion, and accounts for 30% of the US logistics market.

C.H. Robinson is a non-asset logistics supplier, without transportation tools and other fixed assets. The most valuable ones are information networks and shops all over the world, rich customer resources and advanced management experience. C.H. Robinson takes this opportunity to integrate social logistics resources to provide customers with integrated logistics and transportation services.

Case 2: BenNiao: Taking NVOCC (Non-Vehicle Operating Common Carrier) as the Link

The ultimate goal of the BenNiao network of car transportation is to build a road freight data-trading platform linked by non-car carriers, and the scale of the platform should reach first in China. There are three major investors in the BenNiao network of car transportation, namely, China International Shipping Network, freight forwarding enterprises and domestic and foreign investors. BenNiao believes that if freight forwarders are used as NVOCC, big data on freight transport vehicles covering the whole country can be compiled through freight forwarders located all over the country. Supported by this big data, the vehicle cloud trading cloud platform can be successfully built to provide the best logistics solution for domestic road freight transport enterprises.

Through the analysis of the above cases, it can be seen that NVOCC has the following advantages.

Advanced logistics information technology

Through the cases of C.H. Robinson and the BenNiao network of car transportation, we can find that NVOCCs must have advanced logistics information technology and developed information network to grasp the supply information in real time and understand the local supply type and transportation capacity, thus effectively integrating the physical resources and finally combining the physical network with the virtual network.

Rich logistics management experience and resources

This is most obvious in the case of C.H. Robinson. C.H. Robinson has an extensive portfolio covering more than 200 countries and regions in the Americas, Europe and Asia. Over the course of a century of development, C.H. Robinson has accumulated a wealth of resources and management experience, achieving the perfect combination of knowledge-intensive and technology-intensive. Under the knowledge-driven development mode, C.H. Robinson has formed an advanced development concept and management mode, laying a solid foundation for it to become the best modern logistics enterprise.

Agile market response ability

BenNiao big data shows that NVOCCs need to have agile market response capability and be able to respond to market changes in the shortest possible time. Vehicle operating common carriers (VOCCs) must invest a lot of energy in the transportation link and have no time to take care of it when they carry out heavy asset operations; NVOCCs implement an asset-light strategy, focusing on things like market capacity, supply information, organization and allocation of market resources. With big data, it is possible to control the market situation and monitor market changes in real time, thus reacting to market changes in the shortest possible time.

Ability to intensively integrate social logistics resources

C.H. Robinson provides logistics and transportation services for 50,000 enterprises and integrates 1 million trucks in the market. This shows that NVOCCs must have strong integration capabilities, be able to consolidate the scattered logistics resources in society and have the ability to provide integrated logistics and transport services to their customers.

Main problems for NVOCCs

The drawbacks of taxation

The tax law judges whether a subject is a carrier on the basis of whether it has a vehicle or not, which is somewhat contradictory to the contract law, but the actual tax treatment is still subject to the tax law. After the implementation of the move to "replace business tax with value-added tax" in the transportation industry, new business companies in the transportation industry, such as companies that use Internet platforms to carry out truck positioning businesses, transportation process monitoring, and supply chain services, are seen as "freight forwarders" and can only issue invoices with a tax rate of 6% as long as they have no vehicles, while China's road transport industry issues VAT invoices of 11%, which is quite different from foreign countries. For example, in the United States, C.H. Robinson does not need to issue tax invoices at all, only reimbursement invoices.

In addition, as transportation costs are rising, the service quality of individual car owners is continuously improving, and more and more enterprises are unwilling to buy vehicles. Under such circumstances, the inapplicability of the "replace business tax with value-added tax" policy is becoming more and more prominent, resulting in an increasingly unfair competitive situation for the industry as a whole.

The separation of price and tax quotation have made it difficult for competition in the logistics and transportation market. With the implementation of the "replace business tax with value-added tax" policy, actual carrier companies which did not own vehicles were unable to issue invoices with 11% VAT charges, while their affiliated companies that do not undertake the transportation business could. This unreasonable regulation increases the tax burden of transportation enterprises, making the phenomenon of false invoicing and illegal operation in the whole industry increasingly serious.

Vulnerabilities in risk management mechanisms

According to relevant laws and regulations, NTOCCs bear the first responsibility for all losses incurred during transportation. However, the actual situation is that once there is any problem in the transportation of the goods, the owner will file a high claim amount, which makes the NTOCC unable to bear it.

It can be seen from the pilot study of NTOCCs in China, where there is no proper solution to problems such as qualification management and business monitoring of an NTOCC. Other problems such as business authenticity have also not been effectively solved, causing mutual distrust among the entrusting party, the carrier and the actual deliverer. The entrusting party has goods to transport but does not dare to cooperate with the carrier; carriers are on guard against freight drivers and need to pay a large margin, which not only increases the operating cost of NTOCCs but also makes NTOCCs spend time, energy, manpower and material resources to create a trust mechanism, further reducing their profit margin.

The problems to be solved

At present, many small third-party logistics companies and individuals in China assume the role of NTOCCs, but do not really engage in cargo transportation, profiting mainly from the freight difference generated by large-scale "wholesale" transportation. But now, it is difficult for NTOCCs to achieve effective growth in profits only by this price difference collection mode.

NTOCCs make profit mainly through the price difference between suppliers and drivers. Under this profit-making mode, NTOCCs, suppliers and drivers use different settlement methods, resulting in an inadequate supply of funds and failure to improve profits, making it difficult for the whole industry to achieve better development.

Countermeasures and suggestions on developing NTOCCs

Based on the limitations of the above three factors, it is not easy to be an NTOCC since it requires strong financial strength, information gathering ability and management ability.

(1) Capital bottleneck. If an enterprise rashly enters the NTOCC market without strong financial strength, it will have to borrow money from the bank and pay huge loan interest in order to fill the capital gap, making it difficult to obtain ideal income in a short time.
(2) In the era of information explosion, enterprises grasp the initiative when they master the information. The fundamental purpose of

Alibaba's huge investment in the establishment of Cainiao Network is to control information flow and obtain more logistics information. It can be seen that information collection requires enterprises to invest a lot of funds.

(3) The accumulation of management ability requires continuous training of management personnel. The whole process requires a large amount of manpower and material resources, takes a long time and gains income slowly. In addition, another method is to cooperate with large-scale Internet platforms. For example, Log56.com, a platform that has accumulated rich experience in transportation resources, technology and management, is determined to build a non-truck operating common carrying support platform for traditional logistics enterprises. Therefore, enterprises that want to develop a non-truck operating common carrying business can fully cooperate with such platforms.

The identity of NVOCCs is dual; they are both carriers and transport capacity terminals or shippers. Traditional vehicle–cargo matching only provides a distribution service, while NTOCCs not only improve logistics distribution efficiency but also reduce costs. Nowadays, the NTOCC has gradually become the core force of organizing transportation in the transportation market and bears the heavy responsibility of integrating logistics transportation resources and improving logistics transportation efficiency.

In a certain way, NTOCCs really participate in the transportation process; they enable shippers and truck drivers to enjoy high-value platform services and benefit the whole logistics industry. According to the article, China's NTOCCs are facing many difficulties in development at this stage. Solving these difficulties requires a three-pronged approach: the external environment, each company's operations and internal factors. Only by solving these difficulties can NTOCCs achieve stable and sustainable development.

Chapter 2

Unmanned Driving: The Traffic Revolution Sweeping the World

Origin, development and application of unmanned driving technology

Unmanned driving begins a new era of intelligent transportation

Owing to the vigorous development of science and technology, driverless car technology has gradually increased its status in the field of social research. Driverless cars can sense the environment around them, process the captured environmental information and use computer information technology to control and adjust the car's driving speed and direction, thus ensuring that the car drives normally on the road and reaches its destination as planned.

During the course of development, the field of unmanned driving cars is committed to applying more precise information technology to cars, thus promoting the development of human–vehicle interaction, improving the efficiency of this method and reducing the complexity of its operation. Unmanned driving can not only improve the efficiency of car operation and reduce the probability of traffic accidents but also provide travel services for those who do not master car-driving skills.

Development of unmanned driving technology

Autonomous driving is the mainstream trend of automobile development in the long run, and unmanned driving is a specific embodiment of autonomous driving and a crucial part of intelligent transportation. Broadly speaking, driverless cars can be seen as cars that are based on the Internet environment, integrated and applied through computer technology, network communication technology, intelligent control technology and other technologies to achieve autonomous driving, a special kind of mobile intelligent robot, which is the key to what many in the industry call an automatic wheeled mobile robot.

Autonomous self-driving cars can automatically sense the surrounding environment using onboard sensors and grasp the real-time road condition information, and using an intelligent driving device with an intelligent computer system as the core, these cars can drive to their intended destinations without any intervention. While driving, the unmanned car can use the system's safety control function to deal with various emergencies and ensure driving safety.

Application direction for unmanned driving technology

Three directions of application development are on the horizon for unmanned driving technology:

(1) **Unmanned driving systems in an expressway environment:** In China, all expressways have well-placed road signs bearing all the information drivers need to make decisions while on the road. The unmanned driving system applied in this structured environment needs to undertake the functions of tracking road signs and automatically identifying other vehicles. For high-speed automatic driving in this highly standardized environment, developments in unmanned driving systems are committed to reaching Level 4 of autonomous driving: high automation. Although this kind of application is difficult to apply to other environments, research in this direction is being pursued due to the high levels of danger associated with expressway driving and the known relative boredom and/or monotony of driving on expressways, which increases the risk for human drivers on expressways. If fully automatic driving can be achieved, the resulting unmanned cars could reduce these risks, and the value of driverless applications can be fully realized.

(?) **Unmanned driving system in an urban environment:** Compared with expressway driving, unmanned driving in cities requires lower speed and higher safety, implying that it has broad development prospects. In the present stage, it can share the pressure of large-capacity public transportation in cities and relieve the traffic tension in urban areas. Specific application scenarios include airports, industrial parks, parks, campuses and other public places.

(3) **Unmanned driving system in a special environment:** Some countries have mastered advanced unmanned driving car technology and have always been committed to applying unmanned driving technology to military and other special environments. Unmanned driving technology has similarities in its application in expressways and urban environments in these fields, but there are differences in the targeting of technical performance.

Bottleneck of the development of unmanned driving technology

Most unmanned driving cars are in the experimental testing stage. There is still a long way to go before they can take part in the complex real traffic environment, and many bottlenecks exist in their development process, including laws and regulations, technical restrictions, data leakage, ethics, to name a few.

It is hoped that, in the future, unmanned driving cars will be able to think and make decisions like human beings. For now, the safety of the vehicles and their internal passengers is the top priority for driverless cars. Under manual driving conditions, when lives are not at risk, most human drivers will sacrifice themselves to protect the lives of others. For example, imagine a scenario in which there are pedestrians running red lights on the road ahead, other vehicles traveling in the same direction on the left, and roadblocks on the right. In this case, many drivers would rather turn right and hit the roadblocks. Although repairing the car would cost a certain amount of money in such a scenario, it does not threaten the lives of others. If, in this scenario, the cars were unmanned, a self-driving car would have judged the resistance ahead—the pedestrian running a red light—was the least costly scenario, thus directly hitting the pedestrians instead of harming themselves, the vehicles.

Consequently, in the light of the challenges listed above, it is hard to develop unmanned driving technology as it requires not only detailed planning from the government, universities and scientific research institutions, but also the active participation of entrepreneurs and enterprises. Nonetheless, the potential benefits for humankind are still sizeable, and we must speed up its development process with the powerful force of the market so that unmanned driving technology and intelligent transportation can truly benefit hundreds of millions of people.

Future prospects of unmanned driving technology

After the birth of the automobile, the progress of the automobile industry has made positive contributions to the development of the whole society. Unmanned driving relies on advanced technical means to effectively improve the safety and accuracy of driving operations and reduce the probability of traffic accidents while driving. With the further development and maturity of technology, the application scope of unmanned driving in the fields of passenger cars and commercial vehicles will continue to expand, setting off a wave of revolution in the world.

China's huge population base has laid a good market foundation for the development of the automobile industry and occupies a very important position in global automobile development. In recent years, the domestic automobile industry has put in great efforts to create its own brand of products, which has created a good opportunity for the application of new automobile technologies and is conducive to expanding the application scope of new automobile technologies in China's automobile field. Intelligent driving can propel the development of the entire automobile field and promote the progress of commercial vehicles. In terms of passenger cars, commercial vehicles can use intelligent driving technology to help people with their daily life and work, saving them more time and energy and ultimately improving their quality of life.

For example, if the commercial vehicle running on the expressway can be driven unmanned, it can buy more time for drivers to interact with others and inform each other of their current position and expected arrival time. If it is used in the logistics industry, it can improve the distribution efficiency of the logistics center and accelerate the operation of the whole system. In terms of commercial vehicles, the application of unmanned driving can effectively lead to more rest time for drivers, avoid driving fatigue, reduce the probability of traffic accidents and avoid endangering people's lives and damage to property.

Four development stages of unmanned driving technology

In order to adapt to the explosive growth of active safety technology for automobiles, the National Highway Traffic Safety Administration (NHTSA) issued a five-level standard for automobile automation in 2013, dividing the automatic driving function of automobiles into five levels: 0–4.

Level 0: No automation

Level 0 means that the car does not have any automatic driving function, and the driver has full control over all functions of the car. In the process of driving a car, the driver should be responsible for starting, braking and operating the car and observe the surrounding road conditions. As long as people control the car, no matter what auxiliary driving technology is added to the car, it belongs to Level 0. Therefore, although ordinary cars are equipped with forward collision warning, lane departure warning, automatic wiper control, automatic headlight control and other functions, they can only be driven by human control, so they still belong to Level 0.

Level 1: Automation at a single functional level

In Level 1, the driver is responsible for driving safety, but the driver can give up some control rights to the system to manage it. In this stage, some functions have been automated, such as common adaptive cruise, emergency brake assistance, as well as lane keeping. Level 1 has only a single function. During driving, the driver still has to control the vehicle and cannot completely let it go.

Level 2: Partial automation

In Level 2, drivers can share control with cars. In some preset environments, the driver does not need to control and the car can run automatically, but the driver should be on standby, responsible for driving safety and ready to drive the car at any time. In this stage, the key to partial automation of the car is not to have more than two functions, but the driver is no longer the main operator of the car. For example, the car following the function formed by the combination of ACC and LKS and the autopilot function pushed by Tesla all belong to Level 2.

Level 3: Conditional automation

The car can be automatically controlled under limited circumstances in this stage, for example, during automatic driving on high-speed sections or sections with less traffic flow, the driver has enough time to take over the car to ensure driving safety in case of emergency. In this stage, drivers can be freed to the greatest extent, since they are no longer responsible for driving safety and no longer need to monitor road conditions in the course of driving.

Level 4: Fully automated (unmanned driving)

In Level 4, the car can drive to the destination without assistance, as long as the starting point and ending point information are input in advance. In this stage, the car will be responsible for driving safety during the whole process, the dependence on the driver will be reduced to the minimum extent and no one can ride the car when driving.

In addition to NHTSA, the American Society of Automotive Engineers (SAE) has also graded automatic driving by dividing automatic driving technology into six levels from 0 to 5, of which Level 0 to Level 3 are consistent with NHTSA's definition of automatic driving, emphasizing no automation, driving support, partial automation and conditional automation, respectively. As for full automation, the SAE has subdivided it and further emphasized the requirements of driving on roads and differing environments.

According to the SAE's regulations on self-driving Level 4, cars can only drive automatically under specific road conditions, such as closed parks and fixed driving routes. In other words, automatic driving in this stage is highly automatic driving for specific situations. In Level 5, cars can drive automatically in various environments. Moreover, the effective countermeasures are proposed for complex vehicle environment, pedestrian flow environment, as well as road environment.

From four levels to six

To sum up, the functions of different levels of automatic driving are also increasing layer by layer (see Table 2.1).

Table 2.1 Self-driving functions increasing layer by layer.

	Level 0	Level 1	Level 2	Level 3	Level 4	Level 5
NHTSA	Level 0	Level 1	Level 2	Level 3	Level 4	
SAE	Level 0	Level 1	Level 2	Level 3	Level 4	Level 5
	No automation	Driving support	Partial automation	Conditional automation	High automation	Full automation
Functions	Night vision, pedestrian detection, traffic sign recognition, blind spot detection, parallel line assistance, traffic alarm at rear intersection, lane departure warning	Adaptive cruise driving system, automatic emergency braking, parking assistance system, forward–backward collision warning system, body electronic stability system	Lane keeping assistance system	Congestion assistance driving	Automatic parking in parking lot	
Features	Sensing detection and decision alert	Single function (one of the above)	Combined function (Level 1/Level 2 combination)	Specific condition, specific task tasks	Specific condition, all tasks	All conditions, all tasks
		ADSA		Autopilot		

Among them, Level 0 can only realize sensing detection and decision alarm functions, such as night vision system, pedestrian detection, traffic sign identification, as well as lane departure warning.

Level 1 can realize a single control function, such as active emergency braking and adaptive cruise control system.

Level 2 can realize a variety of control functions, such as configuring AEB and LKA for vehicles.

In Level 3, cars can be driven automatically under specific conditions and driven by human drivers beyond specific conditions.

The Level 4, as specified by the SAE, can be unmanned under specified conditions, such as unmanned driving on fixed routes.

The Level 5, as specified by the SAE, refers to completely unmanned driving, which represents the highest level of automatic driving and belongs to the final form of automatic driving. It can be unmanned in any scene.

The advanced driving assistance system (ADAS) is the current highest-possible level of automated driving, belonging to the automatic driving levels 0–2.

Compared with semi-automatic driving cars, fully automatic unmanned driving cars are safer because semi-automatic driving cars may still experience human errors, whereas fully automated driverless cars have no chance for human error. For instance, a survey conducted by the School of Transportation of Virginia Tech University shows that the driver of a Level 3 self-driving vehicle needs 17 seconds to respond to the takeover request of the vehicle. If the vehicle travels at a speed of 65 miles per hour, the vehicle would have already driven 1621 feet, or 494 meters, in those 17 seconds.

From seeing the road object to stepping on the brake, a human driver needs 1.2 seconds, which is much longer than the 0.2 seconds used by an onboard computer. Although the difference between the two is only 1 second, if the car travels at a speed of 120 km/h, the car can drive 40 meters in 1.2 seconds, while the car can only drive 6.7 meters in 0.2 seconds. In case of emergency, the time difference of 1 second can determine the difference between the life and death of a car's passengers. Therefore, for the entire automobile industry, totally unmanned driving is the ultimate development goal of automatic driving.

Evolution path driven by unmanned driving technology

Unmanned driving is a comprehensive technology based on traditional automobile manufacturing technology and integrated with intelligence, automation, electrification, the Internet and other technologies. Unmanned driving vehicles are also called "autonomous vehicles" and "wheeled mobile robots." Through the onboard sensing system, the nearby road environment is sensed, the driving route is reasonably planned and the vehicle is controlled to travel to the reserved target. Unmanned driving vehicles condense many technologies such as automatic control, artificial intelligence, architecture, as well as visual computing. They are the product of the development of computer science, pattern recognition and intelligent control technology to a certain point. They have now been regarded as an important indicator to measure a country's scientific research strength and economic development level and can be widely used in national defense, national economy and other fields in the future.

China has a large population, and the traffic problem is very serious. If unmanned driving can be fully promoted, urban traffic, environmental protection and urban development problems will be solved, industrial manufacturing levels will be effectively improved, and people's lives will be improved, too. As driverless technology matures, traffic management departments must be prepared to promote the integration of unmanned driving technology and intelligent transportation.

In recent years, high-tech enterprises at home and abroad, as well as traditional automobile manufacturers, have been actively deployed in the field of unmanned driving vehicles, giving birth to many products, many of which have passed road tests, some with a mileage of hundreds of thousands of kilometers, laying the foundation for the final commercial mass production. Intelligent Internet-connected vehicles will become the industry with the greatest development potential. According to an analysis of the plans released by major automobile manufacturers and Internet companies, the commercialization of unmanned driving cars will enter a stage of explosive growth.

On the whole, unmanned driving has two development paths, one is ADAS and the other is artificial intelligence. The highest form of the two is the same; both are heading towards achieving completely unmanned driving; that is to say, completely unmanned driving is the result of the development of automation and intelligence to the highest level.

As it is, the automobile industry will continue to develop smarter cars, until eventually, unmanned driving cars become commonplace. Unmanned cars are the solution to reducing traffic accidents, relieving traffic congestion and reducing environmental pollution. However, for unmanned driving cars to achieve their full potential, there are problems such as the level of safe driving the cars can achieve, recognition of the usefulness of unmanned driving, the popularization and acceptance of the idea, as well as legal ethics, which must be overcome. According to experts' predictions, the unmanned driving market will reach US$87 billion by 2030.

The application of unmanned driving technology can meet three potential demands, namely, perceptibility, connectivity and personification of automobiles. In order to realize popularization and application, it is necessary to establish an intelligent automobile standard system and an intelligent transportation system. Finally, it is necessary to realize automobile sharing, alleviate traffic congestion, reduce environmental pollution and realize the overall liberation of human and vehicle productivity.

Application of unmanned driving technology

The application of unmanned driving technology needs to solve three potential demands. The first is the perceptible demand from the real world to the digital world, that is, the demand that can be understood by people and equipment through structured data, specifically including the demand for people to perceive cars, the demand for cars to perceive people, and the demand for cars to perceive the surrounding environment. The second is the connection requirements between different devices, such as smart phones, smart wearable devices, as well as smart cars. The third is the need for the personification of cars. Future cars may develop into intelligent robots, which can not only obey people's instructions but also pre-empt people's needs and recommend services for them.

Unmanned driving technology promotion

To promote unmanned driving technology, we must first establish and improve smart car standards, smart car laws and regulations and intelligent transportation systems. Then, we must enhance the coordination of the surrounding industries of the automobile industry, such as the information industry, electronics industry, transportation industry and Internet industry; fully consider the future development trend of technology; do a good job in software and hardware interfaces, data communication formats and protocols, platform safety construction; interface with international smart car technical standards; and build a smart car standard system with Chinese characteristics. In addition, China should speed up the construction and implementation of pilot demonstration projects of smart cars, build an intelligent transportation network, issue laws and regulations related to smart cars and clarify the responsibility judgment of self-driving cars after traffic accidents.

Unmanned driving technology mission

With the support of unmanned driving technology, shared cars will continue to develop, and cars will have dual function of public transport and services to improve traffic order, reduce traffic accidents and congestion, increase road traffic, reduce unnecessary congestion caused by impoliteness or poor technology, and increase road speed limits and actual traffic speeds. With the continuous popularization of shared cars, people's demand for private cars will continue to decline, traffic congestion and parking difficulties will be effectively alleviated, and greenhouse gas emissions will be greatly reduced. In addition, the operation of shared autonomous cars increases timeliness, safety and accuracy, which can not only reduce the frequency of traffic accidents but also enable the disabled, people without a driver's license, people without cars and the elderly to enjoy the pleasure of driving and traveling, thus fully liberating people's time and productivity.

Unmanned driving's subversion and reconstruction of traffic ecology

It is predicted that, unmanned vehicles will enter the market in an all-round way and the automobile industry will enter a completely new stage of development. According to the estimation of the World Economic Forum, the digital transformation of the automobile industry will create a value of US$67 billion and a social benefit of US$31,000, including improving the interconnection of unmanned vehicles and passengers and improving the ecosystem of the entire transportation industry.

It is estimated that semi-automatic driving cars and fully automatic driving cars have great market development potential in the next few decades. For example, by 2035, the number of self-driving cars in China will reach 8.6 million, including 3.4 million fully automatic driving cars and 5.2 million semi-automatic driving cars.

According to the forecast by industry officials, China's car sales, buses, taxis and related transportation services can generate about US$1.5 trillion per year. According to the prediction of the Boston Consulting Group, it will take at least 15 to 20 years for unmanned vehicles to reach 25% of the global automobile market. In other words, if unmanned vehicles are listed in 2021, it means that their share in the global automobile market will not reach 25% until 2035–2040.

Because unmanned vehicles have had unprecedented influence in the automobile industry, they will bring about great changes. Relevant research shows that with the emergence of unmanned driving cars, expressway safety will be greatly guaranteed and problems such as air pollution and traffic congestion will be effectively alleviated.

Enhance expressway safety

Nowadays, expressway accidents are a big problem perplexing countries all over the world. According to statistics, about 35,000 people die in car accidents every year in the United States, 260,000 people die in car accidents every year in China and 4,000 people die in expressway accidents every year in Japan. According to the statistics of the World Health Organization, the number of people killed in expressway accidents worldwide each year is as high as 1.24 million.

According to statistics, the annual loss caused by fatal car accidents is as high as US$260 billion, the loss caused by car accidents is US$356 billion, and the annual loss caused by expressway accidents is about US$625 billion. According to a survey conducted by RAND Corporation of the United States, drunk driving accounts for 39% of the various causes of car accidents and deaths. In this respect, the popularization and application of unmanned vehicles will significantly improve this situation and reduce or even avoid casualties in car accidents. Among all the traffic accidents in China, 60% of the traffic accidents occur when pedestrians, bicycles and electric bicycles collide with cars and trucks. About 94% of all motor vehicle accidents in the United States are caused by human error.

According to the research of the American Insurance Institute for Highway Safety, after the car is installed with automatic safety devices, the death toll from expressway accidents can be reduced by 31%, and 11,000 people will survive every year. These automatic safety devices include a collision braking system, collision warning system, lane departure warning, blind-spot detection and so on.

Relieve traffic congestion

Traffic congestion is a common problem in big cities. In the United States, every driver is stranded on the road for about 40 hours a year due to traffic jams, which cost about US$121 billion. In Moscow, Rio de Janeiro and other cities, the waste of time caused by traffic congestion is even more serious, with each driver wasting about 100 hours on traffic congestion every year. In China, there are about 35 cities with more than 1 million cars and 10 cities with more than 2 million cars, and about 75% of the roads in the urban areas of big cities are congested. At present, the number of private cars in China has reached 126 million, an increase of 15% year on year.

According to Donald Shoup's research, traffic congestion caused by drivers circling back and forth to find parking spaces accounts for 30% of the traffic congestion in urban areas of big cities, which is the cause of air pollution, because 30% of carbon dioxide is emitted by cars, and carbon dioxide is the main culprit of climate change. In addition, it is estimated that 23–45% of traffic congestion occurs at road intersections. Because the traffic lights and stop signs are stationary and the time interval is set in advance, it is impossible to consider the traffic flow in all directions and difficult to really play the role of traffic flow regulator.

With the increasing proportion of unmanned vehicles in traffic flow, the onboard sensor will be combined with the intelligent transportation system to optimize the traffic flow at road intersections, and the time interval of traffic lights will be automatically adjusted according to the traffic flow in all directions, thus improving the traffic efficiency at road intersections and providing an effective solution to the traffic congestion problem.

Reduce air pollution

Cars are a very important factor causing air pollution. According to RAND Corporation's research, compared with manual driving, unmanned driving technology can improve fuel efficiency by 4–10% through smoother acceleration and deceleration. According to the survey, the smog in the industrial zone is deeply affected by the number of cars. With the increasing number of unmanned cars, air pollution will continue to decline. According to a study, cars emit 40% more emissions when waiting at red lights or in traffic jams than when running normally.

An unmanned vehicle sharing system is conducive to energy conservation and emission reduction. Researchers at the University of Texas at Austin have studied carbon monoxide, sulfur dioxide, nitrogen oxides, volatile organic compounds, fine particles, greenhouse gases and fine particles. The results show that unmanned vehicle sharing systems can not only save energy but also reduce the emission of many pollutants.

Uber found that 30% of passengers in Los Angeles and 50% of passengers in San Francisco choose carpooling. Globally, about 20% of passengers choose carpooling. Whether it is an unmanned car or a traditional car, the more the passengers who choose to carpool, the better the environmental benefits and the more effective the alleviation of traffic congestion. Because carpooling has changed the mode of one person and one car, the air quality has been effectively improved.

Global layout: Grabbing the commanding heights of unmanned driving competition

Competition pattern of global unmanned driving industry

An unmanned driving car is a kind of intelligent car, also known as a wheeled mobile robot, which mainly relies on the intelligent driver in the car to realize unmanned driving.

In a nutshell, unmanned driving cars rely on high-precision maps, supplemented by data collected by onboard sensing equipment, and they make decisions through intelligent algorithm identification and calculation to control vehicles so that the vehicles can realize automatic driving. From the working principle of unmanned driving cars, it can be seen that unmanned driving technology integrates technological achievements in artificial intelligence, vehicle braking, environmental identification and other fields, bringing new development opportunities to markets such as cars, smart chips, sensors and map navigation.

Viewing the pattern of the unmanned driving industry from California road test qualification

At present, California has taken the lead in passing legislation on unmanned driving cars worldwide and is the most important testing base for unmanned driving cars in the world. The U.S. Highway Safety

Administration, which is in charge of U.S. automobile safety, is headquartered in California. Due to its openness, authority and inclusiveness, California has become the world's most important test base for unmanned driving cars.

The California Department of Motor Vehicle (DMV) issues California unmanned driving road test permits to unmanned driving car companies, which can conduct unmanned driving car tests on specific public roads (Table 2.2). In September 2014, the California Department of Motor Vehicle issued the first batch of unmanned driving road test permits (see Figure 2.1). So far, 45 companies have obtained unmanned driving

Table 2.2   California unmanned driving test permit issuance time.

Time of license issue	Name of company
2014	Volkswagen, Mercedes-Benz, Waymo: Goggle Waymo, Delphi, Tesla, Bosch, Nissan
2015	General Motors, BMW, Honda, Ford
2016	Zoox, Drive.al, Faraday Future, Baidu, Wheego, Valeo, NIO, Teleanv, Nvidia
2017	AutoX, Subaru, Udacity, Navya, Renovo, Uber, PlusAI, Nuro, CarOne, Apple, Bauer, Pony.ai, TuSimple, Jingchi, SAIC, Almotive, Nullmax, Samsung, Continental Automotive, Voyage, CYNGN, Roadstar, Changan Auto, Lyft

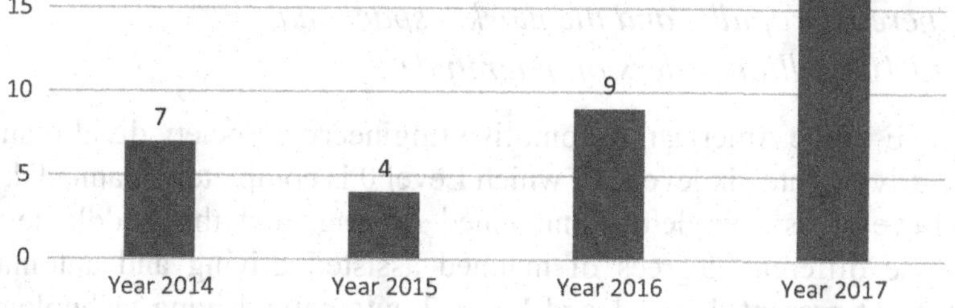

Figure 2.1   Accelerated issuance of driving test permits for unmanned driving in California.

road test permits worldwide, including traditional car companies, parts suppliers, technology giants, start-ups and other different types of enterprises.

The global unmanned driving industry is developing faster and faster. Seven companies obtained California unmanned driving road test permits in 2014, 4 companies obtained permits in 2015, 9 companies in 2016 and 25 companies in 2017. In 2017 alone, the proportion of companies that obtained California unmanned driving road test permits exceeded half of the total, showing explosive growth. This phenomenon shows that the development speed of the unmanned driving industry is increasing. Major companies around the world are focusing on the study of unmanned driving cars, and competition in this field is becoming increasingly fierce.

With the release of the road map of intelligent network connection, the core technology of unmanned driving will be further clarified. The road map of intelligent network connection will help clarify the core technologies required for unmanned driving, and the whole industry will develop into unmanned core technologies such as network connection.

According to the "Analysis Report on the Development Prospect Forecast and Investment Strategic Planning of China's Unmanned Driving Car Industry" released by the Prospective Industry Research Institute, the value of the unmanned driving car market will reach $59.4 billion in 2026. By 2035, the global sales volume of unmanned driving cars will reach 11.8 million, and the compound annual growth rate of unmanned driving cars will reach 48.35% from 2025 to 2035. China's share in the global unmanned driving car market will then reach 24%.

The global penetration rate of autonomous driving will increase rapidly, and the market space may exceed 100 billion orders of magnitude

The SAE of the American Automotive Engineering Society divides automatic driving into six levels, of which Level 0 is completely manned driving, Level 5 is completely unmanned driving, and the middle levels comprise different degrees of manned assisted driving and automatic driving. At present, Level 1 and Level 2 automatic driving technologies

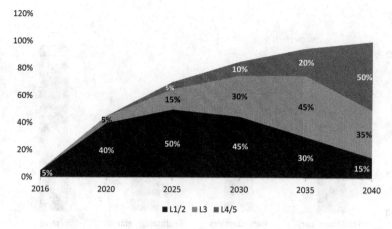

Figure 2.2 Penetration rate of graded self-driving cars.

are relatively mature. Level 3 automatic driving technologies will be mass-produced, and industrialization of Level 5 completely unmanned driving will take more than 10 years. It is judged that the penetration rate of global self-driving will increase rapidly in recent years. It is estimated that by 2020, the penetration rate of Level 1 and Level 2 automatic driving will reach 40%; in 2025, more than 20% of mass-produced cars are expected to achieve different levels of automatic driving; by 2040, all newly produced cars will be equipped with self-driving functions, of which the penetration rate of Level 4 and Level 5 self-driving cars will reach 50%, and the corresponding market size will exceed US$100 billion (see Figure 2.2).

Start-ups have become an important force in the global unmanned driving industry and promoted multi-industry integration

As of 2017, 45 companies have obtained California unmanned driving licenses. Among them, there are 11 traditional automobile manufacturers, including Volkswagen, General Motors, Chang'an and so on. There are 6 auto parts suppliers, including Delphi, Valeo, Mainland China and Bosch, 7 technology giants, such as Apple, Tesla and NVIDIA, and 21 start-up companies, such as Zoox, Drive.ai, Weilai and Pony.ai. (Table 2.1), of

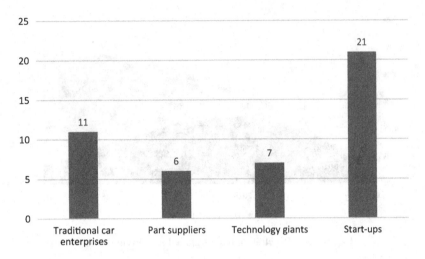

Figure 2.3   The number of start-ups accounts for the largest proportion.

which start-up companies account for 47%, nearly half, becoming important participants in the global unmanned driving industry (Figure 2.3).

Accordingly, it can be judged that future automotive technology is likely to develop in the direction of deep integration of mechanics, electronics, communications and artificial intelligence. Traditional car companies, well-known universities and technology giants will produce more start-up teams, and due to their cross-background, the companies are expected to achieve rapid development.

The rapid development of start-ups has reshaped the competitive pattern of the unmanned driving industry

In 2014 and 2015, no start-up company obtained a California unmanned driving permit; in 2016, 5 companies obtained California unmanned driving permits, accounting for 56%; in 2017, 16 companies obtained California unmanned driving permits, accounting for 64%. It shows a rapid development trend. As start-ups have just entered the industry, the trend of traveling light is expected develop by leaps and bounds. On this basis, we can judge that start-up companies are likely to occupy an important position in the fields of unmanned vehicle manufacturing and operation, system solutions, key components, etc., by virtue of their own advantages.

Development of unmanned driving technology in countries around the world

The continuous development of transportation technology brings many conveniences to people's travel. Cars are being updated and iterated at an increasingly rapid pace. In addition to the requirements of strong power, personalized appearance design and good human–vehicle interaction experience, they also put forward higher requirements in terms of green, safety and intelligence. With this background, unmanned driving technology has broad application prospects and is the mainstream trend of automobile industry development.

Development of unmanned driving technology abroad

The research on unmanned driving cars in developed Western countries began in the 1970s and has made great breakthroughs in feasibility and practicality. However, due to the complexity of the expected objectives and the immature technical conditions, by the end of the 1980s and the beginning of the 1990s, countries had separated themselves from the research projects of unmanned driving vehicles and were beginning to focus on the research of auxiliary driving projects for civilian vehicles on expressways. However, the unmanned driving cars in this period are semi-automatic cars, and there is a big gap between them and the real unmanned driving cars.

Until 1999, the unmanned driving vehicle developed by the Carnegie Mellon University successfully crossed the eastern and western parts of the United States. On the 5000 km intercontinental highway, the vehicle traveled more than 96% of the distance autonomously at a speed of 50–60 km/h. The unmanned driving vehicle project was declared a success.

In 2000, Toyota Motor Corporation developed an unmanned driving bus. Road guidance, rear-end collision prevention, fleet driving, operation management and other parts constitute an automatic driving system. In 2007, Germany introduced the Lux unmanned driving car, which was transformed from ordinary cars. It uses laser sensing technology, intelligent computer and global locator and can handle complex road conditions and drive automatically in urban road systems.

In 2010, Rogas, a professor at the Free University of Berlin in Germany, led the team to transform a Volkswagen Passat. Finally, an unmanned driving car was developed. Even in an underground tunnel, the car could use technologies and equipment such as cameras, laser scanners, thermal sensors, as well as satellite navigation to accurately identify other people and cars on the road and adjust the driving state of the car with traffic lights.

For the purpose of better adopting a more scientific and reasonable driving strategy according to the road conditions, unmanned driving cars usually need to build 3D images in the in-car computer, formulate scientific and reasonable driving routes for cars by analyzing the road conditions, vehicle positions and other data, and provide passengers or controllers with the estimated arrival time.

In 2010, London Heathrow Airport applied an unmanned driving car called "ULTra," which was jointly developed by Bristol University and Advanced Transportation Systems Company, but it had to be driven on special roads.

The "Cycab" unmanned driving car developed by France's INRIA company is relatively mature. The car uses advanced GPS global positioning technology and is equipped with a touch screen. Passengers or controllers can plan their driving routes by using the touch screen. Laser sensors, like human eyes, can help cars avoid roadblocks. At the same time, dual-lens cameras are used to identify road signs accurately. With the help of the Internet of Things and the mobile Internet, vehicles and vehicles, vehicles and roads, and vehicles and people can interact to promote the free flow and sharing of traffic information, relieve traffic congestion and increase the capacity of traffic networks.

Development of unmanned driving technology in China

In China, the National University of Defense Technology developed the first intelligent car in 1989; in 1992, the National University of Defense Technology developed the first truly unmanned driving car; hence, the research and development of unmanned driving car technology in China officially started and entered the exploration stage.

The CyberC3 smart car, an urban unmanned driving car project led by Shanghai Jiaotong University, mainly runs on unstructured roads such as urban non-main roads (road types and environmental backgrounds are complex, and lane lines and road boundaries are unclear), with an average speed of less than 10 km/h, and can realize automatic positioning, navigation, driving, obstacle avoidance, interaction and so on.

Professor Zheng Nanning of Xi'an Jiaotong University set up the unmanned intelligent vehicle project at the end of 2001. In 2002, the unmanned driving car Siyuan No. 1 was launched. In 2005, Siyuan No. 1 successfully completed the campus road environment test. After that, the project team tried to get the Siyuan No. 1 smart car out of the school gate, so that they formulated the "New Silk Road Challenge" plan to make Siyuan No. 1 drive independently from Xi'an to Dunhuang. However, during the actual test, it was found that Siyuan No. 1 was difficult to adapt to the real traffic environment. After more than 10 years of research, Siyuan No. 1 has gradually completed a major breakthrough from specific road sections to complex road sections, from straight driving to overtaking at turning, and from 10–15 km/h to 70–80 km/h.

In 2011, FAW Hongqi HQ3 unmanned driving car completed 286 kilometers of road tests; in 2015, the Baidu unmanned driving car completed the automatic driving test of Beijing open expressway; in 2016, Chang'an's unmanned driving car completed a 2,000 kilometer super unmanned driving test, marking the gradual maturity of China's unmanned driving technology.

With the rapid development of unmanned driving technology, many other new technologies have emerged. According to Thomson Reuters's Intellectual Property and Technology Report, 22,000 patents related to unmanned driving technologies appeared from 2010 to 2015, many of which have been put into use. Especially with the support of deep learning algorithms and cloud service technology, the research and development process of unmanned driving technology is getting faster and faster.

Commercial application prospect of unmanned driving in the world

Because unmanned vehicles need to be equipped with radar, camera and artificial intelligence systems, the early manufacturing cost will be relatively high, and naturally in turn the prices will be higher and unaffordable for ordinary consumers. As a result, some special industries and groups will be the first to use unmanned vehicles, such as the express delivery industry, industrial enterprises, taxis, industries serving the elderly or the disabled.

Public transport

In the future, the public transportation industry will use unmanned vehicles on a large scale. According to Baidu's plan, Baidu will carry out the commercial promotion of unmanned vehicles in a few years and plans to put them into trial operation in domestic cities first. At present, the Baidu unmanned vehicle has been approved by several local regulatory authorities and will be put into trial operation on a predetermined line. In the near future, the Baidu unmanned vehicle will surely realize mass production. In order to promote unmanned vehicles, some cities plan to designate special blocks for unmanned vehicles. There will be no parallel situation of manual vehicles and unmanned vehicles in these blocks. Unmanned driving taxis and shared travel vehicles will assume the responsibility of providing all transportation services for users. In order to create a good operating environment for unmanned driving vehicles, the urban planning department will carry out regional optimization.

The University of Texas at Austin has conducted a study on shared automatic vehicles (SAVs). The results show that one shared SAV can replace 11 conventional vehicles and the operating mileage can be increased by at least 10%, which means that with the popularization and application of SAVs, traffic congestion can be effectively alleviated, environmental degradation can be effectively controlled, and with convenient use, SAVs will become the preferred mode of transportation for people.

Express vehicles and industrial applications

Unmanned vehicles will also be widely used in the express delivery industry and enter the field of lined trucks. With the rapid development of Internet e-commerce, express delivery companies have risen rapidly. Consumers always hope to receive goods in the shortest possible time when shopping online, especially food products such as fresh fruits, and hope that express delivery companies can provide door-to-door service within several hours. According to the data provided by the Ministry of Commerce, in the first half of 2018, the sales volume of China's e-commerce industry reached 4.08 trillion yuan, and the total amount of express parcels exceeded the business volume of the whole year of 2015. Many e-commerce companies promised to deliver them on the same day of purchasing, which further promoted the development of electric vehicle and truck express delivery.

The increase in the number of electric vehicles and trucks has increased the number of traffic accidents to a certain extent. According to the survey, in the United States, truck mileage accounts for 5.6% of the total mileage of motor vehicles, but truck-caused traffic deaths account for 9.5% of traffic deaths. Generally speaking, the production cost for a large truck is more than US$150,000. If cameras and sensors are installed, the production cost of trucks will be even higher. Comparatively speaking, the production cost of small cars is relatively low. Therefore, due to cost constraints, it is difficult to realize the large-scale application of unmanned driving trucks in the early days.

The elderly and the disabled

At present, unmanned vehicles have been widely used among the elderly and the disabled. Due to their physical conditions, both the elderly and the disabled face the problem of inconvenience in getting around. The use of unmanned driving vehicles can help these two groups solve their travel problems.

It is predicted that by 2050, the elderly population in the United States will exceed 80 million, accounting for more than 20% of the total population, and one-third of them will face travel difficulties. This is also the case in China. It is estimated that by 2050, the proportion of China's elderly population in the total population will reach 33%. In Japan, it is estimated that by 2060, the proportion of the elderly population in the total population will reach 40%. At the same time, the scale of the disabled population is also very large. For example, there are about 53 million disabled people in the United States, accounting for 22% of the adult population. Among American adults, about 13% have travel disabilities and 4.6% have visual disabilities.

The disabled and the elderly provide a broad market for the promotion and use of unmanned vehicles. Both groups pursue independence and hope to travel freely. Unmanned vehicles can just meet their needs, allowing them to live independently and maintain a positive and optimistic attitude towards life.

The world's leading unmanned driving R&D enterprise

In recent years, the development of the Internet, artificial intelligence and other technologies have laid a technical foundation for the landing of unmanned driving cars. The world's leading Internet companies and auto giants have built certain competition barriers in the research and development of unmanned driving cars by virtue of their accumulated technological advantages in the field of unmanned driving cars.

Tesla: Plans to achieve "full unmanned driving"

Tesla, an electric vehicle manufacturer, has a leading edge in the fields of driver assistance technology and unmanned driving technology. Elon Musk, CEO of the company, believes that there is vast scope for development in the field of completely unmanned technology. He believes that completely unmanned driving technology can be realized in 2–3 years, while regulatory approval will take 1–5 years. In October 2015, Tesla installed Autopilot software on Model S, which enabled the vehicle to realize automatic steering, lane change and parking. In the summer of 2016, Tesla was criticized after the first traffic death in Autopilot, but Autopilot itself found no safety defects.

After the accident, Tesla cut off its relationship with Mobileye. After that, Tesla began to strengthen its control over the development of radar and camera systems and promised the public to provide semi-unmanned driving and unmanned driving services. Tesla has received 400,000 orders for Model 3. At the same time, Tesla also refused to cooperate with Uber to develop unmanned vehicles.

Since October 2016, all cars produced by Tesla have been equipped with a new sensor and computer software package, Autopilot Hardware 2. When the software matures, cars will be able to realize completely unmanned driving. The system replaces Mobileye's EyeQ3 with Nvidia's DrivePX2, and users must pay for activation if they want to enjoy the completely unmanned function. According to user feedback, the initial application effect of Autopilot 2.0 software was not good, but then the system was updated and improved.

Elon Musk continued its previous style, promised the public a positive timetable for unmanned driving, and released the feature before the end of 2017. The company overturned its previous data collection strategy and used customers' car cameras to collect video information and create a new system. Tesla's unmanned driving user agreement also stipulates that users can only trade on Tesla's network if they want to make profits by sharing vehicles. In addition, Tesla also acquired SolarCity in order to create a complete sustainable transportation ecosystem.

Volvo: Plans to achieve automatic driving by 2021

Volvo has made great progress in the field of self-driving buses. Volvo enjoys a high reputation in the field of safety technology innovation. The technology related to self-driving vehicles is called "intelligent safety" in order to use these functions to reduce the death rate of Volvo vehicles to zero. Previously, Volvo successfully provided XC90SUV with self-driving functions to 100 Swedish customers in 2017, although there were many restrictions in terms of self-driving area, time and conditions.

Volvo said that if the vehicle has an accident while driving automatically, Volvo would take full responsibility and announced that it would extend the pilot program of driving automatically to the United States and China. Volvo keeps up with the development pace of competitors such as BMW and will realize the all-round deployment of self-driving cars.

While keeping up with its competitors, Volvo is also actively looking for partners to set up Zenuity, an autonomous driving joint venture company, in cooperation with Sweden's Autoliv. It plans to take the lead in commercializing the driving assistance system and provide it to other automobile manufacturers.

Baidu plans to divest the self-driving car business and achieve mass production

Starting from 2015, Baidu has conducted public tests on unmanned driving car technology. In November 2016, Baidu invited the public to take electric and self-made unmanned driving cars to conduct an experience test on unmanned driving car technology, which lasted for a week. At the same time, Baidu also obtained an autonomous test license for California unmanned driving cars. In June 2016, Baidu announced that it would realize mass production of self-driving cars within five years. To this end, Baidu set up an AI research laboratory in Silicon Valley. In September 2018, Baidu launched a fund project for developing unmanned driving cars with a total value of US$1.5 billion. Baidu headquarters plans to produce a limited number of unmanned driving cars and plans to mass-produce unmanned driving cars by 2021.

Audi founded autopilot subsidiary

Audi has released a number of self-driving prototype vehicles based on A7 and RS7 models, some of which have already being tested for consumers. At the end of July 2016, Audi set up its own subsidiary, SDS, dedicated to the development of autonomous driving technology. Through this company, Audi joined the competition in the field of autonomous driving. In April 2017, Audi hired the former head of Tesla's automatic navigation program as CTO of its automatic driving department, demonstrating Audi's determination to enter the unmanned driving field.

According to Audi's development plan, the self-driving technology in A8 flagship sedan will be commercialized. The Level 3 self-driving function is called "self-driving under specific conditions," and its commercial application needs to be approved by the regulatory authorities. The entry of Audi, a luxury car brand owned by Volkswagen, into the field of automatic driving is of great significance.

Audi, Daimler and BMW have formed a consortium and spent US$3.1 billion to purchase the assets of Nokia HERE map precision positioning. In recent years, HERE has accelerated its plan to standardize the data collection and transmission of vehicle sensors.

Microsoft: Seeking cooperation with automobile manufacturers

Microsoft began to get involved in the research of self-driving cars. In the initial stage, Microsoft's strategy was to collaborate. For example, in November 2015, Microsoft and Volvo reached a deal to use its HoloLens technology to cooperate with Volvo in the research and development of self-driving cars.

In March 2016, Microsoft announced the expansion of its five-year partnership with Toyota to provide strong support for Toyota's research in robotics, autonomous driving, AI and other fields. As of June 2016, Microsoft's strategy remained to provide technical support to cooperative companies and it had yet to launch its own research and development strategy. Driven by the auto customer business, Microsoft's own Azure cloud business has achieved rapid growth. According to relevant reports, Microsoft is also involved in the HERE HD map service previously held by BMW, Daimler and Volkswagen and holds a certain stake.

Toyota's "guardian angel"

In 2014, Toyota issued a statement claiming that unmanned driving cars will not be developed for safety. Toyota violated this statement and announced in 2015 that it would invest US$1 billion in the research and development of unmanned driving cars. It also established the Toyota Research Institute (TRI) for the research of unmanned driving technologies and hired professors and researchers from Stanford University and Massachusetts Institute of Technology and employees from Jay Bridge Robotics, an unmanned driving car company, to join the research institute. In April 2016, Toyota announced that it would cooperate with the University of Michigan—the third university it cooperated with—to jointly develop unmanned driving cars.

Toyota planned to distribute the research and development tasks of unmanned driving cars among the three universities, of which the University of Michigan was responsible for the research and development of completely unmanned driving cars, Stanford University was responsible for the research and development of some unmanned driving cars and Massachusetts Institute of Technology was responsible for the research of machine learning algorithms. In August 2016, Toyota increased its investment in various schools and invested US$22 million in the University of Michigan to promote research on robots and unmanned driving technologies.

Toyota planned to put "AI car function" on the road in 2021. TRI CEO Gill Pratt has always been supportive of the "guardian angel" system, which will only supervise and intervene in the driver's behavior when the human driver is about to encounter danger or perform wrong operations. At present, TPI is studying the second system, Chauffeur, which will be deployed and applied after Guardian for Level 4 and Level 5 unmanned driving. In March 2017, the Institute showed the public the latest independent research and development platform.

Technical route: Key technologies of unmanned driving industry

Key components of unmanned driving technology

Intelligent vehicles based on artificial intelligence technology have obvious advantages in operability and human–computer interaction and are the mainstream development trend of the automobile industry. With this background, unmanned driving technology has seen a period of rapid development. With the active exploration of universities, scientific research institutions, scientific and technological enterprises and other parties, a large number of unmanned driving car projects have emerged.

According to the report "Analysis Report on Development Prospect Forecast and Investment Strategic Planning of Unmanned Driving Car Industry," released by Prospective Industry Research Institute, it is estimated that in 2035, the global unmanned driving market will reach 600 billion yuan and China's domestic market will be close to 150 billion yuan if the average unmanned driving system costs 50,000 yuan per vehicle. In order to promote the rapid development of the unmanned driving industry, many governments are speeding up the study of relevant laws and regulations.

Onboard sensors enable unmanned driving cars to know the running state of the cars in real time. At the same time, combined with radar, computer vision and other technologies, they can accurately sense the external environment, such as real-time road conditions. Autonomous driving of cars is mainly achieved through artificial intelligence algorithms that simulate human thinking and decision-making processes.

Unmanned driving technology itself is a huge and complex intelligent system, which realizes the organic integration of multiple fields and disciplines. Specifically, the key components of unmanned driving technology include the following:

Automobile architecture

The automobile architecture builds the skeleton for the automobile system and defines the organization principles, integration methods and supporting programs of the software and hardware of the unmanned driving automobile system.

Perception and recognition of the external environment

Artificial intelligence system is data-driven, and unmanned driving vehicle system is no exception. An onboard sensor based on external environment perception and recognition technology is the core means for unmanned driving vehicles to sense the environment and master real-time road condition information. With the blessing of external environment perception and recognition technology, unmanned driving cars can enable onboard intelligent systems to obtain the relative position, distance, speed and other information between road objects (such as pedestrians, cars and obstacles) in real time, providing necessary support for car decision-making and instruction execution.

Positioning and navigation system

In the process of driving an unmanned driving car, the positioning and navigation system will provide a variety of information such as the position, speed and direction of the car, which is the basic software of the unmanned driving car. After years of development, the positioning and navigation technology system has been continuously improved. A variety of positioning and navigation technologies have emerged, such as satellite navigation technology, road sign positioning technology, visual positioning technology, track reckoning technology, map matching technology, as well as inertial navigation technology. Certainly, in practical application scenarios, two or more positioning and navigation technologies are often applied simultaneously in order to improve navigation efficiency and accuracy.

Path planning

Path planning technology in the field of unmanned vehicles refers to the intelligent system of unmanned driving vehicles that designs a safe and efficient driving route between a given starting point and destination by analyzing data such as road conditions, vehicle speed, driving distance, as well as a number of signal lights. It requires the application of statistics, big data, cloud computing and other technologies.

In the aspect of path analysis, when driving a car manually, the driver can make flexible decisions in combination with real-time road conditions. In the unmanned driving state, the intelligent control system needs to use a high-precision three-dimensional road condition model to efficiently calculate the relative position, distance, speed and other information of the car and surrounding things, thus realizing safe driving.

The road condition-thinking model needs to be adjusted in real time. Massive data will be involved in this process. GPU or distributed neural network algorithm must be used to process the data efficiently. It should be pointed out that in order to update the high-precision three-dimensional road condition map in real time, it is necessary to realize data interaction and sharing among intelligent systems of self-driving vehicles in the region. In order to obtain richer and more diversified road condition information, software and hardware equipment such as laser ranging radar, in-vehicle inertial radar and various sensors need to be installed in self-driving vehicles.

In the aspect of path planning, path planning not only needs a high-precision three-dimensional road map but also has a high dependence on high-precision positioning technology. Unmanned driving cars must be able to sense and identify their own positions in real time, implement the optimal route scheme set by the intelligent system, obey the traffic order, avoid obstacles in time, adhere to human safety as the first priority and complete driving tasks safely and efficiently.

The path planning function mainly includes three main points:

(1) Take full account of the overall environment for lane planning and design the optimal route between the starting point and the destination according to the individual needs of passengers.
(2) Integrate lane information by means of navigation, sensors, intelligent algorithms and other means and tools, and select the optimal driving lane.
(3) Understand lane information, make full use of deep learning algorithm and analyze the specific requirements of lanes on speed, steering and other aspects so that the intelligent system can make more scientific and reasonable decisions when controlling the driving of vehicles.

Vehicle control

On the premise of obtaining environmental information, the car should maintain a stable running state through vehicle control technology and an automatic steering control system. During the specific running, the vehicle control technology can control the running speed and distance of the car and can also enable the car to complete driving operations such as overtaking and lane changing. In order to realize these diversified functions, control and operating systems need to be installed on unmanned driving vehicles, such as a satellite navigation system, adaptive cruise control system, emergency braking system, lane departure system, as well as automatic parking system.

(1) **Emergency braking and satellite navigation system:** In case of emergency, the braking system is immediately activated to deal with it in order to ensure that the driverless car is under the effective monitoring of people.

(2) **Adaptive cruise control system:** Ensure a safe distance between the unmanned driving car and the vehicle in front of it so that the car can run safely on the road.

(3) **Lane departure detection system:** To avoid misrouting the car, ensure that the car can follow the guidance of road signs and sounds and quickly adjust the direction when the car shows signs of drifting out of the lane.

(4) **Automatic parking system:** Ensure that the unmanned driving car can automatically park in the correct position and drive out safely.

Perception layer: Collecting environment and driving information

Unmanned cars make full use of the cooperation between software and hardware facilities, including radar, sensors, satellite navigation systems, as well as artificial intelligence computing modules, to drive autonomously without unmanned intervention. Unmanned driving cars will be equipped with a large number of onboard sensors, which is equivalent to allowing cars to have countless eyes, and their safety and reliability are significantly higher than those of ordinary cars.

In the process of unmanned driving, the most important thing is to implement unmanned driving operations on the basis of perceiving the environment. This technology plays a fundamental supporting role in unmanned driving. In addition to environmental perception, it should also be combined with the application of vehicle control technology. In other words, the development of unmanned driving depends on the support of environmental perception and vehicle control technology.

In a relatively perfect unmanned driving system, the information collection network collects the information around the car, then the intelligent algorithm formulates the driving scheme and then the intelligent car-driving controller is used to drive the car to the destination.

The sensing layer is an important channel for unmanned driving cars to obtain external information. At present, the intelligent sensing system for unmanned driving cars to sense the external environment mainly includes three components: vision sensor, laser radar and millimeter-wave radar. Navigation through visual sensors is also called visual navigation. Vehicles will obtain local images of the road-surrounding environment through cameras and then use image recognition and other technologies to realize vehicle positioning and surrounding environment detection.

Laser radar enables unmanned driving vehicles to monitor dynamic obstacles in real time, has strong anti-light interference capability and extremely high detection accuracy and can provide strong support for dynamic obstacle monitoring and motion state evaluation. Laser radar can obtain many surrounding environment parameters such as line number, accuracy, point density, scanning frequency, detection distance, horizontal and vertical viewing angle. It can provide basic information such as position and distance, and at the same time, it can also feed back the density information of the target object so that the algorithm can obtain its reflectivity, which is helpful for in-depth analysis.

A millimeter-wave radar has a frequency range of 30–300 GHz, and the low-frequency band is quite similar to the centimeter band, which can image all the time; a high-frequency band can give full play to the advantages of the high resolution of the infrared wave. The millimeter-wave radar and laser radar follow the same detection principle. They both use the reflection of radar waves by an object to obtain relevant data of target objects an object. However, millimeter-wave radar technology is more mature and has certain advantages in penetration and cost, but the short board is also more prominent. For example, the frequency band has too much influence on the detection distance, it is difficult to perceive pedestrians and it is impossible to realize fine identification of targets.

It is the mainstream trend of unmanned driving car exploration projects to improve the car's perception of its own running state and the surrounding environment through the comprehensive use of a variety of intelligent sensing systems. Generally speaking, the unmanned driving process includes two steps: the first step is to obtain environmental information by using radar and other technologies; the second step is to control the brake system and steering system of the car on the basis of judging the environment to ensure that the car can run safely and stably on the road. By combining the two modules and exerting the synergy between them, the whole process of unmanned driving can be completed.

Using the environment perception technology, the car can capture the relevant information of the current location, roads and surrounding vehicles and obstacles, and send the information content to the onboard center computer, so as to grasp the situation on the way, help the car to formulate and adjust the driving route, and finally drive the car to the destination. Generally speaking, cars can know their own location and surrounding object information through environmental perception technology, judge the attributes of these objects and their distance from themselves, and master the current environmental information from the macro level.

At present, in terms of environmental perception, unmanned driving application technologies mainly include visual sensing, laser sensing and microwave sensing technologies. With the help of these technical means, automobile sensors, in-vehicle communication systems and radar systems can capture environmental information, present two-dimensional or three-dimensional images by using information technology, and send the acquired information to the information processing terminal, and technicians process the three-dimensional images to sense and judge the real-time environment in which the automobile is located. Not only that, different vehicles can also connect information and collect real-time environment and driving information of different vehicles. The application of remote communication technology and Li Yongle wireless network technology in the field of unmanned driving has effectively improved the environmental perception ability of automobiles and promoted the development of unmanned driving as a whole.

Decision-making layer: Route planning and real-time navigation

Unmanned driving decision-making level is responsible for route planning and real-time navigation, which mainly involves high-precision maps, also known as "high-definition digital maps." Unmanned driving cars do not use ordinary navigation maps. They are called "high-precision maps" because they differ significantly from ordinary maps in terms of accuracy and information.

Ordinary maps are relatively rough—because our human cognitive ability is enough to "brain supplement," we can know the direction of the road through the representation of simple two-dimensional lines, and the intersection of lines represents the crossroads—which makes it too difficult for current machines to "brain supplement." The accuracy of high-definition digital maps is generally centimeter level, and it is three-dimensional, including driving auxiliary information such as lane lines and coordinate positions of surrounding facilities.

Another important difference of unmanned high-precision maps compared to the electronic maps currently used by humans is that the high-precision maps capture the intensity of reflections from road LiDAR, a road feature that is of little value to human drivers but significant to "artificial intelligence drivers". Its slow and small variation makes it an ideal feature value to help optical radar locate unmanned driving vehicles. By comparing the information obtained by optical radar scanning with the known high-precision map information, the current vehicle position can be determined.

Unmanned driving decision-making systems need not only independent "intelligent vehicles" but also the support of "intelligent transportation systems," such as V2V. In addition to high-precision maps, another technology supporting path planning is V2X, which is generally believed to be developed on the basis of V2I. V2X means to form an "Internet of Things" between vehicles and the environment, including a series of communication systems such as car-to-car, car-to-infrastructure and car-to-pedestrian.

If the vehicle can directly "get," not just "see" the information of the signal lamp, it can ensure that it will never run the red light. Here "get" means, for example, when the sensor is still "invisible" 100 meters away from the traffic light, the signal light will actively "tell" the vehicle its own signal status and change duration and the unmanned driving vehicle does not need to directly "see" the contents of the signal light. In addition, if the driving intention of the surrounding vehicles can be known in advance, accidents can be avoided to a great extent.

With high-precision digital maps and V2X communication networks, the system can apply search algorithms to evaluate the costs of various driving behaviors, including waiting time for signal lights, road congestion, road maintenance, etc., so as to obtain the best driving path.

Executive layer: Accurately control the operation of the car

The executive layer is also the bottom control system, which is responsible for the specific operations of braking, accelerating and steering of the car. Engineers control the steering wheel and throttle through a special "wire control device" to replace the hands and feet of human drivers and configure a subsystem composed of multiple processors to control the mechanical system of the car stably and accurately.

The vehicle driving controller is the core module to realize vehicle control and automatic driving. Its functions include two types: on the one hand, the vehicle driving parameters are adjusted in combination with the dynamic performance of the automatic driving vehicle and the performance of onboard sensors to ensure safe, efficient and low-energy driving tasks; on the other hand, based on the dynamic performance and sensor recognition performance of unmanned driving vehicles, it allows the car to think and make decisions like a driver with years of driving experience, adjusting the driving state according to real-time road conditions and taking into account various factors such as safety, economy, comfort, ethics and morality, keeping the vehicle in harmony with other vehicles and pedestrians while giving passengers a good travel experience.

Accurate vehicle control is the key point of automatic driving, and the basic principle of vehicle control is to ensure the safety of people and vehicles, which obviously requires strong support from advanced braking systems. When a car is involved in an accident, under the instruction of the intelligent driving controller, the braking system can make accurate and real-time braking to avoid traffic accidents or reduce the negative impact of accidents. After being equipped with a powerful braking system, intelligent driving vehicles need more intelligent control algorithms, which are the main means to endow the braking system with higher control accuracy and robustness.

At this stage, almost all self-driving car projects will use machine learning and other technologies to enable cars to learn and simulate the human driving experience and then combine real-time analysis of intelligent systems to control cars. It is difficult for high-speed cars to avoid emergencies. However, if unmanned driving cars have emergency handling capability, risks can be effectively controlled. Moreover, unlike humans, intelligent systems will not be nervous and flustered when handling emergencies and can make rational and critical decisions. Of course, the premise of all this is to have a powerful "intelligent brain".

Safety is the first issue that unmanned driving cars need to consider. In the manual driving state, there are certain differences in drivers' driving skills, psychological quality, emergency handling ability, as well as operating habits. In the case of emergencies, differentiated countermeasures can be taken, whereas unmanned driving cars have no feelings, and ensuring safety should be the first priority. Most unmanned driving projects are still in the experimental stage and have not yet been verified by the market. Smart cars in the market are mainly semi-automatic driving cars that provide driving assistance services. How to ensure the ride experience of unmanned driving cars in the future is an important topic.

In the future, mature artificial intelligence will be able to analyze the surrounding environment and make decisions like people. When analyzing the driving strategy in a specific scene, it is not necessary to re-analyze it every time. We can use the previous strategy of the vehicle to deal with the scene to control the vehicle or imitate the vehicle in front of us. The impact on the automobile industry will be subversive, and the production and life of human beings will also undergo major changes.

Through the division of labor and cooperation among the above three systems of perception, decision-making and execution, and the clear responsibility to control the operation of the car, the unmanned driving car can have the theoretical "driving" conditions. However, as Woody Lipson and Melba Kuman, authors of *Unmanned Driving*, pointed out, "Although this technology is almost ready, the social environment on which this unique technology depends may not be ready yet." For example, relevant legislation lags behind. However, due to the advantages of efficiency and safety, we have reason to believe that the era of unmanned driving will eventually come.

Chapter 3

From Unmanned Driving to Intelligent Transportation

Intelligent transportation system driven by unmanned driving technology

Development and current situation of the intelligent transportation system in China

Urbanization is accelerating day by day, and people's travel needs are becoming more diverse and personalized. Therefore, how to solve traffic problems such as traffic congestion and frequent accidents has become an important topic in urban construction. The intelligent transportation system, which integrates a variety of advanced technologies, provides new ideas and means for promoting the quality and efficiency of transportation. Its great potential value in solving traffic congestion, inefficient utilization of resources and blocked information circulation is especially worthy of our attention. Among many subsystems of intelligent transportation systems, an unmanned driving system undertakes the important task of vehicle control and management, which has a direct impact on the continuous and stable operation of intelligent transportation systems.

Basic concepts of an intelligent transportation system

An intelligent transportation system (ITS) is a typical cross-domain, covering many fields such as transportation, machinery, electronic information, network and communication. Advanced technologies such as sensor technology, computer technology, information technology, communication technology, automatic control technology, unmanned driving technology and image processing technology are integrated and applied to the transportation management system. The comprehensive transportation and management system with wide coverage, real time, high precision and high efficiency can provide strong support for transportation services.

An intelligent transportation system includes a safety system, traffic management system, vehicle control system, travel demand system, electronic toll collection system, operation management system, operating vehicle operation system, public transportation operation system and other components.

The collection, processing, publishing, exchange, analysis and application of information are the key to the function of an intelligent transportation system. An intelligent transportation system promotes the transformation and upgrading of traditional transportation mode through the application of advanced technology, making transportation service more humanized, personalized and intelligent and creating a better travel experience for the public, which is a direct embodiment of science and technology making life better.

An intelligent transportation system, especially a highway intelligent transportation system, is the key content of government layout in various countries. In the future, cars can realize assisted driving or even unmanned driving under the control of their own intelligent control systems. Real-time monitoring of road conditions is carried out through rich and diversified intelligent detection equipment and systems so as to allocate traffic facilities resources more efficiently. In addition, there are intelligent dispatching systems that specifically serve operating vehicles and intelligent auxiliary systems that guide people to travel intelligently.

Development status of the intelligent transportation system in China

With the support of an information chain, intelligent transportation systems can realize real-time and efficient data circulation. Sensors, monitoring, positioning systems and other equipment are responsible for obtaining data. Data communication is carried out by means of mobile communication, satellite communication, etc. The data are identified, screened, calculated and processed by the central processing unit of the above subsystem and then published on the Internet and other channels. Information feedback and automatic control are used for route planning, traffic signal control, ramp control, etc.

Although China's intelligent transportation system has been developing for a short period of time and is still in the primary stage of development, its momentum is quite rapid and it has received strong support from the government, universities and enterprises. For example, the Ministry of Communications has issued the "Intelligent Transportation Development Strategy for Transportation Industry (2012–2020)," and many cities have basically realized the popularization of electronic toll collection systems and urban signal control systems.

The research fields of China's intelligent transportation system include traffic management system, traffic supervision system, traffic guidance system, electronic toll collection system, traffic signal control and command system, traffic information dynamic display system, public transportation operation command and dispatch system, etc.

The intelligent transportation system has received strong support from the capital. According to the data released by ITS114, in 2016, there were 932 urban intelligent transportation projects in China (all of which have been opened for bidding), with a scale of 15.17 billion yuan. Compared with 2015, the number of projects with a budget of 10 million yuan increased by 58.7% and the scale increased by 55.9%. The year 2017 saw further growth in the intelligent transportation market. Intelligent transportation project monitoring data show that in 2017, the number of urban intelligent transportation projects with a budget of 10 million yuan nationwide was 1,087, with market size of about 19.008 billion yuan. According to data released by ITS114, by the end of December 2017, China's urban intelligent transportation market had won 18 billion yuan, with total market size of 3.67 billion projects.

Problems and countermeasures of intelligent transportation in China

Problems in the intelligent transportation system in China

(1) From the perspective of departmental cooperation, various departments lack communication and interaction in the process of promoting

the development of intelligent transportation systems and the problems of repeated construction and waste of resources are more serious.

(2) Technically, although China has made great progress in the field of intelligent transportation technology, many technologies are still limited to theoretical and experimental levels. Taking the environment perception technology as an example, when the vehicle speed changes greatly in the prior art, the problem of image distortion will occur, and the ability to resist external environment interference needs to be improved. Although radar detection can solve the problem of external environment interference, it has certain visual blind areas, and its practical application is greatly limited.

(3) In terms of cost, although the cost of collecting data through cameras is low, the external environment has a serious impact, image distortion is difficult to be solved effectively, which leads to decision-making mistakes of self-driving vehicles and has high safety risks. Although laser radar or millimeter-wave radar can solve this problem to a certain extent, it is difficult to be applied in self-driving vehicles on a large scale due to the high cost.

Development countermeasures of the intelligent transportation system in China

(1) Establish a sound coordination and organization mechanism. The communication and interaction among organizations such as highways, railways and scientific research institutions are blocked, and there is a serious problem of information asymmetry, which makes it difficult to coordinate with each other. Obviously, it is extremely unfavorable for China to seize the first opportunity in the intelligent transportation outlet, and it will cause a great waste of resources. In the future, the Chinese government should give full play to its leading role in the development of intelligent transportation, speed up the introduction of intelligent transportation development strategies and plans, promote exchanges and cooperation between transportation departments, universities, scientific research institutions and enterprises and make the development of intelligent transportation to a new level with the efforts of all parties.

(2) Establish and improve the training system of intelligent transportation talents. Talent is a necessary resource for the development of intelligent transportation. However, at present, the level of educational talent

training in China is relatively low, with excessive emphasis on theoretical education, neglect of skill training, and insufficient innovation ability of talents. In order to provide sufficient talent support for the development of intelligent transportation, the Chinese government needs to speed up the establishment and improvement of intelligent transportation personnel training system, invest more resources to support personnel training and guide colleges and universities to actively innovate the traditional education model, from focusing on training standardized academic talents to focusing on training diversified applied talents, so as to give full play to the leading role of outstanding talents in the development of intelligent transportation.

(3) Encourage technological innovation. Innovation is an important driving force for economic and social development. Technological innovation produces a very positive impact on solving the pain points of intelligent transportation development and improving the value creation ability of intelligent transportation products and services. Consequently, the Chinese government should encourage technological innovation in the field of intelligent transportation, enhance the transformation of scientific research achievements and offer a steady stream of endogenous power for the development of intelligent transportation.

Development trend of the intelligent transportation system in China

China's intelligent transportation system is developing rapidly, attracting a large number of entrepreneurs and enterprises to compete for layout. In the long run, the development of intelligent transportation systems should take human safety as the first priority, devote itself to creating a higher level of high-quality service for people, attach importance to personnel training and technological innovation, ensure transportation safety, improve efficiency and reduce costs. The development of key technologies such as big data, cloud computing, unmanned driving, sensors and traffic simulation should be emphasized.

Unmanned driving technology is an important supporting technology of intelligent transportation systems. It involves many technologies such as environmental perception, intelligent decision-making, automatic control, coordination between people, vehicles and roads. It has extremely high application value in the construction of intelligent transportation systems. It can be said that only when unmanned driving technology is mature can we truly usher in the era of intelligent transportation.

It is necessary to make full use of subsystems such as the vehicle information service system, traffic dynamic simulation system, traffic flow dispatching control, electronic toll collection system, as well as emergency rescue system for the realization of management and service functions of the intelligent transportation system, promote the integration and application of advanced technologies such as environmental perception, automatic control and intelligent decision-making, promote the large-scale application of intelligent transportation systems in cities and accumulate valuable practical experience for the development of intelligent transportation systems.

To promote the development of intelligent transportation systems with unmanned driving technology as a breakthrough, we need to attach great importance to the standardization and regulation of intelligent transportation systems, and to promote the coordinated development of intelligent transportation systems in the fields of highways, railroads, waterways, airways and pipelines, we need to introduce unified technical and application standards, improve the compatibility of intelligent transportation systems in various regions, levels and sectors, and reduce the waste of resources caused by duplicate construction and give full play to the scale effect.

The development of unmanned driving technology and intelligent transportation systems requires the active participation of all parties. Indeed, the government should play a leading role in the field of transportation, but the power of the government alone is far from enough. It is particularly critical for dynamic and creative entrepreneurs and enterprises to actively participate. Of course, this requires the government to provide strong support in policies, funds and other aspects to create an excellent business environment for enterprises. Driven by the market, unmanned driving technology and intelligent transportation systems can mature in a shorter period of time.

Application of unmanned driving in the intelligent transportation field

Unmanned driving technology is an intelligent control technology for automobiles that endows automobiles with environmental perception, path planning and autonomous control capabilities. Key technologies include environmental perception technology, human–computer interaction technology, intelligent decision-making of automobiles, automatic control, etc. Visual sensors, laser radar, etc., are just like the eyes of a car, which can collect data such as the geographical location and surrounding environment of the car in real time. The central processing unit can carry out three-dimensional modeling according to these data to provide support for route planning, driving, obstacle avoidance, etc., of self-driving cars.

The mainstream unmanned driving car environment perception layer includes the Boss self-driving car environment perception system, the Google self-driving car environment perception system, the Junior self-driving car environment perception system and the Talos self-driving car environment perception system.

An intelligent transportation system takes human safety as the first essence, and in order to ensure human safety in all directions, cars and people need to interact, which requires the use of human–computer interaction technology. Human–computer interaction involves not only the interaction between the car and the people inside the car but also the interaction between the car and the people outside the car. Research on human interaction technology in the field of unmanned driving is currently focused on the interaction between vehicles and pedestrians. By constructing a communication mechanism that enables efficient and convenient interaction between vehicles and people, efficient coordination between people and vehicles can be realized. In the long run, self-driving cars will imitate human behavior patterns when making intelligent decisions in the future.

Efficient and convenient human–computer interaction can bring a better travel experience to users and has a very positive impact on promoting the marketization of unmanned driving. In the absence of human–computer interaction, it is difficult for cars to understand people's needs fully. Self-driving cars will carry out route planning, lane change, obstacle avoidance, parking, etc., through real-time analysis of massive data.

Vehicle intelligent decision-making is an important evaluation index of unmanned vehicle performance. The data obtained by sensors and other equipment will be processed by the processor, and the decision-making optimization will be realized by applying a data model and intelligent algorithm. Of course, this intelligent algorithm should have the ability of autonomous learning and self-improvement so as to meet the actual needs of self-driving cars in various driving scenes. Automatic control is the executor of decision-making instructions, allowing cars to make a series of actions, such as acceleration and deceleration, turning, as well as obstacle avoidance, that have a direct impact on people's travel experience.

In many traffic accidents, traffic accidents caused by human factors account for a high proportion because people will feel tired and have psychological fluctuations stimulated by external factors such as sound and image, thus causing human errors and threatening personal and property safety. However, the intelligent control system based on unmanned driving technology can remain objective and calm for a long time without fatigue and can effectively reduce the number of human traffic accidents.

An anti-lock braking system (ABS system) is one of the relatively mature unmanned driving systems, and it is widely used. Vehicles not equipped with an anti-lock braking system may have their tires locked after emergency braking, thus causing the car to skid. Experienced drivers can avoid tire locking by repeatedly pedaling on the brakes. However, most drivers are easily in a hurry in these few seconds, and there are many drivers who use the accelerator as the brake. However, when a car is installed with an anti-lock system, when it encounters an unexpected accident, effective measures can be taken thanks to the system's real-time monitoring of the tire status before the tire locks up, thereby reducing the possibility of traffic accidents.

A traction or stability control system is also an unmanned driving system that has been applied on a large scale. Compared with the anti-lock braking system, the system is more complex and can monitor the road condition, vehicle speed, driving direction, running state of key components and other information in real time. When it is found that the car may lose control and overturn, effective measures will be taken in time to ensure driving safety. Unmanned driving in the true sense can efficiently and safely enable the car to independently complete the tasks given by passengers or controllers.

The traffic information collection system, information processing and analysis system and information release system are intelligent transportation systems closely related to unmanned driving. Among them, the traffic information collection system is based on global satellite positioning (GPS) technology and various systems, including the infrared radar detection system; information processing and analysis systems are usually applied to GIS application systems, expert systems and other systems; an information publishing system is highly dependent on media technologies such as mobile Internet and mobile phone terminals.

Developed countries such as the United States and Japan, relying on their leading advantages in computer control, network technology, positioning and navigation, artificial intelligence and other fields, can take the lead in building intelligent transportation systems with unmanned driving systems as the core. Self-driving car projects have also emerged in large numbers, and many detours can be avoided in exploration and practice.

Influence of unmanned vehicles on urban traffic flow

In recent years, with the increasing number of urban population and private cars, the problem of urban traffic congestion is becoming more and more serious. In order to plan urban road networks properly and to make the scale and form of urban road construction more reasonable, people began to analyze urban traffic efficiency and the factors affecting it. Many factors affect traffic flow. What role does do unmanned vehicles play in it?

Unmanned vehicles are equipped with onboard sensors to collect environmental data around the vehicles. These sensors are mainly composed of cameras, global positioning systems, laser radar and other parts. At the same time, the intelligent processing module in the unmanned vehicle can effectively control the operating parameters of the unmanned vehicle, such as steering parameters and speed parameters, to ensure that the unmanned vehicle can run safely.

Specifically, this intelligent processing module is composed of a decision module and control module. All kinds of data can be obtained, including video image data collected by the camera, point cloud data collected by laser radar, position data collected by the global positioning system, steering data or speed data output by decision module, execution result data output by the control module, etc.

In many areas, traffic capacity is very limited due to the number of roads and other reasons. Unmanned vehicles realize automatic driving, which can reduce the distance between vehicles, ensure the safety of vehicles, reduce traffic accidents, increase road traffic capacity and improve road traffic capacity.

Analysis of influencing factors

Many factors affect the traffic capacity of motor vehicle lanes. Three factors are listed here, namely, the number of lines, the proportion of unmanned vehicles in all driving vehicles and the peak capacity of roads, so as to obtain their corresponding relationship.

Unmanned vehicles have no driver. If there is an emergency while driving, the driver's reaction time is close to 0 seconds. According to the data, the average driving speed of unmanned vehicles is much faster than that of manual driving. Therefore, the higher the proportion of unmanned vehicles in all driving vehicles, the stronger the road capacity. At the same time, the more road lines, the stronger the road capacity. In addition to these two factors, whether there are intersections on roads also has a great impact on road capacity. The more intersections there are, the worse the road capacity will be.

Traffic flow is not only affected by road capacity but also by other factors, such as geographical location, road network density, road service level, regional vehicle ownership, as well as traffic period. The following is an analysis of these five factors. The more prosperous the area where the road is located, the higher the road network density, the higher the road service level, the more vehicles in the area, and the greater the traffic flow when the traffic period is at the peak of travel.

Analysis of introducing unmanned vehicles into different road sections

Areas with different road network densities have different solutions. First, many factors affect road capacity. If the road has not fundamentally changed, the road capacity will be significantly affected as the proportion of unmanned vehicles continues to increase. In order to deeply understand this impact, some institutions have done relevant research, and the research results are as follows:

First, in smooth road sections, when the proportion of unmanned vehicles is less than 54%, with the increasing proportion of unmanned vehicles, the growth rate of road capacity will continue to slow down; when the proportion of unmanned vehicles is more than 54%, with the increasing proportion of unmanned vehicles, the growth rate of road capacity will accelerate. However, considering the manufacturing price of unmanned vehicles, unmanned vehicles are not suitable for being put on such roads.

Second, in general unobstructed road sections, when the proportion of unmanned vehicles is 40%, unmanned vehicles have the greatest impact on road capacity. As the proportion of unmanned vehicles continues to increase, this impact will become weaker and weaker. Therefore, unmanned vehicles can be introduced into this road section to relieve traffic pressure.

Finally, on congestion-prone roadways, the traffic capacity of the roadway is highest when the percentage of unmanned vehicles reaches 45%. With the increasing proportion, the traffic capacity of road sections declines. The reason for this phenomenon is that the maximum traffic volume of roads prevents the traffic volume from increasing. For such sections, traffic management departments can set up unmanned vehicle lanes to relieve traffic pressure.

Comparing the congested road sections with the actual map, it can be found that the town center has the highest traffic flow, especially at the intersections of the main roads with dense surrounding roads. Opening unmanned vehicle lanes on these road sections can effectively increase the traffic capacity of these road sections and solve the traffic congestion problem.

Intelligent traffic management mode based on unmanned driving

Deep integration of free travel and sharing mode

If self-driving cars want to replace human-driven cars, it is necessary not only to crack technical barriers such as the Internet of Things, big data, cloud computing, sensors and artificial intelligence, but also to make breakthroughs in urban planning adjustment, traffic rules improvement, supervision system construction and other management aspects. From the development practice of many industries, technology and management complement each other. Only when the two develop together can self-driving cars be popularized on a large scale.

Therefore, in exploring the traffic management mode matching self-driving cars, it is too late to explore when the unmanned driving technology is fully mature, and the backwardness in planning, construction and supervision will bring many restrictions to the development of technology.

For example, setting a higher threshold for self-driving cars to go on the road will make them unable to carry out road tests, which will bring great resistance to the development of unmanned driving technology.

Countries around the world have now recognized the important value of intelligent traffic management mode. For example, in August 2014, the Singapore government established the Singapore Autopilot Road Traffic Committee to provide guidance and assistance to the development of self-driving cars from the four dimensions of freight transportation, fixed routes, point-to-point transportation and public facilities operation:

(1) **Freight transportation:** Cargo transportation and delivery are completed through an automatic truck fleet.
(2) **Fixed routes:** These provide transportation services on public transportation lines within and between cities.
(3) **Point-to-point transportation:** This meets the needs of point-to-point travel and short-distance travel through locomotive sharing.
(4) **Public facilities operation:** It provides public services such as plant irrigation, garbage collection and road cleaning.

In December 2017, Beijing Municipal Transportation Commission, in conjunction with the Municipal Public Security Traffic Management Bureau, the Municipal Economic Information Commission and other departments, issued two guiding documents, "Guiding Opinions on Accelerating Road Testing of Self-driving Vehicles" and "Detailed Rules for the Implementation of Road Testing Management of Self-driving Vehicles," which undoubtedly had a very positive impact on the further development of technology and management mode of self-driving vehicles.

The establishment of traffic management mode should be based on people's travel mode. Intelligent transportation mode should highlight its humanization and intelligence and must also fully combine people's travel mode. From the perspective of the number of travel users, we can divide people's travel modes into two categories:

(1) **Free travel:** In the free travel mode, individual travelers have completely independent control and use rights of travel tools. Free use of travel tools and allocation of their internal space facilities can meet people's personalized travel needs.

(2) **Shared travel:** In the shared travel mode, two or more travelers use a travel tool together, which influences each other. The allocation of internal space facilities is restricted to a certain extent, and certain privacy protection issues will be involved. Strictly speaking, only individual self-driving travel can be regarded as free travel.

There is also a special situation between free travel and shared travel. When people take taxis alone, rather than sharing with others, taxi drivers are service providers like taxis. Taxi drivers themselves are independent people, so passengers cannot ignore their existence, and their freedom is restricted to some extent. Personal and property safety can be jeopardized by encounters with bad-tempered drivers.

The advantages of free travel are mainly reflected in convenience, safety and comfort, while the advantages of shared travel are mainly low cost and environmental protection, which can effectively reduce the total number of cars in cities, alleviate traffic congestion and parking difficulties and improve the efficiency of resource utilization. Under certain economic conditions, most people prefer to travel freely, and their awareness of sharing needs to be improved.

From the perspective of the ownership of travel tools, we can divide people's travel modes into private car travel and public travel. When the vehicles people use do not belong to them, they belong to public transportation, such as taxis, online cars, buses, subways, commuter cars, station wagons and private cars transporting family members or friends.

Public travel under manual driving and the travel mode of two or more people taking a private car together do not belong to the category of free travel. Once unmanned driving technology matures, taking self-driving taxis will be similar to self-driven travel and become free travel in the true sense.

In other words, unmanned taxis will realize the deep integration of free travel and public travel so that people can enjoy the convenience, comfort and safety of free travel, while also reaping the benefits of low costs and environmental protection from public transportation. Considering the relatively high price of driverless cars in the early stages of development, limited audience and the fact that self-driving taxis can reduce labor costs, it is only logical that self-driving taxis will be the first to be used on a large scale in the market.

Self-driving taxis and free travel mode

In August 2016, the Singapore taxi start-up nuTonomy conducted a trial operation of self-driving taxis in Singapore. Eligible passengers can obtain services through smart phones. In the trial operation phase, 6 self-driving taxis were put into operation, and 12 passengers obtained experience qualifications. The driving range of taxis was limited to 2.5 square miles of commercial and residential areas, and passengers needed to get on and off at specific locations. In nuTonomy's plan, as more and more self-driving cars are put into use in Singapore in the future, the total number of cars in Singapore will be reduced from 900,000 to 300,000. In October 2017, Delphi Park Electric Company announced that it had completed a wholly owned acquisition of nuTonomy at a price of US$450 million.

For Singapore, a small and economically developed country, the promotion of self-driving taxis is relatively difficult. Its application will bring many conveniences to people's travel and have a very positive impact on improving traffic congestion. It should be pointed out that public transportation is the core component of Singapore's transportation system. The application of self-driving taxis is not to completely replace traditional taxis but to further improve them. In the future transportation development plan released by Singapore, it is estimated that public transportation will be responsible for up to 75% of Singapore's peak travel services by 2025.

Not only Singapore, Uber and other companies have conducted self-driving car tests in California, Michigan, Pittsburgh and other cities to try to introduce self-driving taxi services. Especially for an online car-hailing company like Uber, after applying self-driving taxis, the platform can customize and design perfect plans for people's daily travel. The intelligent system can efficiently allocate vehicle resources. More importantly, it can effectively predict people's travel demand by combining big data and cloud computing technology and adjust the allocation of transport resources in different regions in a targeted manner, so as to better meet the peak travel needs and reduce the no-load rate.

There is a sentence in the slogan of the algorithm competition jointly organized by Didi Research Institute, Udacity and Zhihu: "The dream of changing the world can be realized. Your algorithm will be used in the real world of travel. Maybe one day you can say, 'My algorithm has the final say on which car you take in this city.'" If self-driving taxis can be popularized on a large scale, people will no longer need to purchase, repair and regularly maintain private cars, thus avoiding various problems such as parking difficulties, car insurance, traffic jams, breakdowns and accidents on the way, which is highly consistent with people's yearning for a better life.

Children, the elderly, the disabled and people without driver's licenses can also enjoy free travel through self-driving taxis. Private cars will be greatly reduced, which is more conducive to protecting the environment, reducing traffic accidents and improving travel efficiency and experience.

Scientific research has found that if self-driving taxis can be promoted to the main mode of urban motor transportation, and the number of private cars is strictly limited, the total number of urban vehicles will be reduced by nearly 50%, the parking space occupation will be reduced by 40%, and the accident rate will be reduced by about 90%. If self-driving cars are upgraded to new energy vehicles such as electric power, automobile exhaust emissions will be reduced by about 80%. In this case, the city will have more space to improve the residents' quality of life—for example, setting up more public leisure facilities such as parks and football fields, and widening bicycle lanes.

In order to solve the air pollution problem in the city center, Oslo, the capital of Norway, had aimed to realize "0 private cars" in the city center by 2019; Madrid, Spain, had announced that cars would be banned from entering the city center for about 2 square kilometers by 2020. Of course, in order to meet people's personalized travel needs, private cars will not disappear for a long time. However, it is not necessary to purchase a private car to experience the general freedom of a driving private car. In the future, some service providers may offer long-term rentals of self-driving cars.

Self-driving taxis help the public to enjoy high-quality shared travel services at a lower cost. In Asian markets such as China, India and Singapore, carpooling is favored by a large number of people. This is related to the level of economic development. In economically developed European markets such as Britain, France and Germany, people's acceptance of carpooling is relatively low. However, there are some differences in the acceptance of carpooling among different age groups. In the survey of carpooling willingness for the European market, 45% of respondents under 30 expressed their willingness to carpool, while only 22% of middle-aged and elderly people over 50 expressed their willingness to carpool.

Travel cost has a great influence on the public's willingness of car-pooling; when the travel cost of self-driving taxis was US$20, only 11% of the interviewees were willing to carpool self-driving taxis; when the travel cost of self-driving taxis was reduced by 50% to US$10, the proportion of respondents willing to take self-driving taxis increased to 37%; when the travel cost of self-driving taxis was further reduced by 75% to US$5, the proportion of respondents willing to take self-driving taxis rose to 52%. In addition, many interviewees took the initiative to ask if there were any personal safety facilities such as glass partitions and cameras in the car and said that if they could do this well, they would prefer to take self-driving taxis.

The reason why taxis are used as smaller models instead of large buses is that the miniaturization and decentralization of vehicles have a positive impact on meeting individual travel needs, improving road smoothness, disease prevention and control, safety and anti-terrorism, etc.

Some people say that the public transportation environment can promote interpersonal communication. However, the majority of people prefer to spend their time relaxing and entertaining themselves rather than chatting with strangers who do not share their interests. Therefore, large bus scenes like large buses will not only promote interpersonal communication but also affect people's travel experience.

In the future, as cities continue to grow and the cost of self-driving travel decreases, more and more people will choose to travel together or independently in small self-driving cars.

Intelligent traffic management based on vehicle–road integration

Exploring the intelligent traffic management mode from the perspective of travel mode caters to the people-oriented development concept. A wide range of stakeholders are involved in the creation of a truly intelligent traffic management system, including not only consumers but also government departments, manufacturers, distributors and operators. From the research and development of self-driving cars to their operation, it is a huge and complex project that requires the cooperation and interaction of all parties.

Communication and interaction between cars, cars and roads, and cars and people need to have unified industry standards. At the same time, it is far from enough to rely solely on an Internet travel platform or car company to deeply explore the potential value of big traffic data. It requires enterprise resource sharing and in-depth cooperation. In addition, the definitions of vehicle quality, traffic accidents and other issues are not yet clear, and the high-profile view is that car companies should assume the integrated responsibility of the whole process of self-driving car manufacturing and road operation.

In this case, a car company will be responsible for vehicle research and development, configuration, road construction and management, and finally establish a set of intelligent transportation industry modes of vehicle–road integration and integrated operation to provide strong support for urban transportation development.

For car companies that develop and produce self-driving cars, it is necessary to actively extend to the upstream and downstream of the industrial chain, which helps to improve the value creation ability of the industrial chain and reduce costs and risks. Baidu makes full use of its strengths in resource integration and collaborates extensively with government departments, parts manufacturers, travel service providers, vehicle manufacturers, as well as industry associations, etc., to establish and improve the "smart travel" ecology so that the public can enjoy more convenient and fast transportation services.

In August 2016, California Silicon Valley technology company Velodyne announced that its laser radar company Velodyne LiDAR had received a total investment of US$150 million from Baidu and Ford. With the blessing of capital, the price of laser radar products has been significantly reduced. Thanks to the strong supply capacity of Velodyne LiDAR, the supply price of Velodyne 64-line laser radar has been reduced to 500,000 yuan, compared with 700,000 yuan before. A spokesman for Velodyne LiDAR pointed out that when the order volume of 64-line radar reaches 1 million, its cost will be reduced to US$500.

In other words, price is expected to no longer be an important obstacle to laser radar sales, and the commercialization of unmanned driving is expected to accelerate. At present, many traditional car companies invest in unmanned driving start-up companies in order to seize the opportunity. In order to ensure the safety of self-driving cars and enhance their management and control capabilities, in the future, one enterprise will be responsible for the service supply and operation management of self-driving cars in a certain area. In this case, the target customers that self-driving car enterprises want to strive for will no longer be individual consumers but cities, regions and even countries. From the perspective of industry competition, this will help reduce internal friction in the industry and establish an industry competition pattern dominated by external competition and inter-regional competition.

Autopilot tools such as self-driving taxis are only one of many modes of travel. People can also choose bicycles, electric vehicles, buses, subways and other modes of travel. Moreover, the large-scale application and popularization of mobile Internet and mobile intelligent terminals will attract more outstanding talents in cities and regions with more diversified services and better infrastructure.

From a technical point of view, it is feasible to improve the safety of automatic driving to the level of large-scale application, but after reaching a certain level, for example, after improving the safety from 80% to 99%, it is quite difficult to improve from 99% to 99.99%. It is true that the data analysis capability of big data technology and the computing capability of cloud computing technology can surpass human beings, but new problems emerge one after another. Moreover, to solve the problem, we should comprehensively consider many factors, such as emotion, morality, ethics and law, and we should not only design solutions from a technical point of view.

In the long run, after self-driving vehicles reach the commercial stage, we cannot completely hand over the safety guarantee to self-driving vehicles and systems but should combine more reliable and safe auxiliary means such as classified vehicles and traffic separation.

Classified vehicle

Classified vehicles will carry out differentiated research, development, design and operation management of self-driving vehicles in combination with the actual scene demand characteristics. From different angles, there are many classification methods for self-driving cars:

(1) In terms of the driving interval, they can be divided into short-distance vehicles running at low speeds within cities and long-distance vehicles running at high speeds between cities.
(2) In terms of the load object, they can be divided into buses serving people's travel needs and trucks serving freight transportation.
(3) In terms of the number of passengers, they can be divided into single-person vehicles, double-person vehicles and multi-person vehicles.

(4) In terms of users, they can be divided into police cars, commercial cars, official cars and family cars.

(5) In terms of special scenes, they can be divided into ambulances, fire engines, energy supply vehicles and engineering rescue vehicles.

Classified vehicles are extremely beneficial in reducing resource waste, controlling costs and improving the service quality. For example, those short-distance cars running at low speeds in the city only need to update the local map in real time, which helps to keep more detailed local traffic information, while reducing the total amount of data and improving the speed of the car system; for indoor short-distance cars and inter-city cars, different design schemes can be adopted to differentiate tires, lighting, body materials, sensors and other aspects to reduce waste of resources and improve the utilization rate of resources.

After the vehicle operation interval is defined, the vehicle scale in the area will be effectively controlled, which can improve the efficiency and quality of traffic operation and reduce traffic congestion and traffic accidents. With the popularization of mobile payment and the reform in charging policy, road toll stations will no longer exist in the future and will be replaced by relay stations serving user transfer and cargo transfer.

In the future, transfer or transshipment can be completed without passengers or luggage getting off the bus. For example, passengers can get on and off the bus without stopping after the G-series high-speed train enters the station. For users of self-driving cars, when the road ahead is impassable due to traffic accidents or congestion, the passengers on the opposite side of the road do not have to turn around and return to the original road but can continue to their destination by changing vehicles.

Traffic separation

Traffic separation will set up corresponding travel passages for pedestrians, bicycles, electric vehicles, private cars, buses and other different vehicles and control their driving routes within the passages. At present, expressways and rail transit have basically realized lane separation. In the early stage of the application of self-driving cars, it is necessary to set up special passages for self-driving cars in order to improve safety and reduce the negative impact of accidents.

In the future, when traffic light design is canceled at traffic junctions, traffic separation will be an inevitable choice because it is difficult for ordinary people to judge the driving route of self-driving vehicles, and at the same time, it is difficult for self-driving vehicle systems to find rules in a large number of irregular people. Indeed, with the wide application of the Internet of Things technology, pedestrians can interact with self-driving cars in the future, but passengers in cars may not be willing to compromise, which may lead to unnecessary contradictions and disputes. The separation of people and cars will effectively solve this problem.

In addition, when self-driving cars and manually driven cars share the same road, instructions cannot be fully implemented due to a lack of sufficient binding force on manually driven cars by the intelligent transportation center system with unified dispatching function, and conflicts occur frequently. This is by no means the outcome people want to see.

Policies of unmanned intelligent transportation in countries around the world

In the process of promoting unmanned driving applications and developing intelligent transportation in different cities, there will inevitably be various development paths. Some cities may need to pay higher trial and error costs, which will have different impacts on the public, industry and city managers. The economic and social benefits of self-driving cars are amazing, while the development of a new format will inevitably affect the traditional format, as does the self-driving car industry. Its development will affect the interests of traditional car companies, taxi companies, driving schools and other parties.

Cities must find a set of effective solutions that can balance the interests of all parties, with the improvement of relevant laws and regulations playing a crucial role. At present, governments of various countries are constantly trying and making mistakes and exploring effective solutions in the form of pilot cities. For example, the U.S. Department of Transportation launched the "Smart City Challenge" to solicit automated transportation development plans that make urban transportation safer, more reliable and more convenient and to provide financial support to cities that have achieved certain results.

The Swedish government has launched a strategic innovation plan of "Driving Sweden" to create a new transportation model covering automated transportation for Swedish transportation. Finland's Ministry of Transport studied the legal framework for testing self-driving taxis and set up a working group to guide the promotion. The relevant functional departments of the United States, France, the Netherlands, Austria and many other countries have also made a series of explorations in this respect.

The Chinese government attaches great importance to the development of unmanned driving and intelligent transportation and has drawn up a roadmap for it. For example, in "Made in China 2025," it is emphasized, "By 2020, master the overall technology and key technologies of intelligent assisted driving, and initially establish an independent research and development system and production supporting system of intelligent networked vehicles. By 2025, master the overall technology and key technologies of autonomous driving, establish a relatively perfect independent research and development system, production supporting system and industrial cluster of intelligent networked automobiles, and basically complete the transformation and upgrading of the automobile industry."

The American Institute of Electrical and Electronics Engineers (IEEE) pointed out that self-driving cars are expected to account for 75% of the total number of cars in the United States by 2040. Data show that the death rate per 10,000 vehicles is 0.77 in Japan, 1.1 in the U.K., 1.59 in France and 6.2 in China, which is four to eight times higher than in developed countries. The car accident fatality rate has been the highest in the world for more than 10 consecutive years.

China's transportation demand is huge. Promoting the application of new energy self-driving cars can not only better serve the general public but also help reduce the waste of resources so that the government has more funds to invest in improving education and people's livelihood.

In the future, the Chinese government needs to give strong support to the development of the unmanned driving industry, provide guidance and help for the research and development and landing application of unmanned driving technology from the top-level design level, and guide traditional car companies and Internet companies to cooperate deeply and share resources such as data, technology and talents. At the same time, it needs to speed up the introduction of laws and regulations related to self-driving cars, provide strong support for the testing, operation and management of self-driving cars, and take cities with relatively mature conditions as pilots to explore effective landing solutions.

Unmanned driving is the focus of attention all over the world. Although it is still at an early stage of development, its value has been fully demonstrated. It is an important part of building intelligent transportation and a smart city. Looking ahead, its influence will never be limited to the transportation industry but will burst into amazing energy in many fields such as information, management, social interaction, life, politics, culture, energy, as well as military, profoundly changing all aspects of people's life and work. In the face of this unprecedented huge wave, we should take immediate action and strive to win the development opportunities by taking the lead in layout.

Key factors of unmanned driving from concept to landing

Safety: The inevitable goal of unmanned driving development

The quest for safety is fueling the rapid growth in demand for self-driving vehicles. According to data published by the World Health Organization, around 1.2 million people die in road traffic accidents worldwide every year. In China, traffic accidents caused by human factors account for 93%, and an average of 500 people die in traffic accidents every day. With the emergence of self-driving vehicles, the traditional "man-vehicle-road" ternary control mode will be changed into "vehicle-road" dual control, uncontrollable drivers will be eliminated and "zero regulation violation" will be truly realized, thus greatly improving the operation efficiency and safety of the traffic system, greatly reducing the frequency of traffic accidents, and effectively ensuring driving safety. Research shows that the incidence of rear-end collision can be reduced by 40% if a car is equipped with an automatic braking system; if all motor vehicles are equipped with automatic braking systems, 700,000 traffic accidents can be reduced every year.

The premise of unmanned driving development is safety. Because unmanned driving is still in the stage of testing and perfection, its safety and reliability have not been generally recognized by people. For example, the British regulatory authorities require that self-driving cars must be monitored and can switch to manual driving mode at any time; Germany plans to issue a series of regulatory policies on self-driving cars, including requiring self-driving cars to be equipped with steering wheels and equipped with black boxes similar to civil aviation aircraft, so that relevant investigators can analyze the cause of the accident according to the black boxes and clarify the responsibilities of all parties after the accident.

A survey has been conducted by Sweden's Volvo. The results of the survey show that more than half of the consumers support the installation of steering wheels in self-driving cars. Of all consumers, 80% said that the manufacturer should be responsible for claims if a self-driving car is involved in an accident because the cause of the accident was a malfunction of the self-driving car system. In fact, if self-driving cars run into unexpected situations, users do not believe that the self-driving system can make an effective response, and the fight for control is likely to have extremely serious consequences because while driving self-driving cars, drivers are often relaxed and do not pay attention to the driving conditions. In the face of unexpected situations, they are likely to make wrong judgments and put themselves in danger.

Moreover, in the face of traffic accidents caused by people and vehicles competing for control rights, it is difficult for the transportation department to determine the responsible party. On the contrary, if the driver is required to be vigilant and ready to switch to the manual driving mode while driving the self-driving car, it is better to adopt manual driving directly. This kind of "people and the car itself can both drive" design makes unmanned driving meaningless but also increases the ideological burden of drivers, and all desires for free and comfortable driving are dashed.

Furthermore, in essence, this kind of "people and the car itself can both drive" design is irresponsible when it comes to the safety of self-driving vehicles. With the "route of retreat" of manual driving, relevant personnel will not focus on solving the safety problem of self-driving vehicles, and the unified standard for the design and manufacture of self-driving vehicles cannot be established in a short time; thus, the safety of users cannot be effectively guaranteed.

On May 7, 2016, Tesla Autopilot, which started the automatic driving assistance system, collided with a white trailer truck while driving, and the top of the Autopilot was completely destroyed, and the driver died instantly. Tesla's explanation for the accident was that the white truck was not identified under the blue sky background, and from the perspective of the Autopilot, the side of the trailer truck was suspended on the ground, causing the Autopilot system to misjudge and not start the automatic brake, resulting in the collision between the two cars. At the same time, because the collision location of the vehicle was on the windshield of the Autopilot, the collision safety system failed to perform its function, resulting in the driver's immediate death.

The accident caused quite a stir. Tesla said that a fatal traffic accident occurred every 94 million miles in the United States, and the Autopilot auxiliary driving system had already traveled 130 million miles when the traffic accident occurred. In addition, Tesla also stressed that unmanned driving technology is constantly developing and Autopilot is not perfect. So, who should be responsible for this accident? Some people think that Tesla is to blame, others think that the inattentive driver is to blame, and still others think that the sensor supplier Mobileye is to blame. People's perception of unmanned driving traffic accidents inevitably reminds people of Tesla's AC war with Edison.

In 1880, Tesla invented the first alternating current generator in the world and Edison invented the electric chair in order to make people realize the danger of alternating current. Later, after a fierce confrontation between the two, Tesla's alternating current gained the upper hand and made outstanding contributions to the development of human civilization. It can be seen that all new things are a symbiosis of advantages and disadvantages, and there is no absolute good or bad. Therefore, in the face of a new thing—self-driving cars—we should grasp the development trend and not completely deny it just because of an accident.

Performance: Really realize unmanned driving landing

Because of the huge demand from users, self-driving cars will quickly enter people's lives and become an important part of their daily living space, eventually becoming the primary means of transportation. By then, purely electric driverless cars will become increasingly functional. They will not only be able to drive on the road, but also have direct access to office buildings, residential buildings, and even rooms, becoming office rooms, lounges, reception rooms for users, and possibly fully functional "caravans."

Furthermore, office and residential areas may evolve into giant "saloon cars," nested layer by layer like dolls, with big cars covering medium cars and medium cars covering small cars, giving birth to infinite changes. Of course, pure electric self-driving cars can also be parked in the open air and recharged with solar energy while continuing to provide users with services outside driving.

Self-driving vehicles frequently enter and leave small spaces, which increases the likelihood of scratches and collisions, as well as collisions while driving. In order to reduce scratches and collisions and cushion the injuries caused by accidental collisions, the new concept car is based on the bumper car concept and uses a tough, flexible and environmentally friendly material for the body. Although the traditional metal body is strong and beautiful, it is poor in environmental protection and energy efficiency, not resistant to corrosion, poor in sound insulation, poor in safety and not very practical. Using new flexible materials to make the car body can result in a variety of models such as telescopic cars, deformed cars and water, land and amphibious cars.

Moreover, flexible material is used to make the vehicle body, which makes the storage, assembly and transportation of the vehicle body more convenient. In addition, the structure of the pure electric self-driving vehicle is relatively simple, so vehicle manufacturing will become easier, thus greatly reducing the manufacturing cost. It is possible that in the near future, pure electric self-driving cars of various appearances and sizes will appear on all roads in the world, with spacious carriages, rich and perfect functions, closer-to-nature designs, lower price, greater flexibility and disaster resistance. Self-driving cars will be comparable to housing and even more popular than traditional housing.

In addition, unmanned driving also needs energy convenience. For example, pure electric self-driving vehicles can find charging piles to complete charging ahead of schedule without manual control or use leisure time to charge, and users can use charging time to handle other affairs, so even if pure electric self-driving vehicles cannot realize fast charging at present, there is no need to worry that users will waste time. If it is a fuel-fired self-driving vehicle, the vehicle will automatically go to the gas station to refuel, and the potential safety hazard can be reduced without the presence of passengers. In addition, in an unmanned driving environment, charging stations can reduce the setting of charging piles to lower infrastructure construction costs and maintenance costs.

Although purely electric driverless vehicles have a poorer range than petrol vehicles, they can complete mobile charging while driving, just like refueling in the air, thanks to their greater energy security and greater operational capability. Self-driving vehicles that need mobile charging can turn to special charging service vehicles for help and can also turn to other purely electric unmanned vehicles in the same sector.

The charging method can be direct battery replacement or vehicle-to-vehicle docking charging. No matter which charging method is adopted, the charging of self-driving cars is much simpler than that of manual cars. Private cars and buses are mainly used for mobile charging during driving. Taxi can calculate the driving distance and electricity quantity and arrange passengers to transfer in due course.

Experience: Meet the life and entertainment needs of users

Optimization of appearance modeling, spatial layout and basic functions

Under the condition of unmanned driving, the driver's body posture can be more relaxed; drivers can take not only a sitting posture but also a lying posture, a standing posture, etc. In order to respond to the driver's demand, the carriage must be heightened and enlarged, and the seat in the car should be retracted, so that it can be used by the driver to sit on, flattened into a bed for the driver to lie down, and even folded to allow the driver to stand freely. The raised and widened carriage door can adopt a "walk-in" design, which is much more convenient than the "sit-in" design of traditional cars. In addition, small folding tables can be placed in the carriage to create a simple office space.

In order to save energy and reduce travel costs, self-driving car manufacturers can design a variety of models such as single-person, double-person and multi-person cars according to the needs of users. In fact, single-person self-driving cars are bound to be welcomed by office workers. A single-person self-driving vehicle can be designed as a single-row wide-wheeled vehicle, which looks like a large motorcycle with a canopy. It not only saves space and is more flexible to drive, but also saves energy and protects the environment. Multi-person self-driving cars can be further divided into buses and minibuses that can share space, and pod cars with privacy in space to further improve driving safety. Since the self-driving car is designed according to a unified standard, it can be spliced like a train to form a cart with internal space connectivity. If there are many items to be transported, we can ask other self-driving cars to help and combine them to expand the space inside the car.

In addition, based on the driving environment and tasks, self-driving cars can also be divided into short-distance cars and long-distance cars. Among them, short-distance cars mainly travel in the city. The speed should not be too fast, nor should the functions be complicated, but they should have a strong, comprehensive perception. Long-distance buses mainly run on inter-city expressways. The speed can be designed to be fast, the functions should be appropriately rich, and the comprehensive perception ability can be slightly weakened. This kind of vehicle division can save resources and reduce costs.

Provide communication, office and life entertainment services based on car networking

In self-driving environment, drivers do not need to drive in person and can use their travel time to do other things. According to the estimation of the U.S. Department of Transportation, each person spends about 52 minutes on the way to and from work every day. In self-driving cars, people can use this time more effectively. If the carriage of the self-driving car is large enough, the driving time is long enough, and it is equipped with necessary information equipment, it can create a comfortable office space, make mobile office and mobile home a reality, and truly realize the vision of "car as a service" and "car as a life".

As a result, for users, self-driving cars also involve privacy protection issues, and if they are public servants, they may also involve national security issues. In order to protect personal privacy and provide security, self-driving cars can use non-real-name payment methods. At the same time, the user can turn off the mobile phone's positioning function during the ride, not authenticate with a real name when using the mobile Internet, and even cut off the network connection during the ride. After taking these actions, even if the vehicle is still under the monitoring of the vehicle network, real name correspondence between the vehicle and the user will not occur, and the privacy of the user can be greatly guaranteed. In addition, while driving, the user can manually turn off the camera in the car to avoid breach of privacy.

Of course, taking these measures by users means shielding safety monitoring. In case of an accident, the traffic police department cannot deal with it quickly. After cutting off the network connection, the self-driving car becomes a real "black car." It can neither receive the instructions sent by the command center nor reveal the driver's intentions to the command center. The command center can only monitor it by scrutinizing both sides of the road and using the information provided by the surrounding vehicles. In order to ensure the safety of vehicles, the command center and management department must reserve certain monitoring rights over buses, taxis and other means of transport and adopt automatic detection technology to find dangerous goods and lost goods in time, so as to ensure rider safety and make it easier for passengers to find goods.

How to solve the safety problem of unmanned driving?

To break the shackles of unmanned vehicle manufacturers and scientific research and technical personnel, and to promote the rapid development of deep learning algorithms and unmanned driving technology, enterprises and society must establish fault tolerance, trial and error mechanisms and traffic accident disposal schemes, as well as give self-driving vehicles and R&D designers certain tolerance, because the accident rate of self-driving vehicles is much lower than those driven manually. For example, the transportation department can set accident targets for self-driving car manufacturers. Only when the annual accident rate of all self-driving cars produced by the enterprise is lower than this target can the enterprise continue to operate; otherwise, it will have to pay huge fines, suspend production for rectification, or even be forced to close down.

In order to reduce the number of traffic accidents caused by unmanned driving, self-driving vehicle manufacturers should implement a strict system of regular vehicle return maintenance and emergency handling service, especially a "dual-system" control mode to address the issue of the vehicle network being artificially damaged, such as hacker invasion and virus damage. The main system in the "dual system" refers to the networked open system, while the secondary system refers to the independent closed system. The self-driving vehicle is controlled by the main system and monitored by the subsystem during normal driving. Once the driver finds that the main system is damaged, he can immediately switch to the subsystem, so that the vehicle can resume normal driving and ensure that the driver and passengers get off safely, after which the vehicle can be sent to the maintenance organization for repair.

If the driver does not find any abnormality when the main system is destroyed, for example, the system code is tampered with, and it is found that the obstacle ahead is not detouring but hitting, the driver may not have time to switch the system, resulting in a traffic accident. Therefore, manufacturers and R&D personnel of self-driving vehicles must strengthen system protection and vehicle internal and external interface protection. That is to say, vehicle manufacturers must install protection software for self-driving vehicles so that vehicles can automatically detect, find faults, check and kill viruses, and take responsibility for traffic accidents caused by improper protection, so as to avoid vehicle manufacturers shirking their responsibilities and damaging users' rights and interests when traffic accidents occur. In addition, self-driving vehicle manufacturers should also ensure that the internal and external interfaces of vehicles are difficult to disassemble and change, so as to prevent users and others from artificially damaging vehicles, thus effectively improving the safety performance of vehicles.

In addition, if the transportation department stipulates that self-driving cars must be able to switch to the manual driving mode at any time, the public transportation enterprises and taxi enterprises that are most suitable for introducing self-driving cars will completely lose the advantage of avoiding labor. Because if the enterprise does not equip the self-driving car with a full-time driver, it must check the user's driver's license in advance to find out whether he drinks alcohol, whether he takes drugs, etc. The whole process has not been simplified but has become more complicated, and the desire to enjoy the convenience of a self-driving car may fail.

To sum up, the transportation department should not make the stipulation that "self-driving vehicles must be able to switch to the manual driving mode at any time", otherwise it will lead to unclear standards and responsibilities of the whole industry and plunge the development of the industry into chaos and embarrassment. In other words, for unmanned driving, there is a big loophole in adopting manual assistance to avoid traffic accidents. In order to achieve the ultimate development goal of unmanned driving, the transportation department must reform the current transportation system, clarify the responsibilities of self-driving car manufacturers, unmanned driving system software vendors and self-driving bus companies and the compensation responsibilities of insurance companies, so that users can ride with confidence. Recently, the U.S. Federation and some states have affirmed the legality of self-driving cars. Google's self-driving cars have been affirmed by the U.S. Highway Safety Administration, which has confirmed that the cars are controlled by an automatic driving system instead of the manual control of the owners.

In other words, the previous rule that "self-driving cars must be equipped with steering wheels and brakes" has expired.

In the future, self-driving cars will no longer have steering wheels, pedals, instruments, joysticks, observation mirrors and other equipment. Instead, they will be equipped with panoramic doors and windows, large 3D screens, spacious and open carriages, mobile communication office equipment, etc. Then, riding will no longer be the "connection" of life, vehicles will become an extension of living space, and people's time and energy will be completely liberated and put into more meaningful and valuable things.

According to the survey, 58% of people are willing to take self-driving cars and 69% are willing to take some self-driving cars. From the point of view of age, young people are more willing to spend on self-driving cars, because 63% of the respondents under 29 are willing to take self-driving cars; however, only 46% of the 51-year-old respondents are willing to take self-driving cars. The survey results show that public acceptance of driverless cars will grow over time.

Regionally, Asia has the largest number of users willing to take self-driving cars. For example, 85% of the respondents in India are willing to take self-driving cars, while 75% of the respondents in China are willing to to do so, because these countries have serious traffic congestion, imperfect transportation infrastructure and high traffic accident rate, and they hope to solve these problems with self-driving cars with obvious advantages. On the contrary, users in Japan, Germany, the Netherlands and other countries have relatively low enthusiasm for self-driving cars. Only 36%, 44% and 41% of the respondents in these countries are willing to take self-driving cars, respectively.

Chapter 4

Application of Unmanned Driving Technology in Urban Rail Transit

Application of unmanned driving technology in urban rail transit

Functional characteristics of unmanned driving system in rail transit

In recent years, the development process of urban rail transit has been accelerating, and the corresponding supporting technologies have been rapidly updated. Many first-tier cities with a large population face enormous passenger pressure. For many of them, their only available solutions are to shorten the process of new line construction while increasing the number and departure frequency of shuttle buses on important lines, which will require hiring more crew members, drivers, etc.—undoubtedly increasing investment costs.

In addition, as the frequency of departure increases, the labor intensity of manual operation will increase. If heavy manual labor is performed for a long time, safety accidents will easily occur due to fatigue. In this situation, the urban rail transit industry is paying more and more attention to unmanned driving technology.

Generally speaking, the functional characteristics of unmanned urban rail transit systems are reflected in the following aspects:

(1) Train operation is automated through pre-programming and autonomous machine decision making, which are embodied in many working

links from train start-up, to train alignment, obstacle identification, train and screen door monitoring, as well as marshaling adjustment. Intelligent operation can replace traditional manual operation and realize mechatronics operation.

(2) Improved driving efficiency and comfort while saving energy. Taking the planned timetable as a reference, the running interval and running time of trains are reasonably controlled, the impact rate of traction braking is effectively controlled by the computer and acceleration and deceleration are only carried out when absolutely necessary to achieve the purpose of saving energy. On the basis of analyzing the temporal and spatial distribution of historical passenger flow, the change of real-time cross-section passenger flow and the early warning information of large passenger flow, combined with the original plan, the operation plan is changed to maintain the rationality of train operation intervals and evacuate passengers immediately when necessary.

(3) Make the operation of vehicles, communication and signal systems cooperate with each other, and form relatively perfect subsystems of each part, fully exploiting the role of integrated supervisory control system (ISCS), strengthening the connection between different subsystems and giving full play to the synergy between different systems in train rescue, equipment failure handling and other work. Using the whole network control center (COCC) combined with ISCS, the automatic network operation is jointly implemented to improve the operation efficiency as a whole.

(4) When the train is in normal operation, open the man–machine monitoring interface and the corresponding interface, and send relevant information to operators, passengers and maintenance departments to facilitate the querying and using of demanders; if there is an abnormal situation, the safety program will be automatically activated and early warning will be carried out to determine the degree of impact. The root cause of the problem will be found in automatically or in collaboration with technical personnel. Maintenance personnel will be able to intervene with the help of interface services.

Application advantages of unmanned driving in rail transit

(1) The train control system requires high safety. As an important part of the unmanned driving system, the train control system is responsible

for various safety controls, has multiple functions, and collaborates with the manned driving system. In order to improve the safety of overall operation, it is necessary to deal with related problems on the basis of implementing safety analysis. For example, during the line design process, it is necessary to ensure that the driving environment is not interfered with by external factors, and continuously improve the safety system in the subsequent development process, so as to perceive the safety risks in time through sensors.

(2) Due to the limited number of workers involved in the unmanned driving system, normal operation can only be maintained with sufficient safety, maintainability, reliability and availability. In case of equipment failure or emergency, a remote monitoring system is required to deal with the problem in a timely and effective manner; in addition, the unmanned driving system should be capable of scene analysis and issuing emergency plans in time. In case of an abnormal situation, the formulation of the plan should comprehensively consider the different needs of passengers and prioritize their personal safety.

(3) Communication-based train control (CBTC) mobile block system is widely used in unmanned driving systems. To maintain the normal operation of the system, the most important thing is to use a sound network system. If the synergy between different systems is to be brought into play in the operation process, the value of a sound network system can be highlighted.

(4) The unmanned driving system is a subversion of the traditional manual management mode. Urban rail transit departments are required to change the existing construction mode, adjust the organizational structure, actively learn from the excellent experience of successful projects at home and abroad, formulate more reasonable planning schemes according to the specific and special scenes of Chinese cities, promote the development and improvement of unmanned driving systems from all aspects and improve the management capabilities of relevant departments.

(5) The construction of an unmanned driving system can promote the development of the urban rail transit system from many aspects and improve its automation and intelligence level. In addition to replacing driver's operation with automatic operation, the value of the unmanned driving system is also reflected in the leading level. It is necessary to highlight the shackles of traditional ideas and actively innovate. In the subsequent development process, the unmanned

driving system will focus on dealing with problems in passenger flow, operation, troubleshooting and disaster treatment, using big data and artificial intelligence technology to improve operation strategies and provide high-quality services for passengers and other participants in traffic operations.

Application challenges of unmanned driving in rail transit

(1) **Online detection and monitoring:** Monitoring the running status of vehicles is only part of the online monitoring work of unmanned driving systems. In addition, many systems, including the automatic fare collection system, signal system, passenger information system, as well as fire alarm system, etc., should deal with and solve system failures in time. Obstacle detection is an important part of the unmanned driving system. On the basis of detection, appropriate treatment methods should be adopted. At present, contact detection is a commonly used detection method in the industry. There is a lack of effective non-contact obstacle detection. If obstacles are detected, emergency braking will be adopted to deal with them, which makes it difficult to improve the efficiency of unmanned driving. At the same time, attention should be paid to fireworks detection and treatment methods, anti-terrorism and riot monitoring and treatment methods, and foreign body intrusion monitoring and treatment methods to reduce resistance in unmanned operations.

(2) **Automatic vehicle connection:** If the train breaks down due to unexpected situations during operation, emergency rescue should be started. In the process of implementing emergency rescue, it is necessary to connect the broken-down train with the rescue vehicle. Manual connection is slow and has certain safety risks. An automatic connection can solve this problem. However, in order to quickly complete the one-time automatic connection between the anchored train and the rescue vehicle at the rescue site, it is necessary to improve the relevant technical level. At present, there are many limitations in automatic connection. Only by ensuring that the trains run in the same direction and the doors are in a locked state can all communication trains realize automatic connection. In the future, we should focus on improving the rescue efficiency of train breakdown and reducing the limitation of automatic connection.

(3) **Emergency treatment in operation:** If there is an emergency in the middle of an operation, especially an unexpected situation in the car, such as passengers pressing the emergency brake button of the train in the running interval, and the train is in the full-automatic operation mode without maintenance personnel following the car, there may be a serious crisis. In view of this situation, operation management personnel should formulate targeted solutions. Passengers often violate the subway operation rules in the station—for example, a passenger forcing his way into the platform screen door compartment when the train door is closing or is stuck, thus preventing the train from operating properly. The handling of these situations depends on the station staff, who should predict the relevant risks in advance and put forward effective solutions.

At present, there are still many technical difficulties to be overcome in unmanned driving, such as improvement in the construction of the signal system. Moreover, the subways in the first-tier cities in China are under great pressure of passenger flow, with high departure frequency and high requirements for safety. However, on the basis of continuous technological advancement, the functions of the subway system will be gradually improved, and the difficulties encountered by unmanned driving technology will be gradually overcome. When the development of the operation system gradually tends to be perfected, more and more urban rail transit will introduce unmanned driving technology to promote the rapid development of subway operation.

Rail transit solution based on unmanned driving

As an important part of urban transportation construction, urban rail transit is the primary mode of transportation for urban residents to use daily and has a key impact on their travel experience. In recent years, urban rail transit technology has ushered in a period of rapid development. A large number of unmanned technology application projects have emerged. It provides a new idea for controlling train-operating costs and improving the quality of travel service. It is a hot spot in the field of transportation. Therefore, studying and analyzing the application of unmanned driving technology in urban rail transit and finding effective solutions will have a very positive impact on promoting the large-scale application of unmanned driving technology in the field of urban rail transit.

Facilities and equipment support

Functional guarantee

- **Train function guarantee:** Self-driving trains running normally do not need manual intervention. Trains should not only be able to operate automatically but should also be able to automatically detect their own faults. When there are potential safety hazards or faults in a specific part of a train, it should be able to find out the root causes of the problems, provide effective solutions and take effective measures in time to prevent the situation from expanding and ensure the stable and safe operation of the train.

  It can automatically carry out retrogression positioning. When the self-driving train crosses the parking position, safety accidents can occur easily while boarding and alighting. Therefore, it is necessary to ensure that the self-driving train can carry out retrogression positioning to ensure safe boarding and alighting of passengers.

  It has the function of automatic obstacle detection and processing. When the self-driving train encounters obstacles during operation, major traffic accidents may occur if effective measures are not taken in time. In order to ensure the safety of train operation, the self-driving train must be able to detect and process obstacles automatically.

  The train operation control center can grasp the internal and external conditions of the train in real time with the help of a video monitoring function and a video monitoring system. When there are problems in train operation, the control center can make effective adjustments in time to prevent traffic accidents.

- **Signal:** A signal is an important factor affecting the unmanned operation of trains. Only when the signal system runs stably can the train complete acceleration and deceleration, turning, stopping, opening and closing doors and other operations. When the signal system fails, it can cause dangerous accidents such as door pinch and train derailment. Therefore, automatic detection and maintenance of the signal system is particularly critical.

- **Evacuation platform:** When an accident occurs during the operation of a self-driving train, it poses a greater challenge to accident treatment because staff cannot arrive at the accident site in time for effective treatment. To mitigate the impact of an accident, once the evacuation platform is set up in the tunnel, if the train has an accident, passengers can be transferred to a safe area through the evacuation platform.

Unmanned driving technology itself has a high dependence on supporting software and hardware facilities. When there is a problem with supporting software and hardware facilities and the control center cannot solve it effectively, it must be solved manually. Therefore, the train operation department must check the train supporting facilities and equipment in real time to fully ensure the reliability of unmanned operation of a train.

Innovation of management mode

In some cases, when there is a problem with train operation that cannot be effectively solved by remote control from the control center, a staff member must enter the train to deal with it, but manual handling also has a certain time cost and cannot be dealt with by the crew in a timely manner as in the case of traditional manual trains. Therefore, in order to improve the processing speed of self-driving trains, management mode innovation is an inevitable choice.

There is no driver role in self-driving trains. The driver's function in the traditional manual driving mode is transferred to the dispatching department, which requires the latter to work in a more refined manner, i.e., the dispatching department of driverless trains should have strong communication, coordination and organizational skills and professional driving skills. It should be able to monitor the train passenger flow in real time, respond to feedback from train passengers in the first instance and provide passengers with effective solutions to their problems in the shortest possible time.

In addition, in order to solve the more complex problem of driverless train operation failure, a more perfect maintenance scheduling system should be established to solve the problems when they arise, such as signal system failure and train track damage. Therefore, it is necessary to maintain efficient coordination among maintenance dispatching, traffic dispatching and passenger dispatching, which requires the three to be included in the dispatching system of the control center at the same time.

Personnel quality

The application of unmanned driving technology in the field of urban rail transit is highly dependent on professionals. Although there may no longer be staff inside the train, it does not mean that driverless trains no longer need human support, but rather that the overall qualifications and skills of the staff involved are more demanding.

(1) **Control center:** For example, when a train breaks down, it may previously have required simple handling by the driver, but since there are no crew members on a driverless train, it must be handled by remote control of the control center. At this point, train dispatchers need to have not only dispatching skills but also train accident handling skills, such as appeasing passengers, as well as analyzing and solving train faults. Of course, if train dispatchers want to have these skills, they need professional training.

(2) **Station:** Following the application of unmanned driving technology to the field of urban rail transit, the station must be equipped with more functional personnel with strong professional ability and higher service levels so as to effectively deal with various accidents that may occur on trains.

Passenger cooperation

For a driverless train to operate well, passengers must do a good job of cooperation. On the one hand, human interference in train operation should be reduced. Due to the lack of supervision by crew members, some passengers' interference in train operation cannot be stopped in time, resulting in a significant negative impact on train operation. To avoid this situation, passengers must actively cooperate in addition to severely punishing any interference with train operation. On the other hand, to assist in rescue, it takes some time for the staff to reach the accident site after a train accident, which may cause the team to miss the critical time period for rescue. If passengers can properly follow the requirements of accident handling on their own, it can effectively reduce the potential danger of accidents. It is natural to have high hopes from the application of unmanned driving in the field of rail transit. In order to ensure its rapid and stable development in China, government departments need to make overall plans, grasp key points, guide the safety of unmanned driving technology, standardize application and development, encourage innovation and provide a better business environment for entrepreneurs and enterprises.

Automatic unmanned driving system of urban rail transit

Application survey of metro automation technology at home and abroad

With the continuous improvement in China's economic development, the construction of rail transit systems in various places has obviously accelerated. With the active efforts of universities, scientific research institutions and enterprises, a large number of new urban rail transit technologies have emerged, especially the application of fully automatic unmanned driving technology in the field of urban rail transit, which is of great practical significance in promoting the quality and efficiency of urban rail transit systems, improving the urban rail transit network, and connecting with the standards of rail transit systems in transportation powers.

Advantages of unmanned driving technology

(1) Using fully unmanned driving technology, a subway can automatically perform tasks such as train wake-up, sleep, cleaning, parking, driving, door opening and closing, fault repair, etc. It can set differentiated operation modes such as normal operation, degraded operation, as well as operation interruption to meet personalized needs in different scenes and improve operation safety and riding experience.

(2) Unmanned driving trains start and brake more evenly, providing passengers a high-quality travel experience, and the speed is faster, which can reduce people's travel time.

(3) The fully automatic unmanned subway has a higher level of automation, which can significantly reduce the cost of manpower and material resources. Indeed, the construction of this subway requires a higher cost, but its positive effect on improving the efficiency and quality of operation and reducing the operating cost is obvious.

General situation of application of unmanned driving technology abroad

(1) Paris Metro Line 1. The line was opened to traffic as early as July 1900. It is the busiest and oldest east–west line in the local area, with a total length of 17 km and 25 platforms. It passes through famous scenic spots such as Arc de Triomphe, Louvre, Charles de Gaulle Square and Champs Elysees. In 2011, the line applied unmanned driving trains based on Trainuard MT safety and control system.

(2) The total length of the Barcelona Metro Line 9 in Spain is 41.4 km. Real-time data transmission is realized through spread spectrum radio, and the train is automatically driven through a fully automatic unmanned driving system.

(3) A set of HSST-100 magnetic levitation systems has been built in Aichi Prefecture, Nagoya, Japan. The length of the line is 8.9 km, there are nine platforms, and ATO (automatic train operation) driving mode is adopted.

General situation of application of unmanned driving technology in China

At present, a considerable number of subway lines in China have applied fully automatic unmanned driving technology, such as:

(1) **Beijing Rail Transit Airport Line:** The line uses fully automatic unmanned driving trains, which can optimize and adjust the train operation strategy and operation density in combination with passenger flow. At the same time, it is equipped with a relatively perfect operation auxiliary system, which can locate the train in real time, make the train turn back automatically, shorten the train operation interval and improve the passenger-carrying capacity.

(2) **Shanghai Metro Line 10:** This line is the first line in China to apply unmanned driving technology. The acceleration and deceleration control of the train is more accurate, and the driver's dispatch plan does not need to be considered. Every day, after waking up the train every day, a large number of self-checks are carried out to ensure higher safety and reliability.

(3) **Beijing Rail Transit Yanfang Line:** This line is the first fully automatic subway line independently developed in China and the second

line applying unmanned driving technology after Shanghai Metro Line 10. As of June 2022, a total of 5 metro lines in Shanghai are driverless, namely Shanghai Metro Line 10, Shanghai Metro Line 14, Shanghai Metro Line 15, Shanghai Metro Line 18, and Shanghai Metro Pujiang Line. Line 15 unmanned, as the name implies, is completely free of driver and crew participation, and the train is fully automated under the unified control of the control center. The driverless system automatically realizes functions such as train sleep, wake-up, preparation, self-test, automatic operation, parking and opening and closing of doors, as well as automatic recovery in case of failure, including car washing, which can also be completed without human operation. The train runs smoothly and efficiently, which can provide passengers with a high-quality riding experience and reduce energy consumption by 10–15% compared with ordinary trains.

Thanks to the fact that urban rail transit runs on a specific track, there is less interference from pedestrians and other vehicles, which brings many conveniences to the application of unmanned driving technology. Its research and development will not only promote the improvement of urban rail transit but also provide valuable reference experience for the large-scale application of unmanned driving technology in the transportation field, thus ushering in a new chapter in the era of unmanned driving transportation in human society.

Necessity of developing a fully automatic unmanned subway

The advantages of a fully automatic unmanned subway

A subway automation system has many advantages. With the help of advanced technical means, it can automatically complete many operations such as train start-up, train stop and exit from the parking lot, train cleaning, train door opening and closing, train running, as well as train fault debugging. It can switch between conventional operation, degraded operation, operation interruption and other modes, and improve train transportation capacity on the original basis, accelerate the operation of the whole system and replace traditional manual work with automatic management.

In addition, the application of automation technology can improve the flexibility of train dispatching and separate it from the original line. Specifically, the number of vehicles and frequency of departures will increase during peak hours to provide more convenience to people on their journeys; in exceptional circumstances, the vehicles will run at a steady speed and stop only at designated stops.

Compared with manual driving, the starting and braking of the unmanned subway are more stable, which can reduce the discomfort of passengers in the car and improve their riding experience. If necessary, it can also run trains at 80 kilometers per hour and use technical means to improve train operation efficiency.

In addition, applying high-level automation technology and fully automatic unmanned driving technology can save human resources. In this way, the cost of personnel management and training can be reduced, and the purpose of reducing the overall cost can be achieved. In the early stage of construction, the investment in the construction of an automatic subway is relatively large, but in the later stage, there is no need to invest too much in maintenance cost, which can achieve the purpose of cost saving as a whole.

Today, with the rapid rise of labor costs, the advantages of the automatic subway are becoming more and more obvious. From the perspective of long-term development, it is also the general trend for the traditional driving mode to develop towards the automatic unmanned subway after the reform. As social economy progresses and develops, more and more countries will participate in the construction of automatic subway systems. As a major transportation country, China should also actively develop fully automatic unmanned subways.

The inevitable result of technological development

As science and technology advanced, the fully automatic unmanned driving system was created to meet market demand. In the future, the passenger transportation system will continue to develop under the influence of the unmanned driving system, showing obvious advantages in both technology and safety. Vehicle design technology, civil engineering technology and traffic operation management technology should be used in the development of fully automatic unmanned subways.

If the application of these technologies can be integrated, the realization of automatic subway operation can promote the rapid development of transportation technology and provide boosting force for the development of modern urban rail transit, which is also the reason why many countries around the world build fully automatic subway systems or replace traditional modes with fully automatic modes.

Compared with Western developed countries, China's development in this area is still relatively backward. In order to improve the domestic transportation technology level, it is necessary to increase investment support for technological development and strive to shorten the process of building fully automatic unmanned subways in China.

Only by accelerating the development of fully automatic unmanned driving subways will China be able to shorten the gap with advanced countries in the world. China should actively learn from the excellent experience of other countries in the process of promoting the construction and development of the industry, gradually catch up with the international advanced technical level, gradually improve the technical ability of domestic technicians, promote the development of China's urban rail transit from the technical level, and make efforts to keep pace with the advanced level of world rail transit construction.

Problems and countermeasures of automatic unmanned driving subways

The application of a fully automatic unmanned driving system in an urban rail transit system can achieve breakthrough development in this field and guide the future direction of urban rail transit development. If China wants to improve its transportation technology capability, it must introduce advanced technical means and equipment, vigorously build fully automatic unmanned driving subways, speed up the construction of domestic fully automatic unmanned driving subways from the perspective of technology and safety, and provide boosting power for the development of rail transportation industry.

Nowadays, all countries in the world are paying more attention to the automatic subway in the field of rail transit. So far, many cities, including Singapore and Paris, have started fully automatic subway projects, while Berlin and Marseille are actively carrying out automatic renovation of traditional subways. New York Metro Line 1 is a bridge between Manhattan and Brooklyn in the United States. Automatic control systems have also been applied in this subway.

Dubai Metro, which uses the unmanned driving urban rapid rail transit system, has the world's longest unmanned driving subway. The United Arab Emirates has responded to the country's severe traffic pressure by spending money on the construction of unmanned driving subways. According to the statistics of the World Metro Research Institute, in recent years, the urban population has increased rapidly, and the number of cities with more than one million residents in the world has been increasing, which has increased the capacity burden of subway lines and brought great resistance to the development of rail transit. The development of automatic unmanned driving subways can reduce the pressure on rail transit networks and accelerate the operation of urban transportation systems.

Fully automatic unmanned driving subways

At present, there are four kinds of unmanned autonomous rail transit: automated people mover (APM), automated monorail, advanced rapid transit (ART), as well as automated metro. Among them, the automatic urban subway system is also called the fully automatic unmanned subway.

The fully automatic unmanned driving train system can complete the train driver's operation tasks automatically and centrally control the train operation system. The specific operations include station preparation, train start-up, main train operation, turn-back station return, train cleaning, and dormancy, among others. The automation technology used by this system can undertake train starting, braking, traction and idling, opening and closing doors and screen doors according to program settings, and can also control the station broadcasting system and onboard broadcasting system.

Using the automatic train operation system, the running speed and overall state of trains can be adjusted, braking and accelerating in time can be realized, and automatic management can be realized. The automatic train protection system can control the braking system and determine the opening and closing of train doors.

However, during the operation of the automated subway system, it is necessary to strictly abide by safety rules and use a high-precision engineering control system, which consists of multiple subsystems, such as automatic ticketing system, automatic ticketing system, communication system, as well as rail system. The most suitable places to adopt fully automated subway systems are those with sufficient and stable passenger flow base and short passenger distance, such as traffic between university campuses, a connection between different venues in the exhibition hall of a building, as well as a connection between the main terminal and the satellite terminal in an airport.

Problems and countermeasures

The unmanned driving system in developed Western countries has reached a relatively mature stage. In contrast, although the domestic unmanned driving subway system has also entered the operation stage, there is still an obvious gap between China's unmanned driving subway system and the advanced international level. For example, China's self-driving cars are not as good as those of developed countries in terms of manufacturing, construction, mechanical and electrical equipment, etc., and it is necessary to continue to accumulate experience in the subsequent development process.

In addition, safety and reliability are issues that should be paid close attention to in the development process of unmanned driving systems. Therefore, efforts should be made to build systems engineering that can run smoothly, and China still has a lot of room for development in this area.

From a technical standpoint, technology research in developed countries started earlier; now, they have many years of development experience. By contrast, China's engineering design, construction and operation management have not formed a perfect system, and for further development, China should actively learn from foreign advanced technologies, adjust and optimize them according to China's specific national conditions on the basis of learning their core technologies, gather superior forces to tackle key technical problems, build a theoretical system in line with China's national conditions, and then use advanced theories to continuously improve China's fully automatic unmanned driving subway system.

The fully automatic unmanned driving subway has to go through a long-term development process. It should be built from all aspects. On the basis of ensuring the correct direction, it should be practical and make continuous progress.

From the perspective of safety, only by dealing with safety problems can we open up a development path for the fully automatic unmanned subway system. Therefore, great importance should be attached to safety monitoring and evaluation. Specific evaluation items include track system, store system, control center, civil engineering, station, communication system, as well as broadcasting system. It is necessary to review and inspect the operation of each link, strictly evaluate its safety status and issue an evaluation report for each evaluation project to record the complete evaluation results and provide a true and reliable basis for later inspection work. In order to ensure the normal operation of the unmanned driving subway system, the importance of safety assessment cannot be ignored. For example, Copenhagen's unmanned driving subway system underwent five years of experiments and tests before it was officially put into operation.

Technology and rules of fully automatic unmanned driving subways

(1) **Trains can run automatically:** The railway automatic control system is the key to the fully automatic driving system. It includes two major components: airborne cars and fixed stations. It can obtain rich and diverse information from the track monitoring system and other systems along the line.

(2) **Cab conversion:** During the train turn-back process, the direction can be automatically determined and the intelligent conversion to the driving end can be realized to ensure the safety and reliability of data. When the train switches at the driving end on the platform, the door and screen door are automatically opened; when the train is in various non-platform areas, including non-turn-back lines, the doors are automatically closed.

(3) **Car door and screen door:** Both car door and screen door can be opened and closed automatically, and various emergencies can be handled:

- When there is a problem with the screen door, the system timely reminds to manually close and lock the faulty screen door. The screen door system submits the position information of the screen door to the signal system. The signal system feeds back the information to the train center control system in time. Then the train center control system isolates the problematic screen door. When the train stops, the faulty screen door does not open or close.

- When there is a problem in opening the door, the train automatically closes and locks the faulty door. When the door cannot be closed, the train reminds to manually close and lock the faulty door. At the same time, the door system submits the position information of the faulty door to the signal system and then isolates the faulty door under the control of the train central control system.

- In order to cope with unexpected situations, when the train stops, it should be possible to manually open and close the door. The signal system receives the instruction of manually opening and closing the door and the screen door and judges whether the corresponding conditions are met. After the conditions are met, the door opening and closing operation will be executed. It should be pointed out that when there are various problems related to passenger transfer, the problematic door and coping strategies should be broadcast to passengers by means of the onboard broadcasting system, and the staff should guide passengers to prevent accidents near the problem door.

(4) **Train parking position:** The main train will stop at the station· according to the preset stop procedure. When the train does not stop at the designated position, the train center control system will automatically adjust.

(5) **Evacuation and rescue under special scenes:** In case of unexpected events such as passengers being pinched by doors, fires, hostage-taking by criminals, the train will stop running under the control of the central control system, and monitor the situation, command and coordinate monitoring, security and other systems to carry out emergency evacuation and rescue.

(6) **Auxiliary linkage system:** The train is equipped with an automatic train monitoring system, which makes the control center monitor the platform and related tracks in real time and understand the internal and external conditions of the train, producing a very positive impact on ensuring the normal operation of the train and emergency treatment of accidents. At the same time, the train is equipped with wireless communication facilities so that passengers can talk with the train control center through the special line. In addition, during the train operation, the details in the front track area can be monitored in real time. For example, when people or objects appear, corresponding measures can be taken in time, and an alarm can be sent to the train control center so that the train dispatcher can handle them in time.

(7) **Automatic detection of train derailment:** When the train is about to derail or has derailed, emergency braking shall be carried out in time.

(8) **Automatic detection of door obstacles:** The door system will be equipped with an obstacle detection and protection system. When accidents such as people being pinched by the door occur, the system will automatically open the door, and the train will leave the station after the staff removes the obstacles.

(9) **Automatic alarm:** Automatic alarm equipment and systems will be installed on the train. In case of emergency, an alarm will be issued immediately, and audio and video data of the accident scene will be transmitted to the train control center in real time through the Internet.

Unmanned parking: Start the innovation of intelligent parking mode

New intelligent parking mode based on unattended

Since its entry into the WTO, China's economy has entered a rapid development phase, the urbanization process has been accelerating, the per capita disposable income has been growing, the sales volume of private cars has been rising rapidly, the number of private cars and urban parking spaces has gradually been out of balance, and the problem of parking difficulties has become increasingly prominent. Because there are not enough parking spaces, many car owners have to take the risk of being punished to occupy the road illegally or park on the green space of residential areas, which may cause serious adverse effects. In addition, it is not uncommon for drivers to blindly detour around their destinations in order to find parking spaces, which affects the smoothness of urban traffic to a certain extent and sometimes directly causes road congestion.

In essence, the root of the parking problem is the contradiction between the increasing parking demand and the limited parking space supply. Adams said, "Traffic supply can never meet traffic demand." Therefore, the key to solving the problem of urban parking is not to blindly increase parking facilities, but to make full use of existing parking resources. An intelligent transportation system (ITS) provides an effective solution to the problem of urban parking difficulties. For urban transportation, "stop" and "go" are two eternal themes. In the process of solving the problem of "stop," urban managers should actively introduce intelligent transportation systems to coordinate vehicles with parking lots, parking lot construction and urban development.

Development of an intelligent parking system

In recent years, with the continuous development of intelligent parking systems, it has been applied in more and more parking lots, which has effectively improved the operation efficiency of parking lots and brought great convenience to parking lot management.

Developed Western countries have been conducting research on intelligent parking for a long time. Young and Thompson (1987) developed the earliest intelligent parking system, PARKSM system, which simulated the whole process of vehicles searching for parking spaces in parking lots. After investigating the parking spaces in parking lots, Vander Waerden *et al.* (2003) proposed a selection behavior model for allocating parking spaces according to the characteristics of drivers and parking spaces.

In 1971, the earliest intelligent parking system appeared in Aachen, Germany, and then European countries began to follow suit. In 1986, the urban parking guidance system established in Cologne was a successful example. The system covers 36 large parking lots and 2 P + R facilities, with a total of 17,000 parking spaces. The control center of the system displays the parking space occupation of these parking lots through direction signs and dynamic display boards on the streets. Based on the system, Auckland in the United States has added a parking reservation service, allowing users to reserve parking spaces in advance by telephone or the Internet.

Compared with Western countries such as Germany and the United States, the research on parking guidance in China started late, and the parking guidance system was first applied in the Wangfujing area of Beijing. Up to now, only Beijing, Shanghai, Guangzhou, Shenzhen and other first-tier cities and some provincial capitals in China have established parking guidance systems, which have small coverage, simple functions and serious data errors, and which need to be improved in all aspects.

Characteristics of an unattended intelligent parking system

An unattended intelligent parking system is the core of continuous and stable operation of unattended parking lots and is also the mainstream trend of the development of the parking industry. Specifically, an unmanned intelligent parking system has the following three typical characteristics:

(1) **Unmanned:** Manual parking is a low-tech, repetitive task, whereas labor costs are rising and unattended and self-service payment will gradually become mainstream. Through the establishment of an unattended intelligent charging system, car owners can pay for parking via mobile payment or self-service payment. At the same time, through the installation of intelligent software and hardware facilities such as high-definition cameras, sensors, as well as digital ballot boxes,

license plates can be automatically identified efficiently and accurately, poles can be lifted automatically, and parking waiting time can be reduced.

(2) **Networking:** It is of great practical significance to break the information silo and realize centralized control of the parking lot by networking the parking lot through the Internet of Things and mobile Internet and other technologies to realize the data sharing in the region. Through the establishment of a smart parking Internet of Things platform, the running status of parking lot equipment is monitored in real time, data such as the time of vehicles entering and leaving the parking lot and parking fees are fully collected, and big data analysis is used to provide support for parking lot management decisions. In addition, by installing intelligent ballot boxes and other hardware equipment in the parking lot, car owners can be helped to enter and leave the parking lot more efficiently.

(3) **Customization:** From the perspective of service objects, we can divide parking lots into three categories: public parking lots, special parking lots and equipped parking lots. Different types of parking lots need to be equipped with different software and hardware facilities. After the introduction of the smart parking system, property companies and other units can highly integrate the parking lot data of the property management project to create parking lot big data. On this basis, a series of value-added parking services can be customized and provided according to the characteristics of different parking lots.

The application of an intelligent parking system will not only affect the parking industry itself but also improve the parking efficiency and optimize the parking experience in an all-round way, which will further develop the parking-related industry. For example, with the help of intelligent parking systems, the parking problem of shopping centers will be solved and people's shopping experience will be improved; the owners' and non-owners' license plates will be effectively identified to improve the community security level; and the efficiency of hospital parking and car collection will be improved and the cost of patients' medical time will be effectively reduced.

Importance of smart parking in smart city construction

Smart parking is an important part of building a smart city. Taking smart parking as the starting point and gradually changing all aspects of people's urban life is an effective way to speed up the process of building a smart city.

The realization of smart parking is a concrete manifestation of the achievements of building a smart city, which can effectively improve people's urban life experience. The intelligent parking system is used to realize the information recording, charge calculation, analysis and identification, as well as data collection, etc., of vehicles, effectively control the entry and exit of vehicles, store the big data of vehicle parking in the cloud database, and provide data support for intelligent transportation and smart city construction.

From the angle of urban development, parking will be a rigid demand that continues to expand for a long time; in terms of property service enterprises, the pursuit of lower cost and higher efficiency is eternal; from a car owner's perspective, parking should not only be convenient and fast but also humanized and personalized. In other words, smart parking will be a booming sunrise industry, which will provide a steady stream of development power for the construction of smart cities.

Comparison of advantages and disadvantages between manual charging and electronic charging

With the rapid development of artificial intelligence technology, a large number of concepts related to unmanned and intelligent have emerged, such as unmanned driving, unmanned express delivery, unmanned warehouse, unmanned retail, intelligent transportation, as well as smart city, which have brought far-reaching influence to various industries and will change human production and life profoundly. With the tide of unmanned parking sweeping, intelligent parking has the possibility of landing, and unattended parking lots will usher in a period of rapid development.

With the rapid growth of car ownership, the problem of difficult and expensive parking has become more and more prominent. The traditional supervision method requires high labor costs, and its coverage is quite limited. The problem of arbitrary charges in parking lots cannot be effectively controlled, which has brought a great negative impact on people's travel experience. The unattended intelligent parking scheme provides a new idea to solve this problem.

The parking problem has received extensive attention from all walks of life. In January 2018, in the commentary article "How to Solve the Mess of Bookkeeping of Parking Fees" published in *Jinri Toutiao*, a lot of ink was spent to analyze the current chaos of manual parking fee collection, and it was pointed out that intelligent parking will create great value in parking and urban management in the future.

Manual charging chaos is difficult to supervise

This scene is shared in the article: A car owner spent a lot of time and energy to find a free parking space; before the car was parked, the toll collector came to ask for the parking fee, which was 10 or 20 yuan. The charge was not based on the uniform standard but was judged by the toll collector independently. After asking the car owner about the parking purpose, the price was set according to the parking purpose. For example, the car owner who ate was charged 10 yuan, while the car owner who went to the hospital to see a doctor was charged 30 yuan.

Charges lack effective norms. The subjective consciousness of toll collectors has played too many roles. What's more, the final destination of parking fees is unknown; it is not guaranteed that they will be used for urban construction. Sometimes, people will encounter fake toll collectors. When car owners pay parking fees and drive away, they find a ticket posted on the glass. If they want to complain, they cannot find an effective channel or the cost is too high, so they can only choose to complain in WeChat, microblogs and other media.

The problem of arbitrary parking charges on the roadside is only the tip of the iceberg. For example, parking problems in traditional parking lots such as shopping malls and hospitals have become increasingly prominent. The rapid increase of private cars has further aggravated the shortage of parking spaces, toll collectors have been overburdened for a long time, and the service quality and efficiency have declined. At the same time, toll collectors in parking lots are a continuous labor cost input, with a relatively low cost performance. In this case, it is natural that people favor the intelligent parking mode with high efficiency and low cost.

Electronic toll collection mode is widely sought after by the market

Taking Beijing as an example, on December 26, 2017, 4,086 road test parking spaces in Beijing started the pilot of electronic toll collection and the electronic platform calculated the parking fees uniformly. The majority of car owners can pay through five electronic payment methods, including Alipay, WeChat payment, bank card, ETC and municipal traffic card. The positive impact of this change on car owners and toll collectors is obvious, and parking charges are more convenient and standardized.

The development and application of the Internet of Things, sensors, artificial intelligence and other technologies is rapidly improving the digitalization, automation and intelligence level of parking lots. The parking system will calculate the parking fee according to factors such as vehicle parking time and parking period. The problem of inconsistent parking fees caused by the intervention of manual toll collectors is avoided. At the same time, the application of the cashless charging method enables car owners to pay through their smartphones, and each electronic charge can be tracked, which will effectively solve the problem of unknown parking fees and is conducive to improving the credibility of the government.

At present, China's smart parking industry is still in a phase of rapid development. Smart parking solution providers such as Jeez Technology have developed a systematic, information-based and standardized centralized management and control operation mode. It has many functions such as the real-time transmission of parking lot data and automatic license plate recognition; vehicle information can be entered in time, meeting the rich and diversified application scenarios of parking fees. At the same time, through the electronic charging mode, it creates unattended smart parking lots, promotes the transparency of parking fees behavior and standards, effectively solves the problems of private pricing and fake charging, and greatly facilitates managers to carry out data analysis and real-time monitoring.

Smart parking system in the era of mobile Internet

With the gradual acceleration of urbanization and the rapid development of information technology, intelligent transportation construction projects have been launched in various places, and the whole industry has entered a stage of rapid development. Compared with foreign intelligent and dynamic transportation systems, the overall development level of intelligent domestic transportation is relatively backward. In the era of rapid development of mobile Internet, the combination of intelligent domestic transportation and mobile Internet may be the new direction for the development of the parking industry in the future.

In recent years, the market scale of the urban intelligent transportation industry has been growing, with the rapid development of intelligent public transport, traffic signal control, electronic police, card gates, urban passenger hub information, taxi information service management, traffic video monitoring, GPS and police systems, traffic information collection and distribution and traffic command platforms. A whole PC-side Internet can no longer meet the diversified parking needs of users. Therefore, in the future, China's intelligent transportation market will continue to develop in the direction of mobile Internet.

Relationship between parking lot system and mobile Internet

Car owners' requirements for traffic are to "go" comfortably and "stop" conveniently, but in real life, these needs are often not met. Therefore, the whole industry is looking for solutions to these traffic problems, especially the parking management industry. With the advent of the mobile Internet era, the traditional transportation industry and parking management industry are developing continuously, and a great change is brewing.

Whether it is a smart city or a parking lot system, there are several basic components, namely perception, information transmission, information processing and information application. In the era of mobile Internet, the popularization and application of smartphones have had a certain impact on intelligent transportation, providing effective support for information collection and processing and information services.

The connotation of harmonious transportation is very rich; namely, the transportation system should be harmonious, the composition of the transportation system should be harmonious, the transportation and environment should be harmonious, the transportation and society should be harmonious, the transportation and resources should be harmonious, and besides the harmony of ecological environment, the psychological environment should also be harmonious. Among them, the harmony between traffic and society advocates that traffic development should take people as the core, and the harmony between traffic and resources advocates that people should maintain traffic harmony with the least resources and the least cost.

With the help of the mobile Internet, people can get online information related to mobiles, realize real-time sending and receiving of information, and obtain massive information and diversified services. With the support of these conditions, intelligent transportation can obtain dynamic navigation and real-time road conditions, thus allowing overall traffic analysis.

Mobile Internet is the development direction of parking lot system

The development logic of Internet enterprises is to enter the mobile Internet market, provide services to users, cultivate user groups and make profits. Traditional logistics, taxis, public transportation, parking, etc., are connected with the mobile Internet. Under the guidance of mobile Internet thinking, intelligent and humanized parking lots are constructed to provide intelligent parking services for car owners. Nowadays, for the traditional intelligent transportation industry, innovative development has a very important impact on its revolutionary development.

In a general way, government policies will have a great impact on the business model of some products, but at the same time, they also provide an opportunity to change the management mindset of the industry, sort out the management methods of the industry and solve the historical legacy problems of the industry, especially after the Ministry of Transport has replaced the Ministry of Construction to assume the management functions of urban transportation. There are also some products that cannot be developed without the support of policy departments and industrial enterprises, such as mobile Internet products in the public transportation and parking industries. These products especially need the support of government departments and industrial enterprises in the early stage of development.

In the initial stage of the development of mobile Internet products in the field of dynamic traffic information, its data mainly come from taxi companies, as well as information and data collected by the government. With the continuous development of products, data sources have been updated, data have been collected independently, and the key links of product development have broken the restrictions of other institutions.

In recent years, traditional parking lot enterprises have shifted their focus to mobile Internet intelligent transportation products. Mobile Internet intelligent transportation products for government management departments are constantly emerging, such as mobile operation and maintenance products, mobile command products, mobile control products, as well as mobile video products, providing effective solutions for many problems that cannot be solved by PC-side Internet. Since entering the Internet era, people from all walks of life have been trying to connect with the Internet and mobile Internet. Both PC and mobile terminals are the future of the parking industry and the most effective way to solve parking problems.

Chapter 5

Practical Application of an Unmanned Aerial Vehicle in Intelligent Traffic Management

Application of an unmanned aerial vehicle in an intelligent traffic management system

Intelligent traffic management system in unmanned aerial vehicle era

With the rapid development of the economy and the rapid growth of cities, the number of vehicles in cities is increasing, the transportation network is becoming increasingly complex, and intercity trains, high-speed rail and other means of transportation have also developed rapidly. On the one hand, the gradually developed urban transportation network has brought great convenience to people's daily life; on the other hand, the increasing number of vehicles and increasingly complicated road conditions have created hidden dangers for traffic safety and brought many difficulties to traffic control.

At present, China's traffic control methods are mainly traffic police patrols, fixed-point installation of cameras, etc. The monitoring scope is limited, and the pictures presented by cameras are not very clear. If there is a traffic jam around an accident scene, it is difficult for the management department to obtain the images of the scene in the first instance. If manned aircraft are used to patrol in order to realize the comprehensive monitoring of the traffic network, the fuel consumption alone is

133

unaffordable and extremely costly, and daily real-time surveys cannot be carried out. In addition, the manned aircraft are too large to fly over narrow streets, making it impossible to realize the idea of manned aircraft patrols.

Unlike manned aircraft, the specialty of an unmanned aerial vehicle can be brought into full play in the field of urban traffic management. It can help traffic management departments solve various problems in urban traffic management, implement development plans from the macro level, and also supervise and control road conditions and traffic flow from the micro level, build a three-dimensional traffic management system covering water, land and air to realize all-round monitoring of a certain area, ensure smooth traffic, take effective measures to deal with sudden traffic incidents and implement emergency rescue.

The full name of the unmanned aerial vehicle is "remotely piloted aerial vehicle." In the past, an unmanned aerial vehicle was mainly used in the military to conduct aerial reconnaissance and surveillance, locate targets, organize fire attacks, assess war damage, carry out electronic countermeasures, etc. The unmanned aerial vehicle is mainly composed of carrier aircraft, video transmission, flight control, ground station, communication system, gyro pan-tilt and other components, which can carry out high-definition photography. At present, the flying height of multi-rotor aircraft is no more than 500 meters, which is suitable for various complex environments and can shoot and transmit high-definition images.

In recent years, the rapid development of aviation technology has improved people's cognitive ability in the aviation field. Many cities have serious traffic congestion problems. Passenger and cargo unmanned aerial vehicles using unmanned aerial technology can effectively relieve the traffic pressure in cities, accelerate the operation of urban logistics, introduce new products and services that meet the market demand and further tap the market potential. At the same time, the previous single airspace has become more and more diversified. In order to realize the normal operation of air traffic, it is necessary to improve the ability of airspace management.

With the fast development of society, the application scope of unmanned aerial vehicles continues to expand, playing an important role in the fields of traffic management, agricultural monitoring and public safety management. Aviation emergency operators can use unmanned aerial vehicle technology to obtain data resources, deal with emergencies, complete cargo transportation and so on.

With the increasing frequency of unmanned aerial vehicles, the research and development of passenger unmanned aerial vehicles has also made progress. It is necessary to designate corresponding management departments and specific management and implementation methods. Air Navigation Service Providers (ANSPs) have long been responsible for the supervision of safe travel. However, with the continuous increase in the frequency of manned and unmanned aerial vehicles, the corresponding management workload and difficulty will also increase. In order to ensure the passengers' personal safety and protection against property damage, a perfect safety management system should be formed and continuously improved in the process of development.

Every unmanned aerial vehicle ecosystem stakeholder should pay attention to what problems exist in the system operation process, specific solutions and responsibility allocation, and overcome the difficulties encountered in the development of air traffic on a case-by-case basis. To promote the development of high-altitude travel of passenger unmanned aerial vehicles, it is necessary to speed up the construction of a perfect management system, with special emphasis on the development of unmanned systems. It should be clear that the development of unmanned aerial vehicle systems, automatic unmanned aerial vehicles and vertical take-off and landing flight depends on the construction and development of unmanned aerial vehicle traffic management systems.

For a long time, people in the industry have expressed many views on the problems in the development of unmanned aerial vehicle management systems. Stakeholders and operators have different positions, industries, geographical regions and motives. Operators of different automatic driving projects have different needs, but if these operators want to further tap their mobility potential, they should formulate perfect management system solutions.

The operational efficiency and safety of global aviation are reflected through air traffic management. The development of aviation requires higher safety, so in the process of developing unmanned systems, we should continue to strengthen the construction in this area. Therefore, it is necessary to build a reliable air traffic management system, a perfect communication system, a navigation system, a fully functional communication monitoring system, etc. In order to improve the security of the system and ensure its normal operation, we should also pay attention to relevant testing, establish professional teams and carry out high-quality training.

Application fields of an unmanned aerial vehicle in traffic management

Railway transportation

The mileage of railway construction is generally long, involving a lot of sensitive information along the line. At present, the railway still uses manual attendance, which not only has a heavy workload, but also is easily affected by extreme weather and special terrain, and cannot go deep into special sections for investigation; thus, the quality of project acceptance cannot be effectively guaranteed.

In terms of railway route selection, address survey and ecological evaluation, unmanned aerial vehicles can rely on a 3G network to transmit video remotely in real time and transmit the acquired video images to terminal equipment located all over the world in real time, providing continuous data for railway construction and effectively improving work efficiency. Because of its light fuselage, compact structure and outstanding performance, unmanned aerial vehicles can break the limitations of geography, environment and other factors during use and can fly along and around railways in a complex environment to collect useful information.

After the ground station inputs coordinates, under the control of the ground station, the unmanned aerial vehicle can enter the predetermined flight track and transmit images of the railway and along the line remotely to the ground station to discover hidden problems in time, providing a strong guarantee for the safety of communication equipment and smooth flow of information, reducing the workload of inspectors, improving the inspection efficiency and ensuring the safety of railway operation.

Road transportation

Introducing unmanned aerial vehicles in road transportation can effectively monitor the construction of intelligent transportation. Unmanned aerial vehicles can monitor the road surface in real time. Once traffic accidents and violations occur on the road surface, unmanned aerial vehicles can discover and investigate traffic violations in time to improve traffic management efficiency and ensure smooth roads.

Compared with traditional aerial photography, unmanned aerial vehicle mapping can not only obtain more accurate data but also improve data acquisition efficiency. With the support of an unmanned aerial vehicle system, the traffic management department has created a brand-new way to monitor highway traffic. Unmanned aerial vehicles carry high-definition cameras to take all-round pictures of highways from high altitudes, which can not only obtain more perfect aerial photography data of highways, meet the needs of relevant departments for data, but also provide strong technical support for highway survey and design.

(1) **On-site investigation of serious traffic accidents:** Traditional exploration methods need to consume a lot of manpower, material resources and time and the exploration process is facing great danger, which may lead to secondary accidents or miss the best rescue time due to the slow collection of accident data. Unmanned aerial vehicles are not afraid of danger and can go deep into various areas with a complex environment and terrain for exploration, reach the accident site quickly, collect topographic data, vehicle damage, casualties, etc., of the accident area, comprehensively improve the survey efficiency and guide the rescue work to carry out rapidly.

(2) **Maintain traffic order:** Unmanned aerial vehicles can remotely transmit video and image data to the traffic command center in the shortest possible time. The traffic command center can quickly know the deployment of patrol cars and police officers so that instructions can be given more scientifically, improving the efficiency and quality of traffic management and avoiding traffic congestion at major moments and important occasions. In addition, once an alarm situation is detected by the unmanned aerial vehicle during the patrol, the command center can be quickly notified and the command center can quickly locate and deploy police officers to deal with the situation in the shortest possible time, thus effectively improving the efficiency of traffic management.

If there is traffic congestion on a certain road section, the unmanned aerial vehicle can fly to the scene quickly, find out the cause of the congestion quickly, carry out all-round exploration on the congested roads and the length of the congestion, and transmit the image of the scene to the traffic command center. According to these images, the traffic command center can quickly formulate a diversion plan to restore smooth roads.

Waterway transport

Among all kinds of mainstream modes of transportation, waterway transport appeared the earliest and has taken the longest to develop. Since the reform and opening-up, China's economy has developed rapidly, domestic port throughput has increased, ships have become larger and more specialized and the risk of water pollution has become higher.

At present, the monitoring methods used in water transportation mainly include ship cruises, satellite remote sensing monitoring, the regular cruise of air fixed-wing aircraft and so on. Compared with these traditional monitoring methods, unmanned aerial vehicle (UAV) has lower costs and stronger real-time performance. At the same time, an unmanned aerial vehicle is rainproof and can fly in heavy rain and moderate snowy weather. The waterproof level during flight can reach IPX4, which can effectively cope with the changing weather at sea. In addition, the GPS equipment installed in the unmanned aerial vehicle has high precision. The unmanned aerial vehicle can fly automatically after the route is set on the GPS. The use of an unmanned aerial vehicle for monitoring water traffic can also effectively prevent ships from operating illegally.

Air transport

With the rapid development of the air transport industry, there are increasing demands on airport safety management, and airport safety has become a key concern for governments and the international community. Airports, especially large and medium-sized aviation hub airports, cover a very wide area; they have large flight areas, large terminal buildings, large passenger flow, large cargo flow and large aircraft take-off and landing volume. If safety supervision is carried out only manually, not only is the workload heavy, but it is also ineffective. To improve the quality and efficiency of safety supervision, to detect safety hazards as early as possible and to nip them in the bud, the airport supervision system must introduce advanced technology.

The key monitoring area of the airport is the drop-off area, where the flow of people and vehicles is relatively large, and traffic accidents and disputes occur frequently. Using an unmanned aerial vehicle to carry out cruise monitoring in this area can eliminate the dead monitoring angle of ordinary video monitoring, transmit the captured video images to designated terminals through the network, realize real-time monitoring of this area, reduce drivers' illegal operation behavior, standardize passengers' waiting order and help passengers who have lost items quickly find lost property.

The flight area of the airport is very large, and the search and rescue of accident victims after landing is very difficult. The unmanned aerial vehicle has a flight speed of 80 km/h, a flight altitude of 2,000 meters, a flight radius of 5 km and a one-way flight distance of 10 km, which is very suitable for cruise search and rescue work in large areas such as airports.

Application advantages of the unmanned aerial vehicle in traffic management

(1) **Condescending:** Unmanned aerial vehicles can overlook the traffic flow on the ground from high altitude, help traffic management departments grasp the road conditions in real time, conduct overall command and formulate scientific diversion schemes. Compared with manned general-purpose aircraft and manned helicopters, unmanned aerial vehicles can fly closer to the scene of traffic accidents and can capture clearer images.

(2) **Wide range:** Unmanned aerial vehicles can realize short-distance, high-speed low-altitude flight, can flexibly change the observation angle of view, move in a large range, provide powerful help for traffic management departments to quickly control the situation and do not need to dispatch multiple police cars for a simple task.

(3) **Stay in the air for a longer time:** Compared with manned general-purpose aircraft and manned helicopters, the unmanned aerial vehicle stays in the air for a longer time and urban traffic patrol flights for a longer time, so once the target area is locked, the unmanned aerial vehicle can be sent to perform search missions.

(4) **High efficiency:** Unmanned aerial vehicles can be dispatched at any time without taking a long time to prepare for ground handling and maintenance. Compared with other flying vehicles, the unmanned aerial vehicle has lower investment and higher income.

(5) **Low risk:** The unmanned aerial vehicle is used in urban traffic management and can perform dangerous tasks in disastrous weather and harsh environment. The practice has proved that unmanned aerial vehicle has incomparable advantages in sandstorm detection, chemical pollution and radioactive pollution monitoring, and can complete many tasks that cannot be completed by manned general-purpose aircraft, manned helicopters and other means of transportation.

(6) **Navigation networking:** With the support of aviation networking, the unmanned aerial vehicle can be used online in a way that other conventional aircraft cannot. After selecting the application software and system, the unmanned aerial vehicle can play multiple functions. In addition, in the aviation networking environment, the unmanned aerial vehicle system has the characteristics of high integration, high intelligence and high comprehensive efficiency, which can standardize, serialize and generalize the unmanned aerial vehicle design, enable the vehicle to upgrade on demand, improve its own quality and increase its own functions, promote the stability and practicability of the unmanned aerial vehicle multi-purpose platform, thus making these vehicles low-carbon, green and environmentally friendly and playing an effective leading role in the development of aviation science and technology.

(7) **Replace more with less:** It is not necessary to dispatch too many police forces after the introduction of an unmanned aerial vehicle in urban traffic management. A small number of these vehicles can complete the tasks that a large number of police officers on the ground have to perform, thus saving both labor costs and service costs.

(8) **Flexibility:** Unmanned aerial vehicles can fly over expressways and viaducts in the course of urban management, shuttle between high-rise buildings and even cross tunnels to complete the evidence collection of traffic accident scenes with strong flexibility.

(9) **Emergency rescue:** After natural disasters such as earthquakes, tsunamis and blizzards, the ground traffic in the affected areas will be greatly damaged or even completely paralyzed. In this case, the relevant departments can dispatch unmanned aerial vehicles to go deep into the disaster site for investigation, take pictures of the scene, search for personnel, establish communication relays and deliver first aid items to the victims so as to prepare for the large-scale rescue afterwards.

(10) **Security precautions:** In the process of participating in urban traffic management, if there is a hit-and-run vehicle, the unmanned aerial vehicle can chase the vehicle to obtain evidence, issue a warning to the driver who caused the accident and then release tear gas, catchers and other items at an opportune time to help the traffic police capture the driver who caused the accident.

Technical application of unmanned aerial vehicles in traffic supervision

With the increasing number of motor vehicles and the continuous extension of the urban road network, in order to do a good job in traffic supervision, the traffic police department has continuously increased its investment in traffic technology monitoring equipment, but it still cannot meet the needs of traffic supervision. The introduction of unmanned aerial vehicles can continuously improve the electronic monitoring network, provide a strong guarantee for road traffic management and public security prevention, and play an extremely important role in the process of traffic supervision.

Traffic flow control

(1) The unmanned aerial vehicle is equipped with a high-definition camera or camera, which can collect road information in real time during flight.
(2) The unmanned aerial vehicle is equipped with a picture transmission system, which can transmit the captured video signal or picture signal to the corresponding equipment.
(3) The unmanned aerial vehicle is equipped with a flight control system. With the support of the system, the unmanned aerial vehicle can realize autonomous flight and intelligent monitoring.

Image processing

(1) The design of the image transmission circuit of unmanned aerial vehicles is very stable and sensitive, and the collected images are relatively stable and of good image quality, which can be used in densely populated areas.

(2) The three-axis shock-absorbing flight pan-tilt of unmanned aerial vehicles can carry some airborne equipment, such as visible light and infrared. The grid axis of the pan-tilt is relatively stable and can be corrected automatically.
(3) The high-list digital reflex camera or high-definition cameras carried by unmanned aerial vehicles can capture clear and perfect images.

Flight control system

The unmanned aerial vehicle is equipped with GPS, magnetometer, barometric altimeter, six-degree-of-freedom inertial measurement unit and other sensor devices. The theoretical models of robot control, such as the H infinite algorithm with high robustness and expert system, are optimized. The core module of flight control is more stable and reliable, and the unmanned aerial vehicle system is built into a fully automatic air operation platform. A variety of flight control modes are developed so that the unmanned aerial vehicle can operate in different environments. Even in different altitude modes, this vehicle can keep accurate altitude locking and realize smooth flight.

Strengthening out-of-control protection, even after losing the remote control signal, the unmanned aerial vehicle can hover automatically. When the hover time exceeds 10 seconds, the flight control system can automatically calculate the best return route and send a return instruction to the unmanned aerial vehicle to realize a safe return. Even in windy weather, unmanned aerial vehicles can hover accurately.

Function integration of an unmanned aerial vehicle ground station

The integrated GPS geographic information system can control the unmanned aerial vehicle to fly to the target waypoint accurately, modify the route setting during the flight, give an alarm to the ground station in time in case of positioning error and hover at fixed points during the flight. The telemetry data is recorded to display the flight status of unmanned aerial vehicles, such as flight mileage, flight altitude, flight time, GPS status, as well as voltage.

Unmanned aerial vehicle communication command vehicle

The unmanned aerial vehicle communication command vehicle is equipped with a high-power video receiver, fixed-wing unmanned aerial vehicle ejection frame, telescopic antenna, high-precision real-time kinematic (RTK) and other devices, which can be used for remote monitoring of unmanned aerial vehicles.

Air traffic surveillance system based on an unmanned aerial vehicle

Recently, unmanned aerial vehicles have appeared more and more frequently in the flight field, and there are many "black flying" phenomena, that is, flying at will without monitoring. This kind of flight will induce many traffic accidents and threaten the flight safety and personal safety of civil aviation. To prevent such accidents, it is necessary to establish a complete monitoring system for unmanned aerial vehicle flight and manage it effectively.

At present, the flight of civil aviation aircraft is jointly managed by air traffic control, pilots and dispatchers, where air traffic control and dispatchers are responsible for supervising and commanding the flight of aircraft. Pilots complete the flight by following rules and regulations, obeying the command and ensuring flight safety with the joint efforts of the three parties. The design of unmanned aerial vehicle air traffic monitoring system can learn from the management system of civil aviation aircraft, and the flight of unmanned aerial vehicles is managed by air traffic control, unmanned aerial vehicles and ground stations to ensure flight safety of unmanned aerial vehicles. At the same time, the unmanned aerial vehicle monitoring system can be docked with the air traffic control monitoring system to realize the integration of civil aviation and unmanned aerial vehicle monitoring.

Overall design

The unmanned aerial vehicle air traffic monitoring system consists of air traffic control, unmanned aerial vehicle and ground station. During the flight, the unmanned aerial vehicle sends data such as flight height, flight position and flight altitude to the ground station through the data transmission station. The ground station receives and analyzes these data, and then transmits the new data to the unmanned aerial vehicle through the data transmission radio so as to adjust the flight path and flight altitude of the unmanned aerial vehicle and realize the full-duplex communication between the unmanned aerial vehicle and the ground station.

Because the unmanned aerial vehicle in flight is far away from the air traffic control, ordinary wireless data transmission cannot meet the data transmission requirements between unmanned aerial vehicles and ground stations. Therefore, SIM7100C GSM (4G module) is used to establish a mobile network data transmission channel with the air traffic control, and the flight data of the unmanned aerial vehicle is transmitted to the air traffic control in real time. At the same time, the air traffic control can also use this data transmission channel to send AT instructions to the unmanned aerial vehicle to control the flight altitude, flight route and altitude of the unmanned aerial vehicle. Through the mutual transmission of this data link, the full-duplex communication among air traffic control, ground station and unmanned aerial vehicles is realized.

Module design

(1) **Connection module between flight control and ground station:** Using STM32, MUPU6050, MS5611 and other modules to establish flight control, the information is transmitted to the ground station through the data transmission radio. The proportion integration differentiation (PID) interface of the ground station can fine-tune the flight altitude of the unmanned aerial vehicle, adjust the flight route of the unmanned aerial vehicle and establish full-duplex communication between the unmanned aerial vehicle and the ground station to realize the monitoring and operation of the unmanned aerial vehicle.

(2) **Connection module between unmanned aerial vehicle and air traffic control:** The communication between unmanned aerial vehicles and air traffic control is different from the communication between unmanned aerial vehicles and ground stations. Compared with ground stations, the distance between unmanned aerial vehicles and air traffic control is long, so it is impossible to use ordinary wireless communication to complete communication, and only 4G communication can be used. The 4G module is established by using Sim7100C chip, through which the unmanned aerial vehicle sends flight data to the air traffic control, and the air traffic control can receive the geographical position of the unmanned aerial vehicle by configuring IP to the computer receiving the signal. In the meantime, computers equipped with IP can also send AT commands to unmanned aerial vehicles, control unmanned aerial vehicle flight, and realize

full-duplex communication between unmanned aerial vehicles and air traffic control by applying 4G modules.

Data transmission design

The unmanned aerial vehicle transmits flight data to the ground station through the data transmission station, and the ground station takes out the data from the serial port by using the serial port program, writes the data transmission protocol, establishes a link with the ground station interface, and displays the collected data. Unmanned aerial vehicle data and operator information are transmitted to computers equipped with IP through a 4G network, a database is established, the received data information is sorted out, and then a protocol is written to link with the air traffic control system. Through data link, the flight position of unmanned aerial vehicles can be displayed in the air traffic control interface.

Based on the design of flight control, 4G network, data transmission radio and other modules, this unmanned aerial vehicle air traffic monitoring system can realize full-duplex communication among air traffic control, unmanned aerial vehicle and ground station and realize the flight monitoring of unmanned aerial vehicle through information exchange and cooperation among them. Under the working mode of this unmanned aerial vehicle air traffic monitoring system, these vehicles can send its geographical position, flight altitude, flight route, flight altitude and other information to air traffic control and ground stations during flight.

If the unmanned aerial vehicle deviates from the scheduled flight route, with improper height, improper position and other problems during flight, the air traffic control can contact the ground station in time to adjust the vehicle and provide help for the ground station to control the vehicle to ensure that the unmanned aerial vehicle flies safely and standardly under the joint action of the air traffic control, ground station and unmanned aerial vehicle. At the same time, the combination of this system and the air traffic control monitoring system can promote the integration of air traffic control and unmanned aerial vehicle monitoring.

Specifically, this unmanned aerial vehicle air traffic monitoring system has more practical application value and practical significance:

(1) At present, the existing unmanned aerial vehicle management systems in China are more or less flawed. This unmanned aerial vehicle air

traffic monitoring system can effectively monitor and manage unmanned aerial vehicles, put an end to the phenomena of "black flying" and "flying around" and ensure the safety of civil aviation and personal safety.

(2) At present, there is little research on unmanned aerial vehicle monitoring in China. The above research can make up for the deficiency of unmanned aerial vehicle monitoring system research in China and promote the unmanned aerial vehicle monitoring management system to develop further.

(3) The system combined with ATC (air traffic control) monitoring system can further enhance the monitoring ability of ATC and prevent unmanned aerial vehicles from interfering with the flight of civil aviation aircraft.

(4) In the future, unmanned aerial vehicles will be applied in more and more fields, such as transportation, resource exploration, as well as land survey. To ensure the standard operation of unmanned aerial vehicles, it is necessary to monitor them in real time. This system achieves this and provides a strong guarantee for the normal operation of unmanned aerial vehicle.

(5) This system is stable and has strong adaptability. Loading other modules (such as the environmental measurement module) on unmanned aerial vehicles can enhance the operation capability of unmanned aerial vehicles, control unmanned aerial vehicles to fly into uninhabited areas for environmental investigation and effectively improve its practical utilization value.

Key factors for landing an unmanned aerial vehicle traffic management system

Policy factors: Promote the standardized development of the industry

Up to now, unmanned aerial vehicle has been applied in many commercial and non-commercial fields, and plays an important role. In the past, the application of unmanned aerial vehicles was mainly concentrated in the field of military defense. With the development, the technical level of unmanned aerial vehicles is gradually improving, and many new products will be developed and put out into the market. At present, aerial photography, surveying and mapping in the commercial field have become important positions for unmanned aerial vehicles to play their value. Drone as a service (unmanned aerial vehicle as a service) has received increasingly extensive attention. In the meantime, supportive policies introduced by the government have also strongly promoted the development of unmanned aerial vehicles.

The application scope of unmanned aerial vehicles has gradually expanded in the fields of agriculture, petroleum as well as construction.

In the early stage of development, the application of unmanned aerial vehicles in the commercial field only focused on visual line of sight (VLOS) operation. Nowadays, China, Poland, Australia, New Zealand, Switzerland, Denmark, Canada and some parts of the United States have broadened the application scope of unmanned aerial vehicles through policy regulations, enabling them to play their value in over-the-horizon operations and promoting the innovative application of unmanned aerial vehicles.

The market for unmanned aerial vehicles has enormous potential for growth. Among other things, innovative applications around the consumer are contributing to the growth of the market as a whole. Taking the development of global vertical take-off and landing unmanned aerial vehicles as a typical representative, its market value will continue to rise. ASD's latest market research report, "Unmanned Aerial Vehicle Market from 2013 to 2018," shows that the global unmanned aerial vehicle market is about US$8.351 billion in 2018.

According to the "2018 Global and Chinese Unmanned Aerial Vehicle Traffic Management (UTM) Industry Deep Research Report" released by Newsijie Industry Research, the global unmanned aerial vehicle traffic management system market size is expected to be US$538 million in 2018 and will reach US$1.961 billion by 2025, with a compound annual growth rate of 20.28% between 2018 and 2025. Among them, commercial applications will make great contributions to the rapid growth of the entire industry. In this process, enterprises will improve the efficiency of information acquisition and logistics operations and apply unmanned aerial vehicle technology in cargo handling and distribution. To promote the healthy development of the industry, a mature and well-developed traffic management system is required to achieve a wide range of cooperation from all over the world.

The aviation field will be further developed in the future. A perfect unmanned management system can promote the sustainable development of the market and provide a strong guarantee for aviation safety and public safety. Therefore, we should speed up the construction of a complete management system.

Each operator is required to follow a unified standard to carry out actions, improve the participation enthusiasm of relevant personnel and continuously improve the operation of each operation link in the later construction and development process to get through the operation of each link and improve the end-to-end service on this basis.

It is necessary to focus on airspace management and issue unified standards for stakeholders so as to improve the sustainability of UAV development. For such a purpose of improving the management ability of unmanned aerial vehicle system operation, there is a need to clarify the distribution of responsibilities, optimize the information architecture, establish data exchange protocols, continuously upgrade software functions and improve infrastructure in the process of developing unmanned driving management system.

In order to incorporate the UAV system into the current air traffic management operation system, many difficulties need to be overcome. In the specific implementation process, it is necessary to strengthen the cooperative relationship among data service providers, communication system service providers, regulatory authorities, as well as operators. After mastering the relevant information, the Federal Aviation Administration of the United States and the National Aeronautics and Space Administration (NASA) have joined hands with many relevant organizational structures in the world to jointly carry out problem investigations and formulate solutions, working to introduce unmanned aerial vehicles into airspace and implementing standardized operation and management, so as to build a perfect unmanned management system and reduce the risks of management operations.

In order to promote the development of unmanned aerial vehicle transportation systems, a series of pioneering changes have been implemented in this field, and the autonomous aviation system has been emphatically studied. The Federal Aviation Administration of the United States focuses on analyzing the application of unmanned aerial vehicle system products and their impact. At present, new technologies are being developed and their applications are being promoted in the field of unmanned aerial vehicle transportation. If these activities can be linked with NASA research, the development of value for the entire industry can be promoted.

Safety factors: Improve the safety of traffic management

The development and implementation process of the unmanned driving management system is affected by many factors, and different stakeholders have different expectations for the results of its implementation. In order to improve the operation efficiency of unmanned aerial vehicle systems and the safety of the whole traffic management system, it is necessary to integrate the advantageous resources in related fields and continuously overcome various difficulties in the process of development.

At this stage, the air traffic management services of relevant regulatory authorities are not perfect, and the service development of unmanned driving management systems may rely on the guidance of the commercial market. For example, the regulator has not yet introduced effective management services for the low-altitude operation of small unmanned systems weighing less than 25 kg. In the short term, the regulator will not change the operational authority for airspace and remaining air traffic operations by requiring commercial unmanned projects to apply for authorization.

In order to realize the transformation smoothly, the unmanned management system should adjust the traditional air navigation management mode. Relevant management agencies should assume more responsibilities in the process of operation, including changing airspace classification, formulating instructions and agreements, issuing procedures and specifications, determining coordination areas required by unmanned aerial vehicles, notification areas required by unmanned aerial vehicles, etc., to ensure the smooth development of unmanned aerial vehicle operations.

The importance of manned spaceflight and public safety is obvious. The responsibility for the safety of UAVs operating in the "beyond visual range" lies with commercial UAV operators. At the same time, they are also responsible for tracking unmanned aerial vehicles in the airspace to prevent unmanned aerial vehicles from exceeding the limited airspace. When integrating unmanned aerial vehicles, it is necessary to implement the integration plan on the basis of ensuring that the accident rate does not increase, and at the same time, it is necessary to resolutely avoid introducing more safety risks in the process of planning. In the process of formulating the development plan of unmanned systems, it is important to focus on the deployment of safety and to come up with specific countermeasures.

At this stage, it is difficult to play a practical role in the safety of unmanned aerial vehicles by using monitoring systems, except for identifying the types of unmanned aerial vehicles. By installing sensors on unmanned aerial vehicles and other automatic driving equipment to sense the flying objects in the current airspace or making unmanned aerial vehicles run according to the established route, the probability of accidents can be reduced.

Although the role played is relatively limited, monitoring means are essential to enhance traffic operation safety and improve traffic management efficiency. The automation platform is responsible for collecting solid information, but this method cannot play its role except for those relatively large aircraft that open their own flight information. That is to say, if the unmanned aerial vehicle is small, or if the flight equipment is made of composite materials and plastics, it may not be recognized by the monitoring equipment and collect signals. In order to realize comprehensive and effective surveillance, it is necessary to solve these existing problems, take effective measures to track aircraft and apply all possible tracking methods to the research and development and improvement of surveillance technology.

The lack of mandatory transponders is also the reason for the slow development of surveillance technology. If the aircraft operates in a low-level airspace within 10 meters to 200 meters, it is ineffective to use traditional surveillance radar. Holographic radar can be used to map airspace volume and sense small flying objects, but these operations are not incorporated into the air traffic management system. The provision of monitoring data should be incorporated into the whole operation system in the subsequent development process.

Technical factors: Building a sound infrastructure

Communication, navigation and surveillance systems are the core infrastructure of unmanned management and play a supporting role in unmanned systems. Only with perfect infrastructure can the regulatory authorities or their authorized agencies operate normally.

Communication

All activities of air traffic management are inseparable from the services provided by communication facilities. Air traffic control uses controllers, pilot interfaces, etc. These elements are closely related to communication.

Compared with the previous air traffic management, the application of unmanned aerial vehicles makes the whole traffic management system more involved than in previous air traffic management. In the face of new demands, special attention should be paid to the construction of communication infrastructure, ensuring that control data are uploaded and telemetry data are received through ground stations, and corresponding broadband and operation programs should be equipped for this purpose. At present, wireless hotspots and other low-performance communication devices can be used as information receiving stations in the surrounding areas for signal receiving and data transmission.

As flight distances continue to increase, it is necessary to adopt the information transmission mode that are suitable for the long-distance environment. In the course of development, the digital communication of in traditional aircraft has gradually replaced voice communication. In the future, it is necessary to realize the information communication between unmanned aerial vehicles and traditional aircraft.

It should be noted that the flight plan information involved in unmanned aerial vehicle combat can also be opted out of submission. In the event that the air traffic service provider does not have access to the affected area during a mission, relevant information can be obtained from other parties for effective processing. However, at present, there is not much intersection between the operations of different links, and effective systematic integration has not been realized.

Navigation

For aviation safety, it is essential to prevent collisions and conflicts with other airspace users during the flight of unmanned aerial vehicles. At present, unmanned aerial vehicle equipment cannot effectively sense and bypass other aircraft, and most unmanned aerial vehicles are not equipped with anti-collision systems. Using the navigation system, unmanned aerial vehicles can adjust its flight path according to predefined rules to prevent collision with other aircraft. In addition, in the event of a technical failure, the UAV will not be remotely controlled and there is no solution for this situation at this stage.

Surveillance

The operation process of the air traffic management system must be clear. The industry needs clear procedures and airspace in the development process. For actions beyond the general altitude range and actions carried out in the airspace of densely populated areas, it is necessary to further define clearly, so as to facilitate the implementation of subsequent control actions.

(1) For the normal flight state, the flight data processing system used in the process of air traffic control can detect the flight equipment in the airspace by monitoring the data and analyzing the flight plan information.

(2) Air traffic service providers need various data to support and to complete their own tasks on the basis of using existing procedures and relevant training.

It is very difficult for unmanned aerial vehicles to provide information at this level, and to meet the needs of unmanned aerial vehicle market, it is necessary to connect different elements of unmanned management system infrastructure related to navigation. On the other hand, it is necessary to formulate unified standards and protocols to support the efficient operation of unmanned management systems. In addition, to reduce the difficulty of unmanned traffic management, the air traffic control system should establish a perfect electronic system for collecting flight information in airspace outside the control range.

Data

In the course of the operation of unmanned aerial vehicles, abundant data can be generated, which records the flight path, flight speed and real-time position of unmanned aerial vehicle and can provide effective support for its mission execution. On the basis of data analysis, the best route can be selected, and artificial intelligence and automation technology can be used to ensure that the unmanned aerial vehicle runs according to the established route in a safe and efficient way.

Kennesaw State University started to study the approximate algorithm for the purpose of optimizing the application of unmanned aerial vehicles. The successful launch of this scheme allows logistics enterprises to give full play to the role of unmanned aerial vehicles in transportation and improve the overall transportation efficiency while reducing cost consumption.

Demand factors: Promoting the sustainable development of the industry

The public

All participants should be clear about their own position and responsibilities in the unmanned management system. All stakeholders who serve as one of the components of the whole ecosystem should get rid of their limitations, understand the unmanned aerial vehicle system from the overall level, and strengthen cooperation with other parts.

To be specific, some unmanned aerial vehicle pilots are responsible for transmitting traffic information, some pilots are responsible for transporting medical supplies, while some pilots are responsible for exploring crop growth status, etc. Different operators shoulder different responsibilities. When the application scope of unmanned aerial vehicles is expanding, as human labor is replaced by unmanned aerial vehicles, society may face unemployment.

However, the application of automation technology is also expected to give rise to new jobs. It should reform the traditional management mode of the unmanned management system at an appropriate time, promote the upgrading of the communication system, optimize the training system, and drive the development of the unmanned management system as a whole.

Science and technology

The air traffic management technology at the current stage cannot keep up with the development of unmanned aerial vehicle technology and aircraft technology. Participants who take the lead in the layout in this field are making use of advanced technical means to formulate countermeasures, which will open the way for the future development of unmanned aerial vehicle traffic management. At the same time, it should provide support for the development of self-driving cars through technological innovation.

In this process, safety issues should be especially emphasized. It is necessary to speed up the construction of unmanned management systems and improve the standardization of technology applications after realizing that the development of supervision systems cannot keep up with the needs of technology development and application.

NASA has played a leading role in the development of unmanned management systems and is committed to further promoting the application value of unmanned aerial vehicles in more fields and developing towards tactical application by reducing the impact of the national aviation system on the application of unmanned aerial vehicles in low-altitude airspace.

NASA is implementing a technology transfer program with the purpose of transferring technology to relevant industrial enterprises in the United States and promoting the commercial application of advanced technologies. Uber has established a cooperative relationship with NASA to jointly optimize the management system of flying cars and unmanned aerial vehicles and is committed to accelerating the research and development and application projects of flying taxis.

(1) **EU:** The European Aviation Safety Agency (EASA) will introduce unified unmanned aerial vehicle regulations for the EU. However, at this stage, unmanned aerial vehicles under 150 kg have not been included in this regulation.
(2) **Germany:** According to the newly issued regulations in Germany, operators can operate beyond visual range flights if they can verify the safety flight records. If the weight of the UAV is less than or equal to 25 kg, it can fly in airspace up to a height of 100 meters.
(3) **Australia:** The Civil Aviation Safety Administration (CASA) has relatively loose management of unmanned aerial vehicles, allowing unmanned aerial vehicles weighing less than 2 kg to operate in the air with an altitude of less than 400 feet in uninhabited areas without the approval of relevant departments.

Finance

(1) There are many sources of funds for the construction and development of unmanned management systems, and seed funds from the public sector are one of them.

(2) Enterprises and investors with sufficient cash reserves and are interested in market investment. For example, enterprises represented by Google, Amazon and Uber are committed to developing unmanned system projects. While providing financial support for the implementation of the projects, they can also improve consumers' awareness of unmanned aerial vehicle-related mobile technologies. Most of these enterprises focus on the development of hardware products and service provision.

In addition, many innovative projects serving the operation of unmanned aerial vehicles, such as the construction of unmanned management systems, helicopter airports and other related infrastructure, navigation systems, security software, have also received investment support from some niche enterprises in France, Germany and other countries. Some enterprises use the funds of private angel investors, venture capitalists and private equity to develop navigation and unmanned driving management system technology.

With the rapid development of blockchain and artificial intelligence technology in recent years, the development of unmanned driving management systems may be promoted. Deep Aero is using blockchain technology to develop an artificial intelligence-driven unmanned aerial vehicle system. In this system, blockchain can play an important role in logistics and further improve the functional structure of unmanned management systems. In the specific implementation process, the company will use unified unmanned aerial vehicle registration standards, 3D map data and other technologies to speed up the research and development process.

On the other hand, with the deep deployment of LAANC (Low Altitude Authorization and Notification Capability Program), the Federal Aviation Administration has also participated in the process of supporting the development of unmanned aerial vehicles, vigorously building air traffic facilities and promoting the improvement of related infrastructure.

Market factors: Realizing the industrialization of unmanned aerial vehicle

At present, both unmanned aerial and air vehicles have been showing a boom in development, although a perfect unmanned aerial vehicle flight infrastructure has not yet been established and an effective safety management system is lacking. When more and more unmanned aerial vehicle equipment is put into use, it is necessary to speed up the construction of unmanned management systems so as to improve the sustainability of the development of the entire unmanned aerial vehicle market and provide a safety guarantee for unmanned aerial vehicle flight.

An unmanned aerial vehicle traffic management system needs to cover airspace planning, congestion management, route design, separation management, emergency management, dynamic geographic setting, severe weather management, interval distance, sorting management and many other elements. While providing services for the current unmanned aerial vehicle application, the management system should also take into account the future development in this field, such as the application and development of flying taxis and passenger unmanned aerial vehicles.

An unmanned driving management system can provide a strong guarantee for the development of the unmanned driving industry, promote the development of related enterprises and further tap its market value.

Unmanned system service provider

In the process of carrying out pilot projects and setting standards, unmanned system service providers should join hands with regulatory authorities, communication providers and leading automobile manufacturers to promote the development of hardware and software related to safety traffic management systems. Based on the full application of the core functions of the unmanned aircraft system (UAS) traffic management system, the market for UAS traffic management systems can be expanded to increase profit revenue. American Airlines can require operators to pay subscription fees. In the specific implementation, either a one-time fee or an annual fee could be used. In addition, American Airlines can also require flying vehicle operators to pay service fees after flying.

Unmanned aerial vehicle operator

The demand for unmanned aerial vehicle applications in logistics, forest research and railway inspection will continue to increase. After the establishment of a perfect unmanned driving management system, unmanned aerial vehicle operators can not only fly in the airspace beyond visual range but also perform tasks in areas with large population distribution.

In the process of establishing a traffic management system, unmanned aerial vehicle operators should cooperate. In order to improve the safety of unmanned aerial vehicle operation, attention should be paid to the application of route planning and navigation technology, the emergency management system should be established, navigation software and sensors should be set up to improve the safety of operation and the application scope of unmanned management system network should be gradually expanded. In this process, a perfect unmanned management system can also bring many benefits to unmanned aerial vehicle operators, as well as facilitating communication and interaction between the operator and other stakeholders.

Communication service provider

Communications companies play an important role in the establishment of traffic management systems, as unmanned aerial vehicle interaction and unmanned aerial vehicle tracking rely on the technology provided by these companies, as well as compliance with the technical standards set by them. After the unmanned aerial vehicle traffic management system is put into use, American airlines and unmanned aerial vehicle operators need to pay service fees to communication companies. At present, communication companies that have established cooperative relations with regulatory authorities will take advantage of timing.

Gradually overcoming the difficulties encountered in the development process can prepare the ground for the construction and improvement of the unmanned management system in the later period, so that its development can enter a new period, which can consider the problem from a longer-term perspective and focus on the construction of unified air traffic management. In this process, it is necessary to provide the necessary support for the development of traditional traffic and unmanned aircraft.

Establishing and perfecting a unified air traffic management system to serve the air flight of vertical take-off and landing, unmanned aerial vehicles, etc., can effectively reduce the risk of air traffic. Nowadays, many enterprises have increased their investment support for related development projects and are committed to building air traffic management systems to improve travel efficiency and safety, avoid traffic congestion and reduce traffic accidents as much as possible.

Application and development of an unmanned aerial vehicle in highway surveys

Advantages of an unmanned aerial vehicle in expressway survey

With the rapid development of economic construction, many sectors in China have a large amount of satellite remote sensing images and traditional aerial photography data, but there is also a clear trend of increasing demand for real-time, mobile, high-resolution remote sensing data that are urgently needed everywhere. In comparison with the traditional remote sensing data and image data carried by satellites, large aircraft, total artificial stations and other equipment to obtain a wide range of geographic information, low-altitude unmanned aerial vehicle aerial remote sensing has the advantages of mobility and flexibility. It can carry out large-scale topographic mapping of strip terrain and has good effects in highway surveys, daily maintenance mapping and emergency mapping of geological disasters. Therefore, it has high practicability in highway surveys. Unmanned aerial vehicle aerial survey remote sensing technology is a new technology developed after satellite remote sensing and aircraft remote sensing, which is widely used in emergency surveying and mapping support, land and resources monitoring, major engineering construction and so on. It is a flexible aerial survey technology that can realize quick responses. Low-altitude unmanned aerial vehicle aerial photography remote sensing uses a low-speed unmanned aerial vehicle as the aerial remote sensing operation platform, uses color, black and white, infrared, camera and other technologies to photograph surface features and geomorphic image data from the air, and uses computers to process the image data information. It integrates remote sensing, communication, GPS differential positioning, remote control and other technologies with new application technologies of computer software processing technology.

Expressway engineering has a long engineering interval, in which it is likely to pass through complex, dangerous terrain or encounter some kind of disaster. For example, when the embankment and slope of an expressway are affected by topography, geology and weather, they may collapse and slide, causing danger. In this case, it is necessary to know the geometric shape and earthwork volume of collapse and slide to plan the repair scheme. However, since it is difficult for relevant surveying and mapping personnel and equipment to approach the site of the collapse and slide after the collapse and slide occur, it is important to fly over the site of the collapse and slide quickly without being restricted by the ground. Unmanned aerial vehicle aerial survey with airborne digital cameras for on-site photography is not only simple and fast but also has high safety. The specific advantages are as follows:

(1) **Fast and efficient:** It is easy to obtain the required surveying and mapping images, the equipment is simple and the civilian SLR camera can also be competent.
(2) **Flexibility:** In surveying and mapping work, the quick response ability of low-altitude unmanned aerial vehicles is a powerful guarantee for emergency remote sensing surveying and mapping. Low-altitude unmanned aerial vehicles have been well received and widely used by users because of its light fuselage equipment, flexible transportation, strong off-road capability, low requirements for take-off and landing sites, various take-off and landing modes and quick installation, debugging and take-off operations.
(3) **High resolution and fast processing speed:** The resolution of aerial remote sensing data of low-altitude unmanned aerial vehicles can reach 0.1–0.5 m, which has great advantages over satellite image data.
(4) **Low operating cost:** The aerial remote sensing data of low-altitude unmanned aerial vehicles have not only the value of satellite image data but also the advantage of rapid acquisition of aerial photography of large aircraft. Low-altitude unmanned aerial vehicles do not need professional airport parking and professional pilot teams like large aircraft, and their storage, transportation and flight operations are convenient and fast.
(5) **It is less affected by weather and site:** It can take off without rain and the wind is not too strong, and the runway only needs to be replaced by flat ground.
(6) **The data results are true:** Because the image data can be obtained in a short time, it has strong timeliness and is more realistic to the ground situation.

At present, in the field of expressway engineering construction and geographic information, in order to better meet the needs of "Digital China, Digital City and Digital Life" in China, the aerial photogrammetry mode has been switched from traditional data collection mode to UAV to carry out topographic mapping, oil pipeline patrol, power facilities maintenance, expressway construction, land confirmation, cadastral survey, water conservancy and hydropower construction, farmland information monitoring, national survey, mine resources development, geological monitoring, etc. It has greatly improved the requirements of social development for data update and has become an increasingly important advantage in the construction of the national economy.

Components of an unmanned aerial vehicle photogrammetry system

Application classification

The types of unmanned aerial vehicles are usually divided according to payload and endurance, including the following four types:

(1) **Large unmanned aerial vehicle:** High performance, large payload and long battery life can basically achieve performance similar to that of manned aircraft, but its application is not high because of its high price.

(2) **Medium unmanned aerial vehicle:** The payload is about 20 kg, the battery life can reach 2 hours, and it has a relatively stable flight altitude. Therefore, photographic equipment that needs a stable altitude, such as photographic pan-tilt, can be used, as well as altitude positioning systems. Although relatively expensive, it is ideal as a civil aerial survey platform.

(3) **Small unmanned aerial vehicle:** The flight performance and altitude stability are very low, and the photographic effect is also poor, so the obtained images are difficult to be processed in ordinary photogrammetry workstations. The biggest advantage is the cheap price.

(4) **Ultra-light unmanned aerial vehicle:** In order to save power, delta wings are used. The payload is very small, usually less than 1 kg, the battery life is only about half an hour, and the wind resistance and flight altitude are very poor. The acquired images require special photogrammetric software to process them, which is not possible with ordinary software. However, this problem is gradually being solved thanks to continuous advances in data processing technology

in photogrammetry, and the low price of this system makes it highly adaptable for small engineering projects.

Hardware composition

The unmanned aerial vehicle mapping remote sensing system consists of the unmanned aerial vehicle flight platform, sensors, flight control system, ground monitoring system and ground transportation and support system. The mature flight platforms in China include the "vertical tail" unmanned aerial vehicle, "double-engine" unmanned aerial vehicle and "inverted mast tail" unmanned aerial vehicle, which are equipped with high-end SLR digital cameras. The flight control system of unmanned aerial vehicles mainly includes an autopilot, a GPS navigator, an altitude controller, an altimeter and a barometer.

The key technologies are fixed-point exposure technology, controlled by GPS navigation, and camera rotation correction technology. The ground monitoring system mainly includes the communication system, monitoring software system and maintenance system.

Software composition

Unmanned aerial vehicle aerial photography and image processing are much more complicated than traditional aerial surveys. In order to ensure aerial photography quality, accurate aerial photography planning, rapid aerial photography quality inspection and rapid image preprocessing are needed, and corresponding software should be configured to complete these tasks.

Accurate aerial photography mission planning software is mainly used for aerial photography mission planning. Functions include statistics and mapping of design results, automatic/semi-automatic aerial photography zoning, automatic route laying, automatic adjustment of exposure point spacing and route spacing, ensuring overlap index of stereo observation, modification and editing of the exposure point, route function, route structure, base station layout function, number of films, route length, distance and other statistical reports.

The software of aerial photo quality quick check includes the following technical content: browsing the image quality quickly, checking the overlap index, checking the rotation angle index, automatically forming the photo preview index map, automatically numbering the images in batches, outputting the statistical report of aerial photography quality inspection, and quickly checking the flight data coverage so as to decide on make-up flights and withdrawals.

At the same time, it is directly related to operation efficiency, flight quality inspection and evaluation. The core indexes are the degree of overlap and the angle of rotation, which must meet the requirements of aerial survey specifications. For two adjacent aerial photographs, the degree of overlap and the angle of rotation can be calculated according to the image width through a pair of points with the same name. The pixel number of the original digital aerial photograph is fixed, and the overlap degree can also be calculated for the preview photograph resampled in the same way.

Application of unmanned aerial vehicles in expressway surveys

Unmanned aerial vehicle aerial survey process

The basic process of an unmanned aerial vehicle aerial survey starts from three aspects: calibrating digital cameras from laboratory and field; planning and designing field routes and conducting field flights; and performing field image control measurements. After that, the images obtained from the aerial survey are preprocessed; the procedure includes automatic film arrangement, optimizing the image selection of the survey area, pre-correcting image distortion. After that, the control points are measured and the connection points are automatically extracted. Stereo mapping, DSM generation and orthophoto generation and mosaic are completed by aerial triangulation. In the end, the results are summarized to check the accuracy. The flow is shown in Figure 5.1.

Calibration of digital camera

The azimuth elements and distortion aberrations of the cameras used must be checked prior to the actual aerial survey, as the camera lenses used may have some distortion aberrations. This process is carried out in two ways.

(1) **Calibration in the laboratory:** Calibration whiteboard and calibration software can be used to calibrate the camera in the laboratory. The calibration whiteboard needs special geometric relationship marks, and the software must be capable of automatically detecting

Figure 5.1 Drones flying on the highway, Hangzhou traffic uses "clairvoyance"

Source: http://k.sina.com.cn/article_7505202169_v1bf584bf902000toad.html

the target. Although this method cannot deal with complicated situations, it is very convenient.

(2) **Inspection and calibration on the outdoor site:** In order to deal with the complex situation of an aerial survey site and the common altitude instability of unmanned aerial vehicles, it is necessary to establish a special outdoor calibration field for calibration in addition to the inspection in the laboratory. This calibration method is very similar to the actual aerial survey operation. Regular ground markers are set up on the ground according to the elevation. When flying unmanned aerial vehicles, attention should be paid to high overlap and crossover points. Finally, the calibration parameters are obtained through the overall adjustment of the beam method.

Examples of measurement

For example, when surveying the unstable slopes of mountain roads, an unmanned aerial vehicle aerial survey can be used in order to obtain surveying and mapping data as quickly as possible. In order to test the system accuracy of this technology, GPS surveying and mapping technology can be used to obtain the precise coordinates of some landmark points within

4 cm of accuracy in the survey area. These points can be used to compare the surveying and mapping data of unmanned aerial vehicles as control points and precision checkpoints.

As mentioned earlier, the aerial survey process uses software to design the flight route and calibrate the photographic equipment before the field flight mapping starts. After the completion of the field flight, the image is optimized and selected, and the image is processed by combining GPS navigation data with fast film arrangement software so as to eliminate the blurred image and confirm whether there is any missed shooting phenomenon.

In order to eliminate the distorted image of a camera lens, the original image data obtained by an unmanned aerial vehicle is preprocessed according to the calibration parameters obtained in advance. This is to ensure that connection points can be automatically extracted and that the measurement of control points is accurate. After adjustment, the obtained data are the spatial coordinates and altitude information of the survey area image. After that, stereo mapping is carried out with the special software of photogrammetry, and the large-scale topographic map of the measured area can be obtained. After that, automatic terrain extraction is carried out to obtain DSM. Finally, GIS software is used to make a three-dimensional surface model of the surveying and mapping area.

Accuracy of evaluation of surveying and mapping

The surveying and mapping accuracy of an unmanned aerial vehicle aerial survey can be carried out by using the landmark points previously laid in the survey area, and its accuracy can be divided into plane and elevation. By calculating the root mean square of the two data sets, the plane error and elevation error of the survey area can be calculated. Through the actual data in the past, it can be seen that although there are certain accuracy errors in an aerial survey of unmanned aerial vehicles, they can already meet the operation specifications and are competent for highway surveys of dangerous and complex terrain.

The prospect of an unmanned aerial vehicle aerial survey in expressway engineering is broad. Low cost, fast speed and good effect make it greatly surpass traditional surveying and mapping methods, making expressway surveying and mapping simpler, more efficient and faster. It is believed that the technology of unmanned aerial vehicle survey will mature and play a role in highway surveys.

Chapter 6

Unmanned Ship: The Inevitable Choice of the Strategy of Building a Powerful Maritime Country

Intelligent unmanned ship: Reconstructing the global shipping market pattern

Intelligent unmanned ship: Leading the future of shipping industry

In the future, ships will continue to develop towards using artificial intelligence. In recent years, with the wide application of the Internet of Things, cloud computing, big data, artificial intelligence and other technologies in the field of ships, the automation level of ships has been greatly improved. With the support of advanced science and technology, unmanned ships are very likely to set sail soon.

There are three types of unmanned ships: a fully autonomous unmanned ship, a semi-autonomous unmanned ship and a remotely controlled ship. The former can achieve autonomous planning, autonomous navigation and autonomous perception of the surrounding environment. The latter requires manual remote control and cannot realize autonomous navigation. The second type of semi-autonomous unmanned ships sail according to built-in procedures and perform navigation tasks.

For unmanned ships, various technologies such as ship design, information processing, artificial intelligence, as well as motion control are brought together. The research scope covers multiple fields such as automatic driving, pattern recognition, autonomous obstacle avoidance, autonomous planning and navigation. According to different functions, different modules can be used, different sensors and sensing equipment can be carried, and various tasks can be performed, such as anti-terrorism, mine clearance, surveillance and reconnaissance, intelligence collection, relay communication, search and rescue, anti-submarine, as well as hydrographic surveys.

With the rapid development of communication, artificial intelligence and other technologies, many technical problems that restrict the development of unmanned ships have been resolved. Countries have been investing more and more in the research and development of unmanned ships, which have entered a rapid development stage.

In 2002, the US Navy launched the "Spartan Scout" project.

In 2003, Israel, which has accumulated rich unmanned ship development technology, successfully delivered an unmanned ship—"Protector" to the IDF (national defense force).

In July 2007, the US Navy issued the "Navy Unmanned Surface Boat Master Plan," which divided unmanned boats into four classes: X-Class, Harbor Class, Snorkeler Class and Fleet Class. In the four classes of unmanned boats, the length increased in turn, the endurance decreased in turn, the modules transited from non-standard level to standard level, the tasks transited from a low level to a high level, and different requirements were put forward for the deployment mode and boat type.

In 2008, the unmanned boat "Tianxiang No. 1" developed by Xinguang Company of China was applied during the Olympic Sailing Competition as meteorological emergency equipment to provide meteorological support services for the Olympic Sailing Competition; Yunzhou Intelligent Company uses the unmanned ship independently developed for online water pollution and nuclear pollution monitoring.

In 2013, China has independently developed "Haixun No. 166" unmanned boat built a totally enclosed structure using glass fiber reinforced plastic and diesel engine as a power plant, which had good maneuverability and could resist sinking, wind and waves.

In 2014, Shanghai University developed the "Jinghai" series of unmanned boats equipped with the BeiDou navigation system, which could carry out autonomous positioning, autonomous tracking of navigation trajectory, remote setting of navigation trajectory, autonomous avoidance of obstacles, etc.

In September 2012, eight research institutions, including Fraunhofer CML Company, MARINTEK Company and Chalmers University, jointly launched the "MUNIN" (Maritime Unmanned Navigation through Intelligence in Networks) project. This was the first large-scale unmanned ship research project for unmanned bulk carriers in the world. It was planned to monitor the surrounding environment of the ship through radar, infrared sensors and AIS and then transmit the monitored data to the land control center in real time through satellite communication, which was convenient for land operators to control the ship.

In the past, people thought that unmanned ships was a dream. However, with the continuous development of artificial intelligence and digital communication technology, especially with the emergence of unmanned aerial vehicles and unmanned vehicles, the idea of unmanned ships is now gradually being accepted by people and has attracted countless people to contribute their financial and intellectual resources to the realization of this idea. On November 26, 2021, Oslo, Norway, the world's first fully automated unmanned freighter was unveiled. The 80-metre-long and 3,200-tonnes cargo ship, built by Norwegian fertilizer giant Yara, has begun trial operation.

Unmanned ships represent the future development trend of the entire shipbuilding industry and will have a great subversive effect on the current shipbuilding industry, which means that with the emergence of unmanned ships, the business model and market pattern of ship design, construction, operation, trading and other industries will be completely subverted, hundreds of thousands of ships will face upgrading and millions of crew members will face re-job selection and re-employment. Under the action of unmanned ships, great changes will take place in the entire shipping industry.

Unmanned ships have attracted worldwide attention due to their better safety, higher operational efficiency and lower operating costs. According to a report released by Allianz Insurance in Munich, Germany, 75–96% of accidents during navigation are caused by human factors, most of which are caused by driver fatigue. If the ship can be remotely controlled or is unmanned, such accidents can be greatly reduced and the safety of the ship itself and the safety of the personnel on board can be greatly guaranteed.

Moreover, unmanned ships can potentially prevent pirate attacks. The design of unmanned ships makes it more difficult for pirates to board ships. Even if pirates board ships smoothly, it is difficult for them to enter the control system. Once an unmanned ship perceives pirates on board, the ship's control system can automatically anchor or reduce the speed of the ship and send distress signals to nearby naval vessels, which facilitates quick rescue. Even if an unmanned ship is hijacked by pirates, no hostages can be captured as there are no personnel on board, making it easier for the rescuers to recapture the ship more easily. Therefore, there are fewer chances of the unmanned ships being hijacked.

Unmanned ships can also reduce wind resistance and increase cargo-carrying capacity. As there is no crew on unmanned ships, there is no need to design deck cabins, ventilation systems, heating systems, sewage systems and quarters. This not only reduces the cost of building the ship but also reduces fuel consumption and the running costs of communications.

In addition, in recent years, there have been fewer and fewer maritime professionals, and the emergence of unmanned ships can solve this problem well. There are two reasons for the shortage of marine professionals. First, the ship structure has become more complex, and the requirements for the crew are getting higher; second, sailing is less attractive to young people, and many are unwilling to take up this job. Traditional ships have higher requirements for the professional skills of crew members, while intelligent ships focus on the land operation center. Unmanned ships are usually controlled remotely from land-based operations centers. This naturally attracts highly educated people to work in these centers without the need to set sail.

New change: Development advantages of intelligent unmanned ships

Compared with traditional surface boats, unmanned ships have the following advantages:

(1) Unmanned ships can realize unmanned and intelligent operations. Autonomous navigation and task execution are the most prominent features of unmanned ships. Unmanned ships can carry out autonomous navigation, intelligently avoid obstacles and perform tasks spontaneously as long as the navigation route and task are set in advance, without or with little need for human intervention, liberating a large number of laborers.

(2) The operation efficiency is higher and the standardization degree is higher. At present, the hull length of mature unmanned ships in China is about 1–7.5 meters, and the maximum speed they can reach is 40 knots. This unmanned ship has a small hull, fast speed, strong maneuverability and autonomy. Moreover, the use of this unmanned ship can omit the conventional ship dispatching, chartering, personnel maintenance and other links. With the support of an accurate navigation system, it can be used in various working environments and can perform tasks with high quality and high speed. In addition, the whole operation process is completely controlled by computers, which can ensure the task execution results to be more accurate and standardized.

(3) Unmanned ships can adopt modular design and have various functions. They only need to replace different modules to perform different tasks. Therefore, unmanned ships can perform various tasks by carrying different task modules.

(4) Unmanned ships have fast speed and strong maneuverability. At present, the longest hull of unmanned ships developed by various countries is no more than 12 meters. The maximum displacement is tens of tons, the draft is less than a fraction of that of traditional ships, the sailing speed is about 30 to 40 knots and the maximum speed of some

ships can exceed 40 knots, so they can sail to waters that traditional ships cannot reach to perform tasks in the shortest time, such as narrow roadways and shallow water areas.

(5) Unmanned ships are small and flexible, with good concealment. Unmanned ships are relatively small in shape, which can hidden by using waves, islands and reefs, reducing the probability of damage. They have strong survivability.

(6) Unmanned ships have a low cost of use. As unmanned ships do not need to be equipped with too many personnel, the maintenance cost of personnel is reduced. This allows these ships to be deployed on a large scale and break the constraints of climatic conditions to go out to sea at any time and be on duty around the clock. This greatly reduces the cost of use.

Improvement of efficiency

In the past, watershed sampling, waterway surveying and mapping, and watershed monitoring were carried out manually by hiring large vessels or by using manual positioning and routing. However, due to the excessive size of the vessels, they were unable to act flexibly during operations, resulting in low project development efficiency and poor mapping accuracy. Assuming that the water quality of a reservoir with an area of 1 km^2 is sampled, the environmental monitoring department should set up 10 water quality sampling points, and the whole process takes about 2 hours, but if mature unmanned ships are used, the whole process would take less than 30 minutes.

The compatibility of the platform is good

Unmanned ships are equipped with various interfaces and application software, which can connect many application equipment and instruments to perform different tasks. Generally speaking, unmanned ship systems include propulsion systems, communication systems, water quality monitoring systems, power monitoring systems, navigation systems, RW, PC base station, etc. The navigation board of the hull is equipped with a GPS receiving terminal, a three-axis compass, a three-axis accelerometer and other equipment, supplemented by a built-in navigation algorithm, which can accurately plan the navigation route. In addition, under the action of the wireless communication module, the task data can be transmitted back to the base station for operation and processing at any time.

In addition to the above instruments and equipment, unmanned ships can also be equipped with single-beam sonar, multi-beam sonar, side-scan sonar, shallow surface analysis instruments, water quality monitoring system, small target recognition radar, AIS, weather station, 360-degree full-view pan/tilt, night vision camera and other instruments and equipment, which can provide effective technical support for maritime rescue, cruise, supervision, pollution prevention monitoring, waterway mapping, etc.

Water surface adaptability

An unmanned ship hull has high strength and strong anti-corrosion ability and can work in various waters. Among these ships, the 70 kg and 120 kg series of unmanned ships adopt catamarans, which have strong wind and wave resistance, can cope with various bad weather and drive smoothly; the 120 kg series unmanned ships have faster-sailing speed, greater load and stronger wind and wave resistance; the 300 kg series unmanned ships are trimarans with better stability and greater adaptability to harsh environments.

Endurance

The endurance of the 70 kg series unmanned ships is 80 km, that of the 120 kg series unmanned ships is 100 km and that of the 300 kg unmanned ships uses oil–electricity hybrid system, with endurance exceeding 300 km.

Complementary advantages with an unmanned aerial vehicle

In the 21st century, unmanned driving technology is developing fast and is being used widely. The US think tank RAND has made a comparative analysis of the advantages of unmanned aerial vehicles and unmanned ships. The results show that the performance of unmanned aerial vehicles and unmanned ships is equivalent in terms of power, communication capability, sensing capability, mission module and stealth. Unmanned ships have more advantages in terms of endurance and load capacity, but unmanned aerial vehicles have more advantages in terms of speed and vision.

New technology: Key technology of the intelligent unmanned ship

According to the existing research at home and abroad, the key technologies involved in unmanned ships are as follows:

Automatic route generation and route planning technology

Under normal circumstances, static route automatic generation and path planning technology can be divided into two types. Firstly, the route automatic generation and path planning technology based on an electronic chart is formed. This technology obtains information such as water depth and obstacles through the electronic chart and defines navigable areas and non-navigable areas through this information. Then intelligent search algorithms such as the Dijkstra and AI algorithms are used to find the shortest navigation path in navigable areas.

Of course, this shortest path is not necessarily the actual final navigation route. For example, the planned shortest path may travel in reverse according to the channel recommended by the IMO. In order to solve this problem, automatic route generation and path planning technology based on trajectory analysis came into being. Based on the historical trajectory of ships, this technology uses trajectory compression, trajectory clustering and other methods to plan the feasible navigation path. In addition, it is necessary to provide an effective solution to the problem of local route automatic planning based on dynamic environment awareness.

Communication technology

The communication technology of unmanned ships involves three aspects. They are radio communication, underwater acoustic communication and optical communication. These communication technologies are mainly used between unmanned ships and mother ships, between unmanned ships and unmanned ships. The communication content is mainly the instructions sent by mother ships to unmanned ships, and the feedback of unmanned ships to mother ships is video information, motion state information, etc.

As for communication media, if it is short-range communication, high-frequency communication can be used directly, and if it is long-range communication, satellite communication can be used. UHF (ultra-high-frequency) spread spectrum communication and satellite communication signals often suffer from attenuation or multiple interferences in the process of transmission at sea. In this case, unmanned ship communication should focus on solving the problems of transmission anti-attenuation technology, anti-Doppler frequency shift technology and anti-multiple interference technology.

Autonomous decision-making and obstacle avoidance technology

Unmanned ship navigation has a strong dependence on remote control personnel. The research on unmanned ship technology should reduce this dependence as much as possible, enhance the autonomous decision-making ability and intelligent obstacle avoidance ability of unmanned ships and develop multiple unmanned ships to cooperate in operations so that unmanned ships can independently complete tasks such as remote detection and information collection. To achieve high intelligence and full automation, the unmanned ship must have the ability to make independent decisions and intelligent obstacle avoidance. Many scientific research institutions are currently conducting in-depth discussions on the research of intelligent obstacle avoidance technology for ships.

Technology of object target detection and automatic target recognition on the water surface

As for unmanned ships, the technology of surface object detection and automatic target recognition is the basis of realizing autonomous decision-making and automatic obstacle avoidance. Due to the small hull of the unmanned ship, poor wind and wave resistance and violent six degrees of the freedom movement, the video sent back from the unmanned ship is unstable and the image quality is poor. Therefore, the technology of surface object target detection and automatic target recognition should take the lead in solving the problems of video image stabilization, image quality enhancement and smoothing. Then, it studies the water boundary detection technology suitable for water antenna and water shoreline conditions, the target detection technology suitable for low signal-to-noise ratio and dynamic background conditions, and the water surface target tracking technology formed on the basis of multi-source data association and fusion.

Some researchers have proposed a water surface image processing technology based on light vision. The mean shift search model and Kalman filter prediction model are used to track the target position information in the water surface image. The advantages of the two are combined to greatly improve the tracking speed and greatly reduce its influence on the variation of the target scale.

At present, autonomous technology, collision avoidance technology, threat avoidance technology, automatic target recognition technology, automatic subtask deployment and recovery technology are still in the exploration and research stage. In the application of unmanned ships, water quality collection and single-beam sounding have achieved mature applications, and further research is needed on the retraction and retraction of ship-borne equipment.

New pattern: Changing the design and operation of ships

An unmanned ship is a "new" product with the development of artificial intelligence and digital communication technology. As electronic sensors, computers and communication technologies develop continuously, people have come up with a series of ideas about unmanned driving, such as unmanned aerial vehicles, unmanned vehicles, unmanned ships, as well as unmanned trains. At present, humans already realized the unmanned aerial vehicles and unmanned vehicles, and research institutions around the world have begun to focus on the design and research of unmanned ships.

In April 2016, Rolls-Royce announced an unmanned ship project, the Advanced Unmanned Ship Application Development Plan. Its president, Mikael Makinen, has high expectations for the development of unmanned ships, believing that unmanned ships represent the future of the shipping industry and will bring about pathbreaking changes in the entire ship design and operation industry. In addition, some people believe that the remote control and driving of unmanned ships will also redefine the roles of shipping companies, shipyards, ship equipment suppliers and other shipping industry participants.

Continuous real-time monitoring of ships can better integrate ships into logistics and supply chain systems, improve the operating efficiency of shipping companies around the world, reduce operating costs and increase revenue. In this case, new shipping businesses will emerge, as the times require, such as online freight service business, new alliance creation, asset portfolio and leasing. Some of these businesses are supportive businesses for existing market participants, while others are more subversive and will introduce more new participants to take over the existing market share.

The key capability of unmanned ships is to sense the surrounding situation in real time and transmit the sensed information to the control system or operation center in time, thus completing complex operations, avoiding obstacles accurately and reaching the destination successfully. Rolls-Royce is developing a context awareness system: combining images captured by high-definition visible and infrared cameras with laser radar and radar measurements to draw detailed environmental images around ships. The information is then transmitted to the remote control center, and the captain makes a reasonable decision, or the computer system processes it and makes the next step.

The captain of the remote control ship and the navigation system of the unmanned ship can also obtain more information from sources, such as satellite navigation correction information, weather conditions, as well as position information of other ships, which can be integrated to make reasonable decisions. Crew members have long been accustomed to using data from multiple sources and electronic auxiliary equipment and systems. The system used to monitor the operation of the main equipment of the ship and ensure the normal operation of the engine and other equipment has been widely used on the ship, which can help determine the navigation scheme.

In the future, sensors embedded in the ship's key systems will acquire more data, and the monitoring scope will be greatly expanded to cover the main engine, crane, other deck machinery, propeller, bow propeller, generator, fuel filter device and other equipment. The system can determine whether these devices are operating normally with the aid of this information. Once the key components of the ship fail, the next port can be called immediately to arrange preventive maintenance, and if necessary, the maintenance personnel can be requested to board the ship for maintenance.

Unmanned ships need to deliver the collected data to the shore in time during navigation, and therefore, unmanned ships must be equipped with constant real-time communication links. In this regard, the satellite communication service used by ships on the high seas is very effective, especially the Global Xpress satellite, which can provide a high-speed broadband connection service for unmanned ships around the world in the future.

Countermeasures and suggestions on developing intelligent shipping in China

With the rapid development of Internet technology, great changes have taken place in the traditional commercial format and logistics system. Many traditional physical retailers have withdrawn from the market under the support of the Internet and big data. The pattern of the traditional land transportation industry has also undergone great changes. The role of transportation enterprises in the market has also changed, evolving from market players to followers of logistics platform operators.

Although shipping is only one part of the whole logistics process, it still maintains a leading position as it belongs to the heavy asset industry. However, its relatively backward business model and relatively high operating costs have led to its failure to be recognized by the market. In recent years, large platform operators have made frequent moves to replace the existing freight forwarders and freight platforms of small shipping enterprises. From this point of view, if the shipping industry's own business model does not change, the shipping market can only recover temporarily, and it will never be able to break through the existing difficulties and obtain more benefits.

Whether on a technical level or practical application level, China's fully automated container terminals have always been among the best. The next step is to upgrade the existing technical level, popularize and apply advanced technologies and explore the application methods of artificial intelligence and other technologies in other specialized terminals. The technical obstacles to unmanned cargo ships have now been eliminated, and all that remains are the barriers of perception and acceptance and the balance of interests of the parties involved.

In order to improve awareness and acceptance of unmanned cargo ships, the key lies in making people realize the transportation value of unmanned cargo ships. If unmanned cargo ships can reduce costs and improve efficiency while improving safety and environmental protection, they can be well accepted by society, government and enterprises.

As for the balance of interests of relevant parties, it mainly solves the re-employment problem of seafarers and related practitioners. There will be a gradual evolution from manned ships to unmanned ships, and a number of new occupations and posts will emerge under the new shipping format. With the relative balance of the interests of various stakeholders, the obstacles faced by unmanned cargo ships will be gradually eliminated.

From the perspective of opportunity, the research on unmanned large-scale ship transportation has just begun. The research foundation is rich because China is a big shipping country. A perfect supervision system and service network have been formed in the field of unmanned ships in China with the continuous advancement of information construction, and a large amount of data have been accumulated, creating good conditions for systematic research and development.

Moreover, in the fields of artificial intelligence, cloud computing, big data and the Internet of Things, China's scientific and technological practice ability is constantly improving. Projects such as high-speed rail and self-completed deep-sea exploration projects, which have repeatedly broken world records, have proved that China has strong independent research and development capabilities in key technologies and leading advantages in integration. These projects can provide strong support for the unmanned development of cargo ships from the experience and system levels. In other words, as long as we seize the opportunity, China's intelligent shipping may develop from following to leading.

In terms of motivation, the transformation and upgrading of China's shipping industry and shipbuilding industry have a strong internal driving force. Under the background of the overall promotion of the "the belt and road initiative" strategy and the strategy of a powerful marine country, intelligent shipping will be pushed to a prominent position with the proposal of the strategy of a powerful transportation country and an innovative country, because these strategies can be implemented through intelligent shipping.

In other words, the development of intelligent shipping is not only conducive to the deep-sea shipping industry to carry out self-reform in line with the supply-side structural reform trend, enhance its competitiveness and respond to the construction of a powerful transportation country, but also to build new technological advantages, form new economic growth points, promote the innovative development of related industries and promote the construction of an innovative country.

Moreover, the development of intelligent shipping is also conducive to the construction of a global shipping system and all-round, multi-level and complex transportation network and provides strong support for the construction of "the belt and road initiative." To sum up, at this stage, China should vigorously promote the construction of intelligent shipping so as to promote the strategy of strengthening the country by transportation and jointly build an intelligent shipping power.

The development of intelligent shipping should adhere to several principles:

(1) Take the market as the leading factor and let the government give full play to its guiding role. First of all, establish and improve the promotion mechanism, strengthen overall coordination, carry out planning and guidance, promote the continuous improvement of the policy environment and create favorable conditions for technological innovation, business innovation, as well as capital entry. Secondly, strengthen the dominant position of enterprises, follow market rules and make the market play a decisive role in resource allocation and play a leading role in technology research and development, popularization, as well as application.

(2) System layout, driven by demonstration. Carry out top-level design, make overall plans for the development of intelligent shipping, systematically grasp the strategic tasks in various stages, links and fields, and promote the all-round coordinated development of intelligent shipping. Focus on pilot demonstration, constantly summarize and improve, and carry out risk management to provide a strong guarantee for the orderly development of intelligent shipping.

(3) Lead by science and technology and make breakthroughs in key areas. Focus on the scientific and technological frontier of intelligent shipping, carry out basic research and create forward-looking and leading major achievements. Gather superior resources together, carry out research and development of independent core technologies, overcome difficulties in system integration and seize opportunities to promote the development of intelligent shipping.

(4) Open cooperation and win-win sharing. Encourage cross-industry cooperation in production, education and research, and vigorously promote the research and application of intelligent shipping theory and methods, equipment systems, technology, standards and specifications. Actively introduce advanced technology, cooperate with

developed Western countries, promote the continuous development of global intelligent shipping and share the development achievements.

R&D and application of unmanned ships in the world

Intelligent shipping system for unmanned cargo ship

In recent years, artificial intelligence has developed rapidly and gradually penetrated into all walks of life, including the shipping industry. Intelligent shipping is a new modern shipping system formed by the deep integration of new technologies such as artificial intelligence and shipping. Intelligent shipping system includes five subsystems, namely intelligent ship, intelligent port, intelligent supervision, intelligent navigation guarantee and intelligent shipping service. The following five subsystems of intelligent shipping, the development status of intelligent shipping and the development stage of unmanned freight transportation are analyzed in detail.

Intelligent ship

Intelligent ships automatically sense the data of ships themselves, navigation environment, ports and other aspects by means of the Internet of Things, sensors, communication, Internet and other technologies, and analyze these data by using big data technology, so that ship navigation, cargo transportation, ship management and maintenance can be automated.

Generally speaking, intelligent ships can be divided into three technical levels, namely primary, intermediate and advanced.

The primary intelligent ship only has the auxiliary decision-making function; that is, by making each cabin, instrument and equipment realize data and informationization, the equipment can analyze the perceived information independently and give the best choice to assist human decision-making.

Intermediate intelligent ships can realize partial autonomous operation and remote control, which can not only automatically perceive information and assist humans in making decisions but also automatically execute some commands. Of course, these commands need to be entered in advance by the relevant person, and the machine can only perform those actions that are permitted by the human or will inform the human in charge before automatically performing some actions.

From a technical point of view, all ships can realize unmanned autonomous navigation, but not all ships need to realize unmanned navigation. In the future, cargo ships will inevitably develop in the direction of unmanned. Specifically, the unmanned cargo ship has to go through three stages of development.

(1) **Initial stage:** The unmanned technology of ships is gradually matured. This stage will take at least 5–8 years. During this period, people's cognition of unmanned ships is gradually unified, and the development direction of unmanned ships is gradually clear. The unmanned development emphasizes such aspects as breaking the existing technology, creating new laws and regulations, building an intelligent ship–shore coordination system, as well as implementing skills training for relevant personnel. The unmanned ships will initially have intelligent functions, the technical environment suitable for the development of unmanned ships will become more mature, and experimental unmanned ships will enter trial operation after a series of studies and tests.

(2) **Transitional stage:** Manned ships and unmanned ships coexist. This stage will take at least 15 years. At this stage, with the continuous advancement of research, application and testing, various key technical difficulties of unmanned ships have been gradually overcome. The relevant laws and regulations have been gradually improved, a system to support the autonomous navigation of ships has been gradually established and certain achievements have been made in the technical training of relevant personnel. Shipbuilding enterprises at home and abroad have started to build unmanned ships in batches and put them into use in specific areas, thus forming the phenomenon of unmanned ships coexisting with manned ships.

(3) **Mature stage:** Unmanned cargo ships have gradually become the mainstream. At this stage, the intelligent shipping system has basically taken shape, and the intelligent integration of ship and shore has been widely used in various ports and shipping enterprises. Unmanned cargo ships have gradually taken up the heavy responsibility of cargo transportation.

Intelligent port

Intelligent ports fully integrate new technologies such as artificial intelligence into port management and operation, promote the intelligentization of port production, port service and port management, build a good port format, and enable ports to achieve a high degree of coordination with the entry and exit, landing and offshore of communication, cargo loading and unloading, warehousing, passengers boarding and offshore, thus effectively improving the operational efficiency and safety of the port, maximizing energy conservation and protecting the environment and reduce operating costs.

Intelligent ports can also be divided into three types, namely primary intelligent ports, intermediate intelligent ports and advanced intelligent ports.

(1) Primary intelligent port: The port management has realized informationization, the automatic operation of the production system needs human operators to set it in advance, and some equipment and links have realized intelligent operation.

(2) Intermediate intelligent port: Port management has achieved a high degree of informationization, some equipment and links have basically become intelligent and production operations and management no longer require a large amount of human involvement.

(3) Advanced intelligent port: Artificial intelligence and other technologies are fully integrated into the port business, and a fully automated large-scale professional wharf system has been built, and the field operation has basically been unmanned.

Intelligent navigation guarantee

Intelligent navigation guarantee is called an intelligent navigation support service guarantee system. It refers to relying on sensors, the Internet, the Internet of Things, artificial intelligence, cloud computing, big data and other technologies to build an intelligent shipping information service platform, so that ship positioning and navigation, data processing, communication and other systems are intelligent. From the technical level, it assists unmanned ships in realizing autonomous navigation, and at the same time, it assists relevant personnel in making scientific emergency decisions and necessary administrative interventions through information integration, exchange and analysis, thus building platform shipping services and ensuring information security of intelligent shipping networks. Compared with traditional navigation guarantees, intelligent navigation guarantees should not only upgrade their technology but also expand its functions to meet the operation and development needs of intelligent shipping.

Intelligent shipping supervision

In essence, intelligent shipping service is a kind of e-commerce, which provides shipping services for the demander through an open, standard information system and platform based on a single source or remote information, and conducts service transactions with the demander.

The remarkable feature of an intelligent shipping service is a trading platform, which mainly has two forms, one is Party B's platform and the other is Party C's platform. Party B's platform refers to the platform created by the shipping service provider, while Party C's platform refers to the platform created by the third party, which can simplify shipping selection and transaction links, reduce shipping costs and solve the problems of delayed, unsystematic, incomplete and insufficient service information provision.

Intelligent shipping supervision

Intelligent shipping supervision refers to the use of modern information, mobile communication, artificial intelligence and other technologies to make shipping supervision mode, supervision method, supervision means, evidence collection and emergency decision-making and other corresponding adjustments according to the changes of supervision objects, so as to promote its healthy and orderly development. Intelligent shipping supervision acts on traditional supervision objects, mainly to improve supervision efficiency and effectiveness and reduce management costs; when intelligent shipping supervision acts on new formats, it is necessary to solve the adaptability of supervision means and promote real-time update of supervision basis, supervision mode, supervision standard and supervision mechanism.

Research and development and application of unmanned ships in Europe and America

In the 1960s, the United States and other countries began to apply unmanned boat fleets to the military field. In the past two years, the rapid development of the Internet of Things, big data, artificial intelligence and other technologies have provided strong technical support for the design and development of intelligent ships such as unmanned ships.

The research and development of unmanned ships have been favored by many countries in the world, examples of which are listed below. Norway has set up an unmanned ship experimental zone, South Korea has built a general technology platform for unmanned ships, Denmark has launched a research and development project for unmanned ships and the Netherlands is actively developing floating self-driving unmanned ships capable of carrying people and cargo.

Of course, to promote the sustained and stable development of intelligent shipping industries such as unmanned ships, it is necessary to establish perfect laws and regulations. In February 2017, nine member countries, led by the United States, submitted a legislative plan for unmanned ships to the IMO Maritime Safety Committee. At the 99th meeting of the Maritime Safety Committee of the International Maritime Organization in May 2018, IMO officially announced that it would study and formulate relevant conventions and norms to solve a series of problems such as safety, security and environmental protection of Maritime Autonomous Surface Ships (MASS). At present, the United States, the United Kingdom and other countries have entered the legislative stage of unmanned ships.

Europe is studying the operation regulations of unmanned ships

At present, the construction technology of unmanned ships is mature, and the bigger problem is whether the regulatory agencies allow unmanned ships to sail at sea. At present, all countries in the world have not made clear regulations on unmanned ships, such as whether to allow unmanned ships to sail at sea, how to provide insurance services for unmanned ships and how to determine the responsible person if unmanned ships have accidents during sailing. Currently, the relevant agencies in European countries are working on these issues and discussing the development of regulations for the operation of unmanned ships.

Most of these agencies are members of the AAWA project. One of them is the European Unmanned Maritime System Safety and Supervision Agency (SARUMS), which is composed of seven countries, led by Sweden, and the other is the British Maritime Unmanned Supervision Working Group. These organizations have done a lot of work for the formulation of unmanned ship operation regulations, only hoping that the development of new technologies can be reflected when the International Convention for the Safety of Life at Sea is updated. As for regulators, the safety of unmanned ships is a topic of primary concern. Therefore, engineers are trying to apply various new technologies to the research and development and production of unmanned ships so that unmanned ships can avoid navigation risks to the greatest extent.

Ocean-going unmanned ships have become the norm in 10–15 years

The emergence of unmanned ships is an inevitable trend, but it is only a matter of time. According to the prediction of Rolls-Royce Company, the first completely unmanned ship will appear in recent years. In the beginning, the type of this ship may only be a port tugboat or ferry. As for the popularization and application of completely unmanned ocean-going cargo ships, it will take another 10–15 years. For this reason, Rolls-Royce has established the first cooperation project AAWA in Finland. The development goal of this project is to truly realize the automatic control of ships, enable ships to fully realize automatic operation, and strive for successful application in coastal waters within 10 years.

At the same time, the European Union has also launched the MUNIN project, which is dedicated to the research of unmanned intelligent network navigation systems at sea. The project is led by Fraunhofer Maritime Logistics and Service Center and evaluates the feasibility of unmanned commercial ships operating at sea from three fields: technology, economy and law.

In addition, DNV GL is studying the feasibility of unmanned electric ships running along the Norwegian coastline; China Maritime Safety Administration cooperated with the Wuhan University of Technology to study unmanned multifunctional maritime ships, with a view to applying autonomous ships in both commercial and military fields. The world's first small unmanned cargo ship jointly developed by China Classification Society, Zhuhai Municipal Government, Wuhan University of Technology and Yunzhou Intelligence is expected to be launched by the end of 2018 and will take the lead in commercial operation in 2019.

The Norwegian Maritime Safety Administration and the Norwegian Coastal Administration signed an agreement to allow unmanned ships to conduct sea trials in Trondheim Fjord, making it the first area in the world where unmanned ships can be used for testing. At the same time, the unmanned ship projects of Rolls-Royce and other companies have also attracted the participation of the Finnish Marine Industry Association, the Ministry of Transport and Communications, the Finnish Innovation Funding Agency and other institutions, with a view to carrying out research and exploration in the field of unmanned marine transportation in the Baltic Sea.

Unmanned ships will appear in the next 2–3 years. By 2025, some shipping companies will start operating unmanned ocean-going ships. By 2030, unmanned ships will be widely used. In the long run, with the emergence of unmanned ships, the entire shipping industry will undergo path-breaking changes and a series of changes are still in the gestation stage. With unmanned ships replacing ordinary cargo ships, the operation of the global supply chain will be completely changed and new services will emerge, as the times require.

Research and development and application of unmanned ships in China

No matter what technology and scheme unmanned ships adopt, there are many factors restricting its development, including the safety of information transmission, the stability of remote control and the reliability of power plants. In recent years, with the in-depth application of big data, cloud computing, artificial intelligence, virtual reality and other technologies in all walks of life, unmanned aerial vehicles and unmanned vehicles have appeared one after another and unmanned ships have received extensive attention.

In December 2015, CSSC (China State Shipbuilding Corporation) released a design scheme (I-Dolphin) at the Intelligent Ship Development Forum. The research object of this scheme is a bulk carrier with a dead-weight of 38,800 tons. Big data and information technology are used to monitor the running status of the ship in real time, and its overall performance is evaluated and analyzed so as to formulate the best navigation control scheme and sailing route and minimize the incidence of safety accidents caused by human operation errors.

According to the design scheme announced by CSSC, this unmanned ship is not only equipped with a conventional power system, residential system and operating system, but a real-time communication module has also been added. During the voyage, the ship's driving state and equipment operation can be communicated with the onshore control center through satellite signals, and an expert system is added to analyze the actual operation of the ship so as to formulate a scientific operation plan and make a scientific judgment on whether the equipment on the ship needs maintenance. Theoretically, I-Dolphin can realize autonomous thinking and navigation without human intervention. However, there are some defects in the current communication technology and automation control technology. The ship is still equipped with a crew to deal with the failure of the automation system in a timely manner to ensure the safety of the ship for safe navigation.

In 2017, China once again launched a comprehensive scientific investigation and research activities on the Qinghai-Tibet Plateau again after more than 40 years. In September 2018, the investigation team released the results of the first investigation in Lhasa, which took a solid step on the road of deciphering the "Qinghai-Tibet Code." During the investigation, the application of advanced equipment such as unmanned ships brought many conveniences to the investigation activities.

In fact, intelligent ships such as unmanned ships have become the key research fields of domestic and foreign industries. Projects such as environmental monitoring and regional cruise carried out by unmanned ships have also achieved good practical results. An in-depth analysis of the development status, application advantages, social impact and development path of unmanned ships is of great value for further accelerating the development process of intelligent ship industries such as unmanned ships and enhancing China's scientific research strength and value creation ability.

Improve the layout of European ports

In the "Internet+" action plan, "Made in China 2025" and other documents, the Chinese government pointed out that it is necessary to support and guide strategic emerging industries such as intelligent ships and improve the intelligence level of ships, which will bring a strong thrust to accelerate the digitalization, informationization and intelligence of ships in China.

In 2015, the Ministry of Industry and Information Technology of the People's Republic of China launched the "Top-level Planning of Intelligent Ships" project, and the China Classification Society (CCS) issued the world's first "Code for Intelligent Ships" in the same year,

which clarified the definition, purpose, function, technical requirements and application scope of intelligent ships. In 2016, the Ministry of Industry and Information Technology of the People's Republic of China launched the "Intelligent Ship 1.0" project to study and design demonstration ships such as super-large container ships, super-large ore ships and super-large crude oil ships.

On January 12, 2023, the world's first intelligent unmanned system research mother ship "Zhuhai Cloud" was delivered for use. "Zhuhai Cloud" is manufactured by Guangdong Laboratory of Marine Science and Engineering of South China (Zhuhai), the ship is the world's first intelligent marine research vessel with autonomous navigation function and remote control function, and has obtained the first intelligent ship certificate issued by China Classification Society, and the power system, propulsion system, intelligent system, dynamic positioning system and survey operation support system are all independently developed by China. Its unmanned system can avoid obstacles and plan its own path. With a length of 88.5 meters, a beam of 14.0 meters and a depth of 6.1 meters, the "Zhuhai Cloud" has a design displacement of about 2,100 tons, a maximum speed of 18 knots and an economic speed of 13 knots. On November 28, 2017, CSSC I-Dolphin, 38,800-ton intelligent bulk carrier, the world's first intelligent ship built by China State Shipbuilding Corporation, was named and delivered. The ship has many functions such as engine room assistant decision-making, ship health management and intelligent navigation. Previously, Rolls-Royce's vice president thought that the trial of full-size unmanned ships at sea would not be realized until at least 2020. In any case, unmanned ships have to solve three major problems before their successful advent, which have been mentioned earlier, and these three major problems will be elaborated on in detail below.

Case: Rolls-Royce unmanned ship project

In March 2016, the Stril Luna offshore vessel, owned by the renowned British aero-engine company Rolls-Royce, was launched, which successfully applies the "smart bridge building" concept developed by Rolls-Royce. In addition, Rolls-Royce has completed the test of remote navigation virtual reality system in Norway, which is primarily used on ships and enables all-round monitoring of the ship with the help of cameras and sensors installed onboard. The monitoring video and pictures are transmitted to the control center in time, and these pictures are displayed through 3D animation and virtual reality technology on a terminal display screen so that the ship operator can operate the ship through the operating handle, such as controlling the ship's engine and transporting goods. In fact, in a sense, the world's first unmanned ship has come out, that is, the Stril Luna offshore ship.

In April 2016, Rolls-Royce released the operation version of the shore-based control center of unmanned cargo ships, which once again showed the concept of "unmanned shipping" to the world. According to the videos and pictures released by Rolls-Royce, this version shows a small shore-based monitoring and control center, which can accommodate 7–14 people. It can monitor the fleet around the world through interactive intelligent screens, speech recognition systems, holograms and unmanned aerial vehicles, and know the operation of the fleet and what is happening on and around the ship in real time.

For unmanned ships, a land operation center is essential, and unmanned ships need someone to control them onshore during sailing. Different types of ships or different stages of navigation require different levels of supervision and control. Cargo ships sailing in the open sea need less manpower supervision, and a captain can monitor multiple ships at the same time, while ships sailing in coastal waters and ships entering and leaving ports require a lot of manpower supervision to avoid collisions or other accidents. Therefore, a reliable remote control system is needed for unmanned ship navigation.

In order to do a good job in the research and development of this remote control system, Rolls-Royce draws on the experience of aviation, nuclear energy, space exploration and sailor simulation training system construction and combines with ergonomics, practicability and ease of use of the system, and devotes itself to the research and development of remote control system and remote control center. Rolls-Royce has accumulated some experience in this field. Prior to this, engineers from Rolls-Royce Company designed the Unified Bridge, which completely subverted the traditional bridge style and created a more comfortable, cleaner and safer environment for the crew. Unified Bridge was born in 2014. Up to now, it has been applied in tugboats, large yachts, polar research ships and other different types of ships.

Strategies and paths for China to build an intelligent shipping power

Path 1: Solve the security of information transmission

Security is the key for unmanned ships to become the mainstream direction of the shipbuilding industry in various countries. The shipbuilding industry is facing a serious problem of homogeneous competition, Overcapacity and price wars are rampant, and more efficient, safe, green and intelligent ship types have become a strategy for shipping enterprises to break the situation. Under this background, the advantages of low cost and safety of unmanned ships are fully reflected, which will lead to the transformation and upgrading of infrastructure, industrial cooperation and management mode of the shipbuilding industry.

The equipment on ships such as fire-fighting, pollution prevention, living facilities and other equipment in ships mainly serve the ship's staff, while unmanned ships do not need human involvement in their operation. This equipment can be removed directly, which can reduce the weight and manufacturing cost of ships, reduce energy consumption and have more space for loading goods. Rolls-Royce notes that unmanned ships will save 12–15% of fuel due to their advantages in lower mass and less air resistance.

From a technical point of view, the full integration of real-time dynamic data from ships and ports can help companies optimize and improve their supply chain and logistics solutions and significantly increase transport efficiency.

In addition, among the many factors causing marine accidents on ships, human decision-making and operational errors are undoubtedly one of the main factors. In April 2018, the report on ship and port accidents released by Japan P&I Association pointed out that nearly 80–90% of accidents are caused by human factors, and these accidents are not caused by a single error but a series of errors. The operation of unmanned ships will be controlled by an intelligent expert decision-making system and a remote control system. When human intervention is needed, the controller can also operate remotely in an onshore control center in a better operating environment, which will significantly improve the safety of ship operation.

Before the unmanned ship is put into commercial operation, the security problem of information transmission must be solved.

Unmanned ships use real-time data transmission, remote control, artificial intelligence and other technologies, which not only facilitate ship driving but also provide diversified choices for pirate robbery. At the RSA Encryption Algorithm Security Conference held in March 2016, the Verizon RISK security team told an incident. Pirates hijacked a cargo ship; instead of hijacking the people on board for ransom, they quickly found the container and robbed all the valuables in the container.

According to the investigation of the Verizon RISK security team, pirates invaded the bill of the lading management system of the company in advance and learned the types of goods transported by the cargo ship, thus locking the robbery target in advance and carrying out an efficient robbery. Through this incident, we can see that in the future, pirates may not resort to violent robberies but rather hack into the ship's control system in advance and take control of the ship before carrying out the robbery.

In the future, information and data security must be considered in the development of the shipping industry. Human beings have accumulated rich experience in the prevention of land Internet systems, and the unmanned ship control system can learn from these experiences to prevent hackers from invading and ensure the safety of data transmission. Of course, shipping enterprises should also maintain the security of their own information systems and enhance the security level of information systems besides the ship control system. Many shipping enterprises have now been equipped with advanced network management systems, which can check the running status of ships in real time, determine whether the cargo is safe or not, and even monitor the running status of certain equipment. However, in the process of practical application, most of these systems are in a "streaking" state, and their functions cannot be effectively played.

If pirates cannot invade the control system of unmanned ships successfully, they can also attack the fleet management system of shipping enterprises and select ships with mechanical equipment failure through data analysis, thus increasing the success rate of boarding and robbing them.

Path 2: Improve the stability of the power plant

Compared with manned ships, unmanned ships have some obvious advantages.

First of all, a manned ship has a large number of crewmembers, so it is necessary to equip the crew with a lot of equipment, such as life-saving equipment, firefighting equipment, as well as living facilities. Not only does this equipment take up a lot of space, but it also increases the cost of operating the ship. This is because most of the equipment is relatively underutilized, such as life-saving equipment and anti-pollution equipment, but in order to ensure that this equipment is used properly, shipping companies have to maintain it on a regular basis, which is costly. As unmanned ships have no crew, this equipment naturally does not need to be equipped, which not only saves a lot of space but also saves a lot of money on equipment purchase and maintenance, which is a significant economic benefit.

Secondly, as the ship performance is getting better and better, the professional requirements of operation are getting higher and higher, and the fatigue driving and bad mood of the crew have gradually become the main factors that induce navigation accidents. Unmanned ships are controlled by operators in shore control centers through expert decision-making systems and remote control systems, thus minimizing the adverse effects of human factors on the safety of ship navigation.

At the technical level, unmanned ships should also solve the stability problem of ship power plant operation and ensure ship navigation safety through continuous and stable propulsion power. While an unmanned vehicle can be repaired in time if a fault occurs during the driving process, an unmanned ship cannot be easily repaired once a fault occurs when sailing at sea, so it is very important for an unmanned ship to ensure the stability of its power unit.

At present, the most commonly used power plant for civil ships is a low-speed diesel engine, which has a very complex motion structure, slow speed and poor stability. Seafarers still need to operate manually when encountering bad sea conditions and low-speed navigation, especially when equipment fails. From this point of view, the low-speed diesel engine is difficult to meet the requirements of unmanned ships for power plant stability and is not suitable for use on unmanned ships.

In comparison with the conventional cargo ship with a single engine and single slurry, the power plant of the ship with a double engine and double propeller is more stable and has more advantages in propulsion redundancy. However, once the load suddenly changes, the low-speed diesel engine cannot run stably at all due to the limitation of the working principle.

In terms of unmanned ships, the best power layout scheme may be the combination of different types of diesel engines and vehicle-driven thrusters. This kind of ship will use two different types of main engines and drive thrusters, and use low-speed two-stroke diesel engines to drive when sea conditions are normal, which is more economical; if the main propulsion diesel engine fails, the four-stroke diesel engine can be started immediately, which is more reliable and can provide continuous power for ship navigation.

In addition, unmanned ships can also use electric propulsion. Compared with the scheme of diesel engine directly driving propeller, electric propulsion is more stable, more redundant and easier to realize remote control. However, because the labor costs of sailing are acceptable at present, it is better for shipping companies to hire crew members to operate directly, saving time and effort, instead of investing an extra fee to add a propulsion system or using electric propulsion.

Path 3: Enhance the reliability of remote control

As for unmanned ships, the reliability of remote control needs to be solved in future development. Because of the harsh marine environment and the influence of seawater resistance, it is difficult for ships to operate flexibly like cars and airplanes. Airplanes, cars and trains have already been driven by a single person, but ships have been delayed. Among several existing means of transportation, ships are regarded as the most difficult means of transportation to drive.

The unmanned ship "Stril Luna" is an offshore ship, which can travel under severe sea conditions. Its hull is thin and more flexible to travel. It is equipped with a high-power propulsion system and end-to-end auxiliary propulsion device, which has strong maneuverability and is easier to realize remote control. Restricted by economic conditions, the maneuverability of ordinary ocean-going freighters is much worse and the operation process is more complicated in comparison with offshore ships equipped with various advanced equipment. Therefore, large ships make decisions based on the experience of the captain during navigation and control the running state of the ship. If artificial intelligence or remote control is adopted, the navigation risk of the ship will inevitably increase.

The technologies of "unmanned engine room" and "one-person bridge building" can be regarded as the precursors of the concept of the unmanned ship. Through the practical experience of these two technologies in ocean-going ships, we can know that the realization of ocean-going unmanned cargo ships needs requires continuous exploration and practice, and this process may take quite a long time.

The unmanned engine room is also called periodic unattended machine space. It replaces the traditional engine managers with various sensors and signal control systems, which monitor and control the operation of the equipment in the cabin. At present, it is widely being used in most ocean-going freighters. Although the engine room equipment of this kind of ship is highly automated, mechanical faults that need to be eliminated manually may still occur during the navigation of the ship. In order to ensure the normal operation of the ship, the captain usually arranges the crew to rotate to respond in time when the faults occur.

"One-person bridge building" is a bridge automation design concept, which mainly adopts electronic integration technology to arrange the ship control panel within reach of the driver so that the ship operator can control the ship as flexibly as the aircraft driver and the automobile driver. However, the handling actions required by ship driving are more complicated compared with airplanes and cars, and it is difficult for one person to complete them independently. In order to ensure the safety of ship navigation, even if the ship is equipped with a "one person bridge building," two operators will be arranged on duty.

In the future development of "unmanned ship." even if the three major problems that restrict its development, including information transmission security, power plant stability and remote operation reliability, can be solved smoothly, the recognition of unmanned ships by the shipping industry and shipping-related industries will not be greatly increased for safety reasons. Even though unmanned ships can avoid the risks caused by human factors, many unpredictable risks will arise. In addition, in the short term, the maritime laws and regulations on unmanned ships will not be issued, so it will be difficult for unmanned ships to be effectively applied in the shipping industry for a long time to come. However, as the level of ship automation continues to improve, ship manning will be gradually reduced, which is a general trend of the development of the shipping industry.

Path 4: Give full play to the function of the navigation support service

In essence, an unmanned ship is a fully automatic surface robot, which can independently complete driving, maintenance and other work without the need for manual control. As the mainstream transportation mode of international logistics, shipping bears more than two-thirds of the freight volume of international trade, and the market prospect of unmanned ships is very promising and has received close attention from governments, enterprises and capital around the world.

As the era of unmanned ships is approaching, traditional means such as providing navigation aid service information through visual navigation marks and VHF voice will no longer be applicable. It is common practice to provide customized navigation aid services in combination with the working characteristics, task requirements and navigation surrounding the environment of the unmanned ship control system.

In this case, for the purpose of giving full play to the navigation support service function, it is necessary to identify the unmanned ship control system efficiently and accurately; provide radio navigation marks or visual navigation marks with strong machine vision recognition ability; improve the construction of maritime communication infrastructure, especially to create a maritime communication link with large bandwidth, high frequency, high efficiency and high reliability; create a communication platform that meets the information exchange needs of ships; customize and design routes for ships by analyzing ship types, water intake, water depth, meteorological data, etc., and simultaneously provide safety information services such as hydrometeorology, navigation notices and warnings during ship navigation; establish a simulation navigation platform to simulate the real navigation environment; and improve the technical performance and emergency handling ability of unmanned ships.

Navigation mark service

The unmanned ship is effectively controlled through the cooperation of radar, camera, infrared sensor and land control center. Therefore, more emphasis should be placed on using radio navigation marks such as radar beacon, radar transponder, radio navigation station, radio beacon, propagation automatic identification system, differential global positioning system and visual navigation marks using machine identification technology when providing navigation mark service for unmanned ships.

At present, the base station signals of the automatic ship identification system have basically covered the main navigable waters along the coast of China, the Yangtze River trunk line, the high-grade inland waterways of Grade 4 and above, and some closed waters. Supported by the base station of the automatic ship identification system, the virtual navigation mark of automatic ship identification system has the advantages of low cost, convenient setting and low difficulty in identifying and analyzing marine electronic charts, which will create great value when the unmanned ship market explodes in the future.

Communication services

Unmanned ship navigation mainly depends on electronic navigation, which determines that it must interact with shore-based systems more frequently, thus making the business and application demand of offshore communication platforms usher in explosive growth. The mother ship and other unmanned ships are the main objects of communication between unmanned ships. In this process, unmanned ships can receive various instructions from the mother ship and information provided by other unmanned ships, and at the same time, feed back information such as their navigation status, surrounding environment and other information to the mother ship and other unmanned ships.

Nowadays, most maritime communication platforms have a single service type, limited bandwidth and data storage space and low data processing efficiency, which has made it difficult to meet the needs of marine information system expansion and caused many obstacles to improving the functions and services of marine application systems. In order to better meet the era of unmanned ships, the following three points need to be done in improving communication services.

(1) Further improve the construction of maritime communication links such as satellite communication, very small aperture satellite terminal station (VSAT) and very high frequency data exchange system (VDES), and improve the bandwidth, frequency, efficiency and reliability of maritime communication services.
(2) Build a perfect maritime cloud communication platform. The cloud computing platform, the research focus of all countries in the world, integrates distributed computing, parallel network computing, virtual technology and other technologies, efficiently configures multiple information resources and hardware structures, and endows the system with higher computing capacity, transmission efficiency and storage performance.

    The cloud computing platform uses standardized Web service technology supported by standard service technology to communicate, which makes the communication of all parties more convenient, fast and low-cost. In recent years, following the introduction of e-navigation strategies in various countries around the world, shielding data sources and providing on-demand services have become the mainstream trend of maritime services. In this case, service demanders do not need to know who provides information for themselves through what channels and equipment, but only how to obtain the required information conveniently and quickly.

    Of course, this requires the collection and transmission of ship information data based on the standard and unified protocol model. At the same time, data transmission should be convenient for users to identify each other. China has already started research and exploration related to building a "smart maritime cloud" through cloud computing technology. In the maritime cloud, there will be standardized protocols for functions such as authentication, encryption and management, and service discovery; the creation of a service-oriented communication system to allow global developers to participate in the development of maritime service solutions; and the establishment of an open supplier-neutral platform that uses communication channels such as satellite, wireless communication and the Internet to enable real-time interaction between all parties and facilitate the flow and sharing of information and other resources.

Onshore heterogeneous software systems based on maritime cloud, smartphones, tablet computers, and personal computers, etc., can interact with heterogeneous software systems of various ships and offshore structures efficiently and at low cost through standardized interfaces, protocols and access control rights.

(3) Expand the functions of the automatic ship identification system. For example, for the automatic ship identification system based on VHF communication frequency band and SOTDMA communication protocol, there are some shortcomings in system capacity and transmission bandwidth of communication system, which can no longer meet the needs of information interaction between ships and between ships and shore with ever-expanding scale and rapidly increasing frequency. However, it is expected to solve this problem effectively by using automatic identification technology based on mobile IP technology of public network GPRS/CDMA/3G communication system.

Constructing a unified deployment of maritime information sharing platform

If there is no unified maritime information sharing platform, some shore commanders may ask it to accelerate from the left to surpass the ship in front when a sailing ship encounters an emergency, while others ask it to accelerate from the right to bypass the ship in front, resulting in confusion in decision making.

The existence of water control problem by many leaders makes China's maritime supervision and service departments perform their own duties alone and makes it difficult to circulate and share data resources and give full play to their potential value. Moreover, the problem of repeated construction also causes serious waste of resources, which makes it difficult to provide efficient and convenient maritime safety information services for ships.

When there is a unified deployment of a maritime information-sharing platform, we can collect ship route information, improve the efficiency of data resources utilization, and better provide safety information services for ship navigation. For example, we can comprehensively apply ship automatic identification system, electronic chart display and information system, water depth data model, environmental management tools, etc., for ship route customization design; collect, integrate, analyze, exchange and apply all kinds of maritime information (such as waterways, ports, navigation marks, sea conditions, shipping management, goods, shipping markets, as well as public services); establish an information resource pool based on massive data; and basically achieve comprehensive coverage of wading activities, thus realizing the in-depth exploration of the potential value of data.

Of course, before establishing the platform, it is necessary to establish a unified data source standard for the basic architecture specification of E HNA system and integrate the source data output from the data center into the information systems of different agencies, such as maritime, port and shipping, by combining the differentiated needs of each agency. On this basis, the data will be analyzed by applying technologies such as big data and cloud computing, and customized services will be provided to users through channels such as public networks, satellite links and VHF on platforms such as portals, apps and WeChat public service platforms.

Research and development of "unmanned ship simulation and virtual training system"

At present, the mainstream computer simulation system positions people as bystanders, which cannot make the output content of the system adjust effectively with the difference of users' perspectives, and the interactivity is poor, making it difficult for users to have a sense of immersion and immersion, requiring people to compromise with the computer. With the development and application of virtual reality simulation technology, human–computer interaction ushered in a new era. In a virtual reality simulation system, people get more respect and can dominate the virtual environment, integrating into it in a certain role and having a better interactive experience.

In essence, virtual reality technology is a computer simulation system that can create a simulation environment integrating vision, hearing and touch for users, and provides a near-realistic feeling and experience for the user through natural communication and interaction with objects in the virtual environment through various devices equipped with sensors. Specific to the unmanned ship field, the simulation and virtual training system suitable for unmanned ships will build a virtual display training system by applying advanced equipment such as stereo glasses and audio, large screen display equipment, advanced 3D graphics accelerator card, position and orientation tracking equipment, and a variety of new technologies, such as collision detection, audio virtualization, as well as image panoramic modeling, so that the unmanned ship intelligent system and remote operators can carry out practical training.

With the support of an electronic map, the aviation insurance department can expand the service comprehensively; for example, unmanned ships can obtain the real-life model of virtual water environment in real time; with the image-based panoramic modeling technology, it makes the scene model more three-dimensional and realistic, and a typical application scenario is to take a series of real-life photos in the target water area by the digital camera, and then generate 360-degree panoramic pictures by smoothing, splicing and other technologies. When users observe from different perspectives, they can digitally deform the pictures from the corresponding positions and project them into the virtual scene where users are located.

Path 5: Improve the maritime laws and regulations system

Unmanned ships will lead the shipbuilding industry into a new era. Just like smartphones subvert the mobile phone industry, smart ships will also bring far-reaching influence to the shipbuilding industry and reconstruct the market structure of the industry. Of course, the development of unmanned ships requires innovation in existing shipping mode, operation management, norms and standards, laws and regulations, etc.

The development of unmanned ships drives the new ship businesses such as online freight services, ship-shore integrated communication, and cargo supervision and control to develop in a rapid way. It will not only improve the existing business efficiency but also open up more new markets after collecting and analyzing massive unmanned ship automatic driving operation data. Unmanned ships transmit instructions to control ship operation through the network, and network security will become the top priority of risk prevention and control.

With the continuous research and application of unmanned ship technology, data resources such as ports and maritime affairs will be highly integrated, which can provide many conveniences for route planning, logistics and transportation, and maritime supervision. In addition, the definition of ship operation responsibility and insurance claims rules need to be adjusted accordingly due to the lack of crew participation.

It is necessary to speed up the study of new maritime laws and regulations to ensure the sustained and stable development of unmanned ships. To be specific, such laws and regulations include three aspects.

(1) Ship safety laws and regulations, for example, revise and improve the relevant provisions of the "International Convention for the Safety of Life at Sea" (SLOAS), such as life-saving equipment, manning of fire-fighting ships, signal and alarm requirements, and revise and improve the relevant provisions of the "International Rules for Preventing Collisions at Sea" (COLREG), such as observation navigation decision-making and light signal interaction;

(2) Crew management regulations, for example, add unmanned ship clauses to laws and regulations such as "International Labor Convention," "Minimum Safe Manning Rules for Ships," and "International Convention on Standards of Training, Certification and Watchkeeping for Seafarers" (STCW);

(3) Laws and regulations on maritime rights and liabilities, for example, perfect the provisions of captain's liability, salvage at sea, legal subject and insurance liability.

Unmanned ships cannot have a crew to carry out routine maintenance during the voyage as traditional ships do, which requires higher reliability of the ship's systems and a comprehensive ship equipment health management system, matched with onshore support such as remote management and operation and maintenance support.

With a highly integrated unmanned vessel system and networking and collaboration with shore-based agencies such as customs, border guards, flag states and port states will be able to enforce the law remotely by automatically obtaining information in real time instead of boarding the vessel. Ports and waterways should set up infrastructure to match the operation of unmanned ships and provide effective management schemes. As for standards and specifications, relevant departments and trade associations should speed up the research and formulation of basic technical standards, safety standards, management standards, inspection and evaluation standards that are in line with unmanned ships.

Need all-round support

Unmanned ships have very broad development prospects; however, the development of unmanned ships is not a simple matter, and there are a series of pain points such as technology, law, operation and management. To break the development dilemma of unmanned ships, it is necessary to make the government, shipping enterprises, classification societies, scientific research institutions, ports, solution providers and other subjects participate actively in providing all-round support for the unmanned ship industry.

Research and innovate shipping management and ship operation mode, guide the transformation and upgrading of shipping enterprises, value the new challenges posed by ship–shore integration to ship safety, and guide and standardize the innovative formats of unmanned ships under the tide of sharing economy.

In the establishment of unmanned ship maritime laws and regulations system, it is encouraged to pursue entrepreneurial innovation, ensure safety and order, guide enterprises to carry out healthy competition, improve the applicability of existing maritime laws and regulations, and explore effective unmanned ship operation supervision policies in combination with the shipping characteristics and needs of domestic and foreign ships.

An unmanned ship can realize high integration and real-time sharing of information. If unmanned ship operation can be brought into the large logistics circulation system, it will have a very positive impact on improving logistics efficiency. For example, developers help logistics providers to provide technical solutions such as cargo status monitoring and shipping space reservation in real time so as to improve transaction security and reliability, which is of great value in building a freight credit system based on the unmanned ship operation mode.

To reduce the cost of trial and error, it is necessary to establish an unmanned ship test area in an area with suitable conditions. When determining the pilot area, various factors such as meteorology, signal strength, navigation density, hydrological conditions and demonstration effect must be comprehensively considered to accumulate operation and management experience gradually and lay a solid foundation for the popularization of unmanned ships nationwide.

Chapter 7

Unmanned Port: Application of Electrical Automation in Ports

Development status and strategy of port electrical automation in China

Development status of port electrical automation in China

A port is a very important transportation hub connecting land and water transportation where ships can safely enter, exit and berth. It plays a positive role in promoting economic development. As China opens to the outside world, ports are playing an increasingly important role. It is now essential to ensure the healthy development of ports in order to promote social stability and sustainable development. In this respect, the electrification of ports is an important measure. Realizing the development of port electrification can not only intelligently control the port electrical equipment but also improve the operational efficiency of the port and promote the better development of the social economy.

After joining the World Trade Organization, the speed of construction and development of electrical automation in domestic ports has increased. However, the level of development of electrical automation in Chinese ports is still not comparable to that of developed countries. Up until now, although China has devoted itself to the exploration and research of computer automatic monitoring and management systems, specialized wharf management systems, bulk grain automation systems and other aspects, it has been unable to effectively promote the development and realize the universal application of electrical automation due to the limited condition of electrical equipment and the backward technology level in China. In addition, many traditional ports have not yet realized information management and are still using old equipment, which makes the development of port electrical automation in China slow to make obvious progress, and there is still an obvious gap between China and developed countries. In other words, the development of port electrical automation in China still has great potential for development, so there is an urgent need to improve the availability of port electrical equipment, give full play to its practical application value, improve the efficiency of port operation in China on the original basis and enhance the overall management ability.

At present, the electrification of China's ports is developing at a rapid pace, with many ports having been electrified and the operational efficiency of ports having been effectively improved. In the case of the electrification of container terminals, China has been vigorously developing container transport and has developed CC, RTG and other equipment since the mid-1970s, which effectively met the needs of port operation.

Although the development of port electrification in China has made some achievements in recent years, compared with Europe and the United States and other developed countries in the West, the development level of port electrification in China needs to be improved. On the one hand, many electrical equipment in China are imported, and there are few independently developed devices, some of which are relatively backward and cannot keep up with the pace of development of the times. On the other hand, the development level of electrical automation in China has been delayed due to the limitation of technical level and hardware conditions such as electrical equipment, and it has not been widely popularized and applied, resulting in low efficiency of port work. Although the development level of port electrical automation in China is not high at present, there is a lot of room for future development.

Advanced automation technology and information technology are adopted, which has accelerated the development of port electrical automation in China. As a result, it should focus on the current situation, emphasize key projects, dare to break through the shackles of traditional thinking concepts and improve the automation level of port electrical operation by implementing strong reforms. In the specific reform process, the following two things should be done:

(1) Integrate hardware construction with software construction, clarify the key points of construction and give full play to the synergy

between them. During the construction of port electrical automation, it is necessary to adopt consistent standard electrical equipment and electrical system, improve the efficiency of electrical automation development and promote the construction of port electrical automation in China on an overall level. At the same time, it is necessary to focus on technical research and application, pay attention to the development of port electrical management system and continuously narrow the gap between China and developed countries.

(2) Concentrate superior forces to develop integrated terminal management, integrated dispatching and other related software, rely on its own strength to establish a well-structured software system gradually to reduce the dependence on foreign core technologies. In this process, advanced technical means should be used, modern docks and loading and unloading equipment should be adopted, management systems should be optimized and the development of electrical automation in China's ports should be promoted from all aspects in order to rank among the advanced international ranks.

To sum up, the application scope of electrical automation control technology in the domestic industrial field will be gradually broadened with the development, and its application can improve the modernization level of domestic industrial development. Therefore, more attention should be paid to electrical automation control technology and its value should be fully recognized.

Development significance of port electrical automation in China

The implementation of automatic management and control of port electrical equipment is also known as the construction and development of port electrical automation. In the past, the port control system realized the connection among contacts, contactors, timers and different relays through wires on the basis of following a certain logical relationship. Automation can realize the transformation of a control system to automation and intelligence and realize centralized control. Automation has obvious advantages, can play an important role in port electrical management and has a broad development market. This can make the development of the whole industry keep up with the pace of the information age.

The port occupies a very important position in all kinds of transportation infrastructure, which not only is conducive to the realization of an export-oriented economy but also plays a positive role in promoting the development of national economic construction and foreign trade. In recent years, with the support of the policy of "further opening to the outside world," the scale of China's import and export trade has been growing, and the port and container throughput have been increasing continuously. With this trend, China's foreign trade is developing faster and faster, the role of ports is becoming more and more important, and the requirements for ports are getting higher and higher.

In the past, the port has always adopted traditional management means, and the efficiency of cargo handling is relatively low. To further promote the development of the port economy, it is necessary to change this traditional mode of operation, and port electrification is a good choice. Port electrification is to automate the management and operation of port electrical equipment and control port equipment automatically so as to reduce port operation cost, improve operation efficiency, increase port throughput and play a strong role in promoting port economic development.

The construction and development of port electrical automation cannot be separated from the support of core technologies. In terms of core technology, developed Western countries have more advantages in development. In the process of developing port electrical automation in China, we should actively learn from the core automation technology of developed countries, improve our independent research and development ability and develop port electrical automation technology suitable for the national conditions of China. Specifically, developed Western countries have mastered automatic scheduling management technology, wireless data communication technology, frequency conversion speed regulation drive technology and automatic process control technology.

In the case of frequency conversion speed regulation drive technology, this technology relies on continuous transportation and loading machinery technology and total variable product technology, which can effectively accelerate the operation of port electrical equipment and implement efficient system management. On the basis of continuous improvement of the technical level, the management ability of port electrical equipment will be gradually improved, and the production cost will be saved. In addition, the programmable logic controller (PLC) can also effectively promote the development of port electrical automation. Specifically, the PLC can control different types of machinery by analog or digital means, which can play its value in many links of port operation and management, reduce the labor burden of production personnel, complete more workload at the same time and effectively promote the development of port electrical automation.

Port electrical automation is the mainstream direction of future development and a long-term development goal for China. It is necessary to tackle key technical problems and break through the shackles of traditional thinking in the process of implementing the reform of port electrical automation. While understanding the development status of port electrical automation in China, we should recognize its future development trend and comprehensively consider various factors. In the specific development process, we should make full use of the existing superior resources and environmental conditions, persistently carry out learning, innovation and breakthroughs, constantly accelerate the pace of port electrical automation development, and strive to become a country with a higher level of port electrical automation development in the international scope.

Practical application of electrical automation in ports

With the rapid update and iteration of science and technology, related application equipment and management systems also need to be reformed. Many industries are now committed to the development of automation, digitalization and modernization. However, in the specific development process, only by fully considering the specific conditions of ports can the optimal allocation and efficient utilization of resources be realized.

As an important logistics distribution center, the modernization of port needs to give full play to the advantages of knowledge resources. Therefore, it is necessary to focus on the training of port staff and vigorously introduce modern technology and equipment to promote the development of a port in the direction of modernization. Here, the practical application of electrical automation in ports is analyzed and combed.

Automation of port loading and unloading system

The port loading and unloading transportation system plays a prominent role in the process of port operation, so the port loading and unloading speed is closely associated with the automation and scientific level of the system. Usually, bulk cargo terminals are equipped with two types of systems: centralized control systems and distributed systems.

In the centralized control system, there is only one control host, by whom all logical operations and data processing tasks of the system are carried out and to which the control system is connected remotely or locally. There are many hosts in the distributed control system. Different hosts take on different equipment control tasks. The hosts send data information by means of network communication. Whether it is a centralized or a distributed control system, the automatic network task is undertaken by the control level network.

In addition, the operation of the port can also be monitored by applying the automatic control system. In the process of monitoring, the control equipment and monitoring personnel of the port will collect the operation data of the port field equipment and transmit it to the relevant management departments. The development of port loading and unloading system automation can also optimize the work of each link of port and improve its overall operation efficiency instead of only strengthening the management and monitoring of port operation.

Automation of the port power system

In the analysis of the modernization of the port, the port can be considered to have achieved a shift towards automation if the value of the application of computers is effectively reflected in the control of the power system. By analyzing the specific use methods of computers, it can be seen that in order to integrate the data generated by the control link with the protective data in the system, the computers in the power system are connected with the middle line of the network in a distributed structure, thus optimizing the functions undertaken by the port and accelerating the operation of the whole system.

In addition, it is necessary to use advanced technology to equip the power system with efficient management and protection devices and give full play to the functions of the central signal system, integrated operation screen and analog screen in the process of developing modern monitoring. Moreover, it can also apply computer technology in substation management, control the operation of equipment in power supply systems through network diagnosis and professional operation and complete online self-inspection, which fully reflects the value of power systems in monitoring and management.

Automation of the integrated wharf system

To improve the modernization level of port management, it is necessary to promote the universal application of automation technology, information technology and computer technology in all aspects and then improve the economic benefits of port operation. From the point of view of port container work, it is difficult to speed up the overall operation efficiency fundamentally only through single machine automation equipment. If an automatic container crane is adopted, the automation device of this equipment can be used to speed up the operation of the wharf.

By analyzing the operation of the container crane at the present stage, it can be seen that it is impossible to move and lift the container smoothly, which can cause damage to the goods and threaten the personal safety of workers. In view of this situation, it is necessary to improve the control theory and improve the stability of existing devices so as to reduce the probability of risks in the operation of this link.

In addition, wharf work focuses on operational efficiency and should pay attention to the research and development of relevant technologies to improve the efficiency of container cranes through the implementation of technological innovation, thereby accelerating the operation of terminal automation. In terms of logic control, emphasis can be placed on theoretical updates and technological iterations to improve the positioning accuracy of cranes. Comprehensive use of various advanced theories and equipment, optimizing power supply equipment, improving the management and monitoring capabilities of the entire system, thereby improving the level of automation of the entire terminal operation, reducing the risks of various tasks and achieving improved efficiency.

Development strategy of port electrical automation in China

Increase technical research and investment

In order to promote better economic development, China's ports must be electrified on priority. The key to port electrification lies in continuously increasing investment in technology research and development. Technology is the core for the realization of port electrical automation. Only by relying on advanced technology can the level of port electrical automation be continuously improved and the development of port electrical automation be truly realized. Therefore, relevant departments should make a deep understanding of the development of China's ports, increase investment in electrical automation research from both manpower and material resources, actively learn from foreign experience in port electrical automation and introduce advanced equipment so that the technical level of port electrical automation in China can be continuously improved.

Take PLC technology as an example. The PLC is a programmable controller, which replaces intermediate and time relay with software, and the remaining hardware components related to input and output are reduced from 1/10 to 1/100 of the relay control system through wiring, reducing the incidence of faults caused by poor contact. In addition, the PLC replaces the intermediate relay, counter, time relay and other components in the relay control system with software, which reduces the workload of control cabinet design, installation, wiring and other links, and greatly improves the operation efficiency of electrical equipment, promoting the working efficiency of the whole port.

Establish a unified electrical automation control system

With the increasing frequency of port trade and the continuous growth of port equipment, port management is facing more and more problems. In order to carry out comprehensive management of port equipment and improve management efficiency, China's port management departments must base themselves on the present and further promote reform.

First of all, each port should establish a unified electrical automation control system according to its own actual situation so as to promote the coordination of software and hardware construction. The construction of an automation control system should cover all aspects of ports and establish a unified electrical system in all ports to effectively control all ports and promote the development of port electrical automation.

Secondly, all ports should do a good job in comprehensive management, further develop relevant application software, build a completely independent software system in combination with the actual situation of Chinese ports, and introduce high-tech to improve the operation and management level of container terminals and loading and unloading equipment, enhance the development level of electrical automation in Chinese ports and be in line with international standards.

Increase the training of electrical automation professionals

The development of port electrical automation cannot be separated from the support of professionals. In recent years, many high-tech products and equipment have been introduced into China's ports, and the operation, repair and maintenance of this equipment cannot be separated from professionals. Therefore, the development of port electrical automation must emphasize personnel training.

On the one hand, the existing staff must be trained to improve their electrical operation skills and strengthen their professional ability, so that their professional ability and level can be effectively improved. On the other hand, electrical automation professionals should be actively introduced, combined with the existing talents of enterprises, to jointly form a professional team to promote the better development of port electrical automation.

To sum up, the development of port electrical automation is an inevitable choice in line with the rapid development trend of modern society. The development and realization of port electrification are beneficial to promote better economic growth and enhance the comprehensive management ability of China's ports. In order to realize the electrical automation of China's ports, China must combine the current situation of port development, increase the investment in the research and development of port automation technology, actively introduce foreign advanced electrical automation technology to continuously improve the level of electrical automation in China's ports and make the level of electrical automation in China's ports reach the international standards.

Electrical automation control technology and application of ports in China

Control technology of port electrical automation in China

In recent years, the domestic electrical automation field has shown a vigorous development trend. After analysis, it is not difficult to find that its development has advantages but also faces many challenges. So, what is the specific development of electrical automation in China at present?

Through continuous efforts, the gap between China's development in the field of industrialization and that of advanced international countries has gradually narrowed, and the scope of application of automation technology in the industry has been expanding, with high-tech industries being particularly obvious. Many enterprises have begun to operate around electrical automation control technology, actively promoting the transformation and upgrading of enterprises and transforming traditional manual operation into automation control, which not only reduces the cost consumption of enterprises but also improves the sustainability of enterprise development.

The application of electrical automation control technology can improve the modernization level of industrial development, reduce the cost of human resources with the help of automation technology, improve the accuracy of industrial operation, achieve the improvement of production quality, accelerate the overall production and operation of enterprises and increase their economic benefits. Many colleges and universities have set up electrical automation control technology majors in order to meet the needs of industrial development, aiming at accelerating social and economic development by relying on electrical automation technology, satisfying people's pursuit of high-quality life and then mobilizing people's enthusiasm for participation.

Characteristics of electrical automation control technology

In the process of application and development, the electrical automation technology embodies different characteristics that are different from other technical methods, which are not possessed by the latter. Specifically, these characteristics mainly include the following four aspects:

(1) The electrical automation control technology has high speed, high accuracy, limited actual control and little information, so it usually does not need to carry out the high-frequency operation.
(2) Electrical automation technology can realize the transmission and reception of signals in time, complete the overall control task quickly and is suitable for remote operation.
(3) Different from the traditional control system, electrical automation control technology can reduce the control time and effectively improve the operation efficiency. In addition, data acquisition and remote control can be successfully completed, which is the core feature of electrical automation control.

Development status of electrical automation control technology

In recent years, the development of electrical automation control technology has made a very obvious breakthrough. The development level of electrical automation control technology is increasing day by day after the high integrated circuit is put into use. From the current stage, the development of electrical automation control technology is mainly reflected in the following three points:

(1) In the current industrial production field, electrical automation control technology occupies a dominant position, which can meet the production needs of users.
(2) Electrical automation control technology is now widely used in many related fields.
(3) In the development process of industrial production, electrical automation control technology has played a positive role in promoting the process. On the basis of macro analysis, many enterprises, driven by the implementation of modern reforms, have gradually broadened the application of electrical automation control technology and accelerated the development process.

System function of electrical automation control technology

Electrical automation technology is equipped with some characteristics that are different from other technologies. On the premise of electrical control, electrical automation control technology can operate circuit breakers in electrical systems and has to have certain functions in order to achieve this control. Generally speaking, electrical automation control technology should have the following functions. It can operate the outlet isolating switch between transformer and generator, add magnetization and demagnetization, switch between different control modes and operate excitation transformer.

Design concept of electrical automation control technology system

Electrical automation control technology adopts three design modes of remote detection, centralized monitoring and monitoring bus in the process of system design and follows the following design concepts in the design process:

(1) When implementing remote monitoring, the electrical automation control technology will obtain remote signals in time, transmit them and find the control signals to be corrected from the feedback information to complete the task of remote monitoring.

(2) When implementing centralized monitoring, electrical automation control technology can control all links through a single processor. This design mode has low complexity and loose requirements for protection, which can reduce the difficulty of later maintenance.

(3) When implementing bus monitoring, electrical automation control technology can integrate different integration functions and combine different control methods to improve the overall monitoring operation effect. Based on the analysis of macroscopic structure, the design concept adopted in the design system of electrical automation control technology has high-practical value and has achieved certain results in application. Therefore, on the basis of understanding the specific situation, we should choose the appropriate scheme to complete the design of the electrical automation control technology system.

Intelligent port based on information technology

Waterway and land transportation should be connected by ports. For foreign trade and import and export of goods, agricultural and industrial products should also be distributed through ports, which reflects the importance of ports. China is currently carrying out intelligent port construction, reforming traditional ports by relying on advanced technologies such as cloud computing and the Internet of Things so as to transform and upgrade them to an intelligent direction.

As a container distribution port, the Shenzhen Chiwan Port not only promotes the development of trade in the Pearl River Delta region but also is an important single container terminal in China; the annual throughput of the Port of Rizhao is as high as 1.2 tons, and its scale ranks first among all coal and iron ore powder terminals in China. In recent years, many ports have actively introduced big data, cloud computing and Internet of Things technologies and are committed to building intelligent ports. Unmanned is a new development period that intelligent ports are about to enter.

Under the traditional mode, the operation of ports is slow, the production efficiency is low and regional traffic congestion occurs frequently. Workers use paper and pen to collect all kinds of operation information, but different people have different levels information collection efficiency. Weather factors, environmental factors and so on also have an impact on information collection, which reduces the guarantee of the accuracy of information. In addition, the port has a large number of operations, so the traditional information collection method cannot complete all the recording work in a short time, requiring the operators to wait in line. Moreover, the information collectors sometimes need to perform multiple operations at the same time, making them unable to concentrate and reduces their job security.

After the informationization construction, the port will apply GPS, vehicle-mounted terminals, as well as handheld terminal equipment, etc., to realize automatic operation in many links, which can speed up the operation of each link. Using modern information technology, the port can automatically identify the cargo box number through camera equipment, use an industrial computer to let the working vehicles receive the operation instructions quickly and then execute the operation instructions after multi-party data confirmation to complete the loading or unloading tasks of containers and avoid wasting labor resources due to information errors. At the same time, providing operation time arrangement for operation vehicles, combining with the application of a global positioning system and navigation system, reasonable scheduling and arrangement of operation vehicles can alleviate regional traffic congestion at the wharf.

The Chiwan Port and Rizhao Port have achieved comprehensive coverage of information terminal equipment, that is, each container and bulk cargo equipment is equipped with corresponding information terminals according to transportation needs, replacing traditional manual labor with automatic operation and reducing tally personnel to the original 25%. In comparison with the traditional mode, automatic operation can speed up the loading, unloading and stacking of goods and reduce the waiting time of people in line. The fuel consumption of each equipment is expressed digitally, which is convenient for workers to provide energy for the equipment in time.

Currently, more and more fields are carrying out "Internet+," and port construction has begun to use Internet thinking to manage the data of shippers, freight forwarders, ships, etc., through a comprehensive platform so as to realize the optimal scheduling of equipment resources and location information in the port and reduce the cost consumption of terminal management. Using advanced technical means, we can provide operation information to freight-forwarding companies, provide an accurate reference for freight-forwarding companies to make operation plans and upload company information, driver information and vehicle information to mobile terminals.

The whole process of port operation under the environment of the Internet of Things

After a period of intelligent construction, the whole operation process of the Shenzhen Chiwan Port has been made intelligent, including delivery, container stacking, goods going out to sea and production allocation.

Before the goods enter the port, the wharf production management system collects the goods information, box number and other data, and after determining the shipment time, the lender is notified by the wharf; after the vehicles transporting goods arrive at the port gate, the radio frequency identification technology is used to identify the cargo box number and get the driver's relevant information in real time—for example, which logistics company does the driver work for. If the container truck itself is equipped with an onboard computer, it can also submit relevant information to the industrial computer controlling the gate when it is about to reach the port gate, and the industrial computer compares the operating system with the data obtained by it. After confirming that the box number, car number and personnel information are correct, the gate is opened, and the automatic acquisition terminal is used instead of people to record information, thus improving the operation efficiency.

In the traditional model, the port operated with staff going ashore to check and record the box numbers. All loading and unloading equipment used in ports is now equipped with a global positioning system. After the packing vehicle enters the gate, the loading and unloading equipment can receive information immediately, and the closest equipment will load and unload the vehicle. This automatic dispatching mode can fully realize the full utilization and optimal allocation of loading and unloading equipment resources. Using automation instead of the traditional operation mode can better deal with the problem of wrong box loading.

In the concrete implementation process, the cargo box number for lifting operation will be compared with the operation data provided by the industrial computer, and geographic mapping will be carried out in combination with the global positioning system. If the wrong box is loaded, the spreader will stop the subsequent packing operation. When stacking goods, the driver can adopt reasonable stacking methods according to the guidance of the operation management system.

After that, the shipment operation will be carried out. The nearest trailer will transport the goods to the shore, and the stowage system installed on the ship will analyze and process the data to determine the specific cabin where the goods of different types, weights and properties should be placed, and complete the loading by bridge crane.

When the ship arrives at the port and needs to be unloaded, it will also provide cargo data to the wharf. The trailer used for loading will receive the operation information from the production management system, arrange for the driver to drive the car to the corresponding yard and complete the packing work of the yard. When the customs department completes the cargo audit, the freight-forwarding company can enter the port for cargo transportation.

Nowadays, the Port of Rizhao can also use a computer system to transmit the operation plan and provide operation instructions to drivers so that they can confirm the information. The stacking position of the bulk cargo terminal is not fixed, which may lead to operational errors. Once the driver has arrived at his destination based on the location alert information, he must reconfirm the information before loading and unloading to avoid any errors. The central control room also uses the global positioning system to rationalize tasks according to the driver's work.

Application of port electrical automation based on PLC technology

Current situation and characteristics of PLC technology for electrical automation

The value of technological innovation has been fully affirmed by all sectors of society, and the application of new technologies in various industries has brought a powerful impetus to promote the transformation and upgrading of traditional enterprises and improve productivity. Port electrical automation is the mainstream trend of modern ports, and it is an effective means to improve port throughput and reduce operating costs.

The application of PLC technology to the field of port electrical automation can effectively improve the operation efficiency of port electrical automation and reduce accidents. On the one hand, PLC technology can enable managers to control the operation intensity of port electrical automation more accurately and improve the operation stability; on the other hand, it promotes the efficient allocation of port manpower, material resources and other resources to improve production efficiency.

PLC refers to an editable logic controller, which is characterized by the use of editable memory to store internal programs and execute various instructions, such as sequence control, logic operation, as well as arithmetic operation. At the same time, PLC can control mechanized equipment by analog input and output and digital input and output at the same time. With the support of current technical conditions, the PLC can be widely used in the field of industrial control.

The hardware structure of the PLC consists of a power supply device, memory, central processing unit, function module, input/output interface circuit, as well as communication module, etc. From the perspective of PLC development, the current performance of PLC equipment used in the field of industrial control has diverse characteristics, which are mainly manifested in the following aspects:

(1) **Simple programming, convenient use and strong operability:** After introducing PLC, the programming language is mainly a ladder diagram or logic diagram, which is simple in programming, short in the development cycle and can be debugged on site. At the same time, with the help of an online scheme, the program can be scientifically adjusted to avoid adverse effects on hardware.

(2) **Diversified functions and high cost performance:** Up until now, PLC products have had the characteristics of standardization, serialization and modularization. Users can use various hardware devices flexibly to configure the system and build a system with personalized characteristics in scale and function.

(3) **Simple installation, with the advantage of load:** The installation and wiring of PLC products are very simple. As long as the external wiring is normal, the system can run normally. At the same time, PLC equipment also has the advantage of carrying a load, which can drive conventional solenoid valves and AC contactors to work normally.

With the economic globalization and the rapid growth of cross-border trade, the value of ports, especially large ports with high management level, has been fully reflected, and accelerating the realization of port electrical automation has become an inevitable choice for modern ports. Therefore, it is necessary to make full use of a series of technologies such as power electronics, information processing, system engineering, control theory and computer technology. PLC technology has high application value in the field of port electrical automation. The application scenarios of PLC technology are very diverse, and its powerful control performance has been fully reflected in many projects. Moreover, because of its own programmable system, the staff can further optimize and improve the control system according to the actual needs.

In the field of port electrical automation, PLCs have a high degree of fit with practical work needs and a wide range of applications, which is highly practical. After the management module is standardized, the control operation in a specific scene can be completed by inputting it into the PLC and writing specific code in the system. At the same time, PLC application and maintenance are convenient and quick. The PLC can automatically respond to the problem when there is a problem, which can effectively reduce the negative impact caused by accidents.

In practical application, PLC programming is simple, and staff can complete program preset according to need by inputting simple language application, which is of great value in reducing resource waste and improving the efficiency of port electrification operation.

The practice has proved that the introduction of PLC into port electrical automation and its integration with key equipment in port electrical automation systems can promote the efficient and stable development of port electrical automation. At the same time, the introduction of the PLC into the field of port electrical automation can also reduce labor intensity and improve labor productivity and comprehensive benefits. The following is a systematic analysis and discussion on the application of the PLC in the field of port electrical automation.

Application advantages and prospects of electrical automation PLC

Application advantages of the PLC in port electrical automation

(1) **Simple operation and strong practicability:** Workers can develop the programming system with lower time cost and debug it on site so that they can customize the programming scheme according to specific application scenarios and can obviously improve the production efficiency of port electrical automation.

(2) **Multiple functions and high cost performance:** PLC product development has entered the stage of standardization and modularization, which can realize multiple functions through the differentiated combination of different modules, thus flexibly applying to various practical scenes.

Application of PLC in port electrical automation

At present, the application of PLC technology in the field of port electrical automation has achieved preliminary results. For example, after applying PLC to the belt conveyor, workers can control and monitor the running system of the machine in real time and accurately.

The PLC can realize distributed control and bring a lot of convenience to field control and centralized control. For example, the centralized control device is arranged in the central control room, and then with the help of sensors, information control and TCP/IP protocol, the staff can interact with the field control station conveniently and quickly in real time, which has an obvious positive impact on improving production efficiency and emergency treatment of accidents productivity and the emergency response to accidents.

Cargo loading and unloading is an important function of the port terminal. Developing port electrical automation can reduce labor costs and improve port operation efficiency. Gantry cranes are widely used in the process of port cargo handling. This kind of equipment is upgraded from bridge cranes, which is especially suitable for port operations and has the advantages of strong practicability and wide operation range.

In the process of port operation, the gantry crane can respond and execute instructions in a short time, which can effectively improve the efficiency of cargo handling. Of course, gantry cranes do not work independently, and they are usually equipped with a series of supporting equipment. PLC technology can also be used in gantry cranes, which can improve the efficiency and accuracy of the current distribution of gantry cranes. After the control loop and DC power supply are connected, workers can simply operate on the master controller to complete related operations.

PLC technology can also be applied to port transport aircraft. In the centralized control system of port transport aircraft, a supervision and control network based on dispatching telephone and TV systems is built.

At the same time, the advantages of PLC control systems, such as flexibility, stability and high efficiency, are brought into full play to speed up the circulation speed of goods in the port and significantly improve the overall operation efficiency of the port.

Development prospect of PLC in port electrical automation

PLC technology has a very broad application prospect in the field of port electrical automation. In the future, with the further development of PLC technology, its application scenarios will become more diversified, the cost will be further reduced and efficiency will be further improved. For example, the integration of PLC technology and computer-aided assembly into the field of port electrical automation will promote the latter to further develop in the direction of digitalization and distribution.

With the continuous development of port trade, higher requirements will be put forward for its electrical automation level, pursuing higher safety and stability and emphasizing stronger cost control, which requires further improvement in the application of technologies such as PLC. PLC technology has created considerable value in the application of port electrical automation, but there are also many problems in this process. For example, when in a special environment such as a strong magnetic field, the PLC is prone to system errors, which cannot guarantee the accuracy of data and may lead to wrong instructions from output equipment, thus causing a series of problems.

Therefore, in the future, we need to further improve the application stability and safety of the PLC in the field of port electrical automation, improve its technical performance, make it adapt to various special scenarios and lay a solid foundation for building a world-class port cluster in China.

Application of PLC in port electrical automation field

Application of PLC in electrical automation of portal crane

Cargo loading and unloading is the most common work in ports and docks, and gantry cranes are the most commonly used equipment for cargo loading and unloading. At present, the most common gantry cranes in the market are mainly composed of a walking mechanism, luffing mechanism, rotating mechanism and lifting mechanism. If grab operations are required on site, the lifting mechanism should be equipped with two sets of symmetrical equipment, namely, support and opening and closing, to ensure the opening and closing effect of grab. For the application of gantry cranes in ports, the following conclusions can be drawn in combination with the technical characteristics of gantry cranes: For gantry cranes, stability performance is very important. In addition, gantry cranes often operate frequently in port applications. In order to meet the needs of frequent start-stop, gantry cranes equipped with frequency converters, switchgear, contactors and other equipment must have the function of supporting frequent start–stop operations.

The driving mode of the gantry crane running mechanism is best based on a three-phase AC wound asynchronous motor, and the driving mode can be single driving or joint driving. The PLC is used in gantry cranes, and its driving operation principle is as follows. The power supply passes through the wharf power grid operation system, passes through the cable drum slip ring in the middle, flows through the central slip ring and then transmits to the automatic air circuit breaker device of the power distribution cabinet in the machine room, and each operation system distributes the current reasonably through the isolating switch device. At the same time, the DC power supply flows directly into the control loop and the gantry crane operator inputs the PLC through the control of the master controller. The output port covers an overvoltage circuit, overlimit circuit, interlock circuit, overcurrent circuit and other related circuits. In this driving mode, if the peripheral output signal of the PLC corresponding to the gantry crane is normal and the output signal of the PLC is 24.0 V, it can drive the coil of a small relay device, trigger the contactor coil and start the relevant operation mechanism. With the intervention of the PLC, the gantry crane will not be overworked, the labor intensity can be effectively controlled and the labor efficiency is greatly improved.

Application of PLC in electrical automation of port belt conveyor

The belt conveyor has great application value in the port work site, which shows that the belt conveyor can scientifically monitor the operation of the whole control system. With the help of existing technology, PLC control is gradually developing to PCC control, which is mainly manifested in the establishment of a supervision and control network based on the

PLC centralized control system and the integration of the dispatching telephone system and industrial television system. The operation system of the belt conveyor has a strong dependence on the flexible application of the PLC control system, which can effectively improve the operation efficiency of port cargo and reduce the failure rate of the belt conveyor during operation.

After introducing the PLC into the belt conveyor, its electrical automation system mainly adopts a distributed control structure, which consists of two parts: one is the field control system, including a control station, a detection device and a field control device; the other is the centralized control system, including a server device, a monitoring center, an operator device, a site monitoring screen and so on. The centralized control device is installed in the central control room and uses TCP/IP protocol and Ethernet to interact and communicate with the field control station. If the distance between the central control room and the field control station exceeds 1200 meters, it is necessary not only to connect with Ethernet but also to add repeaters to consolidate the results of the data interaction.

With the rapid progress of modern science and technology, the application advantages of PLC control systems can be further developed, and the development performance can be further improved. In this situation, the PLC control system has been widely used in all walks of life, especially in the field of port electrical automation. In order to make full use of the PLC control system, the person in charge of port electrical automation should accumulate work experience, absorb and learn from foreign advanced PLC technology and constantly improve their skills so as to promote the all-round development of port electrical automation through flexible application of PLC technology.

Chapter 8

Unmanned Wharf: Disruptive Change in the Automatic Wharf

Development status and trend of the intelligent automatic wharf

Development status and main problems of ports in China

Ports play an increasingly important role in the global collection and distribution network and undertake more and more functions (including the distribution of import and export goods, international logistics and transportation, global resource allocation and the construction of global value chains, etc.) with the continuous advancement of global economic integration, the continuous growth of the total world economy and the rapid development of international trade.

In recent years, in order to cope with the global environmental degradation, China has comprehensively promoted the construction of a "resource-saving and environment-friendly society" and made a series of arrangements for the development of a green, low-carbon and circular economy. In line with this situation, China's port construction and equipment renewal should be fully automated, efficient and environmentally friendly as much as possible.

With the rapid development of computer and Internet technologies, all industries have made intelligence and automation their development goals, and ports and docks are no exception. Using advanced technology to build an automated wharf can realize not only intelligent operation but also low-carbon operation.

Current situation of port development in China

(1) **Large throughput:** From the beginning of the 21st century, China's economy has been growing at a rapid rate and the scale of import and export has been expanding as well. Ports along the route have seized this opportunity to achieve rapid development. According to the "Global Port Development Report" released by the Shanghai International Shipping Center, the Dalian Port, Qingdao Port, Yingkou Port, Quanzhou Port, Tianjin Port, Nanjing Port and Kaohsiung Port rank among the top 20 ports in the world. In the cumulative cargo throughput of the top 10 ports in the world, China's port throughput has accounted for more than 85%, and its position is becoming increasingly stable. In addition, according to the latest data released by the National Development and Reform Commission, from January to July 2018, the cargo throughput of ports above designated size in China reached 7,667.72 million tons, of which 2,427.61 million tons of foreign trade cargo throughput and 142,284,400 TEU of container throughput were completed, and these throughputs continued to grow.

(2) **The overall growth rate is fast, and the situation of "strong in the north and weak in the south" is obvious:** As of the first half of 2018, among the top 20 ports in terms of cargo throughput, 8 ports were located in the north of China, such as the Tangshan Port, Qingdao Port, Tianjin Port, Dalian Port, Rizhao Port, Yantai Port and Yingkou Port, and 6 ports were located in the south of China, such as the Shanghai Port, Suzhou Port and Guangzhou Port. From the perspective of regional ports, the ports around the Bohai Sea have the largest throughput and the fastest average growth rate. In other words, in terms of port throughput and its growth rate, China's ports are characterized by a "strong north and weak south."

Analysis of problems existing in port development in China

Since the reform and opening-up, China's ports have developed at a rare speed in the world and made remarkable achievements, so China has become a major port country in the world. However, if China wants to upgrade from a world port major power to a world port powerful nation, it still needs to overcome many difficulties, which are mainly manifested in the following aspects:

(1) **The port layout planning and management are unscientific, and the utilization rate of shoreline resources is low:** Some coastal areas in China carry out the strategy of "developing cities with ports" and regard the construction of large ports as the goal of urban development. Some cities also propose to build international shipping centers, which leads to dense ports, unreasonable port site selection, port scale and wharf layout in China. At the same time, because the port construction is greatly promoted in some areas, port expansion has taken up many shorelines, which leads to the low utilization rate of the shoreline and fails to form economic utilization.

(2) **There is continuous construction of port infrastructure, conflict in the economic hinterland, and fierce competition:** As a result of the vigorous promotion of port construction, the infrastructure of many ports is redundant and the utilization rate of port throughput capacity is not high. For example, the utilization rate of port throughput capacity is about 78%, while that of the Tianjin Port and Qingdao Port is even lower, which are 55% and 68%, respectively. Moreover, there is conflict in the economic hinterland of many ports, and the competition between them is very fierce, which is not conducive to the overall coordinated development.

(3) **The overall energy level of the port is low, the service function is not strong, and the economic benefit is not high:** There are many freight terminals in China's ports, with single functions and no developed logistics industry chain. The main profit sources are cargo loading and unloading, warehousing and transportation, and the development level is low. In addition, the port logistics industry and other industries (such as port industry, port and shipping service industry, as well as tourism) failed to achieve a high degree of integration, which led to the port failing to play a role in driving regional development and falling short of a modern international integrated port.

(4) **With the rapid development of the port industry, the deterioration of the port ecological environment is increasing:** At present, there are many petrochemical, iron and steel enterprises in the coastal areas in China that are prone to environmental pollution and are not conducive to the environmental protection of coastal waters. In addition, the machinery and equipment of many ports and docks are outdated, with low fuel utilization rate and large carbon emissions, which not only cause serious waste of resources but also induces very serious environmental pollution problems.

The existence of these problems is inconsistent with the sustainable development strategy, and the construction of automated wharf has changed the old operation mode of the port wharf, which not only improves the operation efficiency of the port wharf but also enhances the competitiveness of the port and narrows the gap between China's port wharf and comprehensive international ports.

Concept, technology and function of the automated wharf

Concept of the automated wharf

The automated wharf makes use of advanced technology to make the mechanical equipment of wharf run by itself without human intervention. The automated wharf consists of four parts, namely, automated yard operation machinery, automated horizontal transportation machinery, automated shore operation machinery and automated control system. Among other things, the automated control system is central to the entire automated wharf, with a high level of technology and reliable operating processes.

With the gradual expansion and application of cloud computing, wireless communication and intelligent manufacturing in wharves, automated wharves will be more intelligent, reliable and stable, operating costs will be greatly reduced and equipment utilization will be effectively improved compared to traditional wharves.

Function division of the automated wharf

The automated wharf mainly has three functional divisions.

(1) **Shore operation area:** The quayside container crane is arranged in front of the wharf to complete the loading and unloading of ships. The crane can carry the imported containers directly onto the chassis truck, which is then towed by the container tractor to the yard for parking, and then the container tractor drags the car out of the yard and comes out directly. For export containers, the container tractor parks the chassis loaded with containers in the yard. When the ship arrives, the container tractor tows the chassis to the dock, and the container crane hoists the container to the ship. The main feature of this system is that the container stays on the chassis from beginning to end.

(2) **Horizontal transportation area:** Through the horizontal transportation area, goods can be automatically transported between the shore operation area and the yard operation area. At present, container trucks or fully automatic unmanned automatic guided vehicles (AGVs) are mainly used in the wharf to transport containers horizontally, in which container trucks are controlled by drivers and AGVs are completely controlled by a central computer system. AGV technology was born in the 1980s. It has the functions of unmanned driving, precise positioning, automatic navigation, route optimization, safe obstacle avoidance, etc. It can replace trucks as the most important horizontal transportation tool in the horizontal transportation of docks.

(3) **Yard operation area:** At present, the most commonly used operation mode of container yards is RTG (rubber-tired gantry) crane or RMG (rail-mounted transtainer). The process loading and unloading system of container trucks is manually operated and the loading and unloading are carried out by manual labor. At present, the automatic unmanned empty container yard used in Shanghai Waigaoqiao Wharf uses a relay loading and unloading system with a combination of high- and low-level RMGs and buffer platforms.

The automatic yard operation area is mainly equipped with the following kinds of equipment:

- **CRMG:** The main function of this equipment is to take out the container from the container truck and put it on the middle platform of the buffer zone, or take out the container from the transit platform of the buffer zone and put it on the container truck. In short, it is responsible for loading and unloading the container.
- **DRMG:** The main function of this equipment is to take out containers from the buffer transfer platform and put them in the storage yard, or take out containers from the storage yard and put them in the buffer transfer platform. In short, it is responsible for loading and unloading trucks.
- **Buffer platform:** The buffer platform is located at both ends of the loading and unloading operation line, and its function is mainly to store containers temporarily so that the loading and unloading capacity of incoming and outgoing containers is balanced. At the same time, under the action of guide plate structure, containers can be quickly placed, effectively regulating the position of incoming and outgoing containers and effectively improving the extraction efficiency of RMG containers.

- **Container truck:** The function of this equipment is to transport containers horizontally at the wharf. Container trucks operating in the yard can be divided into two types: the outer container truck, that is, the container truck in the society, and the inner container truck, that is, the container truck inside the wharf.

Development status and trend of automated terminal abroad

Automatic quay crane runs in parallel with AGV and automatic track crane

This type of operation mode is typical of Rotterdam Port in the Netherlands. The ECT of Rotterdam Port uses a semi-automatic quayside crane, automatic yard track crane and AGV, in which the driving speed of the AGV is 3 m/s. Among them, the semi-autmatic quayside bridge is mainly responsible for ship loading and unloading, and the driver only needs to do a good job of box matching, and other work can be completed automatically. The AGV is mainly responsible for the horizontal transportation of containers between the wharf front and the storage yard. The AGV is equipped with ultrasonic detection devices and other auxiliary safety collision avoidance devices, which can sensitively sense obstacles in the process of deceleration to avoid collision in the process of movement. The operation of the AGV and automatic crane (ASC) is controlled by the production process control system (PCS) in the central control room of the wharf, which basically realizes complete automation. The yard tire crane can also operate automatically under unmanned control.

The CTA of Hamburg Port uses the semi-automatic quayside bridge with double boxes and double trolleys of ZPMC port machinery, the double-track crane with one high and one low stacking and taking box, and the double box traction AGV, in which the driving speed of the AGV is 5.8 m/s.

The terminal configuration of Euromax Port in Rotterdam is completely consistent with the previous one, but with a much higher speed of 20 m/s for the AGVs and a more advanced management software system. The wharf has the dual advantages of ECT automated wharf and HHLA wharf, with high operation level, high degree of informationization and more accurate positioning. In addition, the wharf adopts a double-box and double-trolley quay bridge, which is faster and more accurate than the first generation of double-trolley quay bridges in positioning. The rear trolley is pulled by wire rope, which solves the problem of trolley skidding under high-speed driving conditions. The improved double-box and double-trolley quay bridge is more suitable for use in the automatic wharf.

Parallel operation of automatic quay bridge, straddle carrier and automatic track crane

Typical examples of this mode are the APMT Wharf in Virginia and the HJS-TTI Wharf in Spain, in which the APMT Wharf is equipped with eight quayside bridges, which use chassis vehicles for horizontal transportation and ARMG technology for a storage yard. There are 15 box areas perpendicular to the wharf behind the wharf, and each box area is equipped with two ARMGs. Each ARMG has a lifting capacity of 40 TEU, a stack height of six floors and a length of 60 TEUs.

Development status and trend of the domestic automated wharf

In 2005, the Shanghai International Port Group and ZPMC cooperated to develop the first automated yard in China. Two RMGs are installed on a loading and unloading line of the container yard. These two RMGs have different heights, and relay operation is carried out through the ground transfer platform. The high RMG is responsible for loading and unloading containers in the container stacking area, and the low RMG is responsible for loading and unloading container trucks to ensure that the track crane on the unmanned track can accurately dock the container trucks. The whole loading and unloading process is automated, which effectively improves the operation efficiency of the container yard.

In October 2014, China's first automated container terminal entered into trial operation. The terminal puts terminal loading and unloading completely on the track and is driven by electric drive instead of a traditional internal combustion engine. In addition, the terminal can also realize the unmanned operation of the yard. The whole system is controlled by the computer in the central control room, which is a truly fully automated terminal system. The labor cost of the wharf has been greatly reduced and the level of safe operation has been greatly improved with the support of the system, which provides an effective solution to the problems of loud noise, environmental pollution and excessive emission.

At present, all countries in the world are facing a serious energy crisis and are demanding good environmental protection. For this reason, China has put forward a sustainable development strategy. Under this situation, China's automated wharf is bound to develop in the direction of unmanned operation, low carbon use, energy saving, high efficiency, safety and reliability, and environmental protection.

The above-mentioned horizontal transportation mode, which replaces the traditional internal combustion engine drive with an electric drive and puts the wharf loading and unloading completely on the track, has been applied in the Xiamen Ocean Gate Automated Wharf, which not only reduces noise but also realizes energy saving and emission reduction. It is estimated that the use of electric drive at Jane Gege Wharf will save at least 25% of energy and reduce carbon emissions by at least 16%.

After the offshore wharf enters the trial operation stage, a single bridge can transport 37–38 natural containers per hour. The work efficiency has been greatly improved in comparison with manual operation, and the annual throughput of the wharf can reach 780,000–910,000 TEUs, which has also achieved a substantial increase.

In terms of operating costs, the investigation shows that after the full automation of berth 14 of the Xiamen Ocean Gate Container Terminal, the annual operating costs have dropped to 25.64 million yuan, while the annual operating costs of conventional terminals are about 40.39 million yuan, a decrease of 37%. In terms of labor cost, the fully automated wharf only needs to pay 18.72 million yuan per year and the conventional wharf needs to pay 30.72 million yuan per year.

The operation of the Xiamen Ocean Gate Wharf has had great influence on the local port, with labor costs at the wharf being significantly reduced, the whole operation being safer and the level of operation being significantly improved. In addition, the Xiamen Ocean Gate Wharf covers a small area, with faster loading and unloading speed of ships and higher operation efficiency of the wharf. At the same time, harmonious development has been achieved in port areas, people and natural environment under the coordination of the automated wharf. A more harmonious ecological environment has been constructed, which makes the economic benefit acquisition and environmental impact reach a balance, responds well to the concept of sustainable development, greatly improves the resource utilization rate of port economic activities, minimizes the adverse impact of the port area on the environment and obtains social, economic and environmental benefits at the same time.

System reform of automated container terminal yard

Limitations of traditional container terminal yard system

The construction of automated container terminals has become an important part of the transformation and upgrading of coastal ports in China. By learning from experience and introducing equipment and technology from developed countries in Europe and America, the construction of automated container terminals in China's ports has achieved good practical results in the overall planning, equipment research and development, but there is still much room for improvement in terms of business management and process. Among them, the shortcomings exposed in the design of automated container terminal yard systems need to be focused on.

Limitations of traditional container terminal yard system

With the advantages of low cost, simple and flexible equipment operation of equipment, easy damage to containers and high efficiency of site utilization, the traditional container terminal yard system of "tire crane + stacker (forklift)" has been widely used in China's coastal ports for quite a long time. After years of development and improvement, the traditional container terminal yard system has formed a set of relatively mature management processes and rules. At the same time, the application of mathematical models and simulation technology in the port operation field makes the advantages of the system further developed. However, with the popularization of automated container terminals in developed countries, China has gradually realized that there are many shortcomings in the traditional container terminal yard system.

(1) **System inputs and outputs are unpredictable:** Traditional container terminal yard system is difficult to effectively evaluate the entry of export containers, so it is necessary to make container entry and exit plans manually, which requires higher experience and will increase labor costs. At the same time, the manual formulation of the traditional container terminal yard plan is restricted by the subsequent ship stowage and lacks flexibility. For example, before the formulation of the yard plan, the staff cannot predict the number of start-up operations, the number of shells of export containers on the ship and other information. Similar problems exist in imported containers. Although

information such as import ship map can be obtained first, key information such as transit second-way ship and customer container lifting cannot be obtained without an import container unloading yard plan.

(2) **Constraints and conflicts coexist:** Traditional container terminal yard planning is easy to cause "balance trap." When the export container yard is highly dispersed, it is necessary to use a variety of machines for related operations, which brings about a serious waste of mechanical resources; while when the export container yard is highly concentrated, it tends to cause confusion in the operation road and reduce operational efficiency.

To a great extent, this problem is caused by the fact that the traditional container terminal yard system cannot accurately predict the subsequent ship open circuit and stowage, and it is difficult to effectively allocate the export container area according to the actual number of ships open circuits, so the yard plan can only be made according to historical data and working experience.

In the traditional container terminal yard system, containers of the same port or the same ton class are piled up centrally in the same container area, but there are some differences in the order of instructions of different containers, which is easy to produce a large number of repeated operations. At the same time, the same container area contains two or more operation roads, which will bring many negative effects on yard planning.

The traditional process mode of tire crane receiving and dispatching boxes in container terminal yard requires that the operation of receiving and dispatching boxes in the same box position should be concentrated, and after one box position is completed, the tire crane should go to the nearby box position for operation. At present, although the development of communication technology can enable truck drivers to obtain information on the location of picking up and receiving boxes with the support of wireless terminals, the length of the truck is much greater than the length of box positions, and trucks with different box positions or different operation routes will interfere with each other when they work in the same box area at the same time, thus increasing the operation cost and reducing the operation efficiency.

(3) **The contradiction between benefit and efficiency is prominent:** The traditional operation mode of the container terminal yard system needs a tire crane to drive back and forth to send and receive

containers, with high turnaround rates and long waiting times. At the same time, imported containers cannot be stacked in separate tickets or based on two-way ships. When the import container has a large number of tickets, and the container with the same ticket cannot be unloaded at the same time, it is necessary to stack the container in several different boxes by driving back and forth with a tire crane, which will significantly reduce the operation efficiency of the import container.

In addition, before making the plan of the import container yard, it is impossible to accurately predict the customer's ship lifting and second-way ship loading. In this case, it is necessary to use a tire crane to drive back and forth to complete the container delivery, which brings many troubles to the operation.

(4) **The yard planning rules are complex:** Traditional container terminal yard planning is limited by many factors, such as position-by-position, arrangement-by-arrangement, heavy (light) pressure-by-pressure, ship-by-ship, port-by-port as well as tonnage-by-tonnage. However, yard planners mainly design schemes subjectively according to their own experience, which may lead to various problems in practice.

Characteristics of automatic container terminal yard system

An automated rail-mounted gantry (ARMG) crane is widely used in automated container terminals both at home and abroad. Its operation principle is using an automated guided vehicle (AGV) to connect ARMG on the seaside with a quay bridge to form a seaside propagation loading and unloading system of the wharf; the ARMG on the land side is connected with the outer container truck to form the roadside operation system of the wharf. Finally, an ARMG operation area composed of seaside and road tests is formed. Specifically, the characteristics of the automated container terminal yard system mainly include the following three points.

(1) **The collection box point is fixed:** The container collection point in the traditional container terminal yard is not fixed but should be adjusted to operate the box positions according to the tire crane. It is

necessary for the container truck to go to the box position in the instruction to collect containers. In contrast, a fully enclosed automatic container terminal yard takes the two ends of the box area as fixed container collection points.

(2) **The dual-machine configuration forms a "buffer-relay" operation mode:** Taking the unloading operation of imported containers as an example, the "buffer-relay" operation mode is as follows. After the seaside ARMG collects the imported containers from AGV, the land-side ARMG will be responsible for relay transportation, transport them to the land-side storage area and send them to the external container.

(3) **Fully enclosed double-machine operation:** The fully enclosed yard of automated container terminal can effectively solve the operation contradiction of horizontal transportation machinery in the same container area, between container areas and between containers; moreover, the design of double-machine buffer operation provides an effective scheme for solving the operation of receiving and dispatching containers.

System reform of automated container terminal yard

The junction point of tire crane and container truck in the traditional container terminal yard is dynamically changing, and the previous instruction position of collecting container is the starting position of the next instruction. However, the box collection points fixed at both ends of the box area can keep different loading and unloading instructions independently and will not be disturbed by the previous instruction, and can accurately evaluate the time and capital cost required to complete each instruction.

In the traditional container terminal yard system, similar containers are stacked in the same container area as much as possible so as to reduce the driving distance of the tire crane, control the cost and improve efficiency. The automatic container terminal yard system, however, does not need to worry about the mutual influence of different operation instructions and usually only needs to stack containers of the same kind (containers on the same ship, voyage and tonnage) and in the same row in order to avoid ARMG turning over containers, without being bound by other rules.

Adhering to the principle of tonnage is a key point of traditional container terminal yard planning but is no longer applicable in automated container terminal yards. The principle of tonnage-by-tonnage is to classify export containers according to their quality in order to improve the stability and safety of ships during stacking. For example, containers of 1 to 10 tons or less are Grade 1, containers of 10 to 20 tons are Grade 2, etc. Of course, different ports have different methods of classification, with some ports having Grade 1 representing containers of 1 to 5 tons.

However, there are obvious flaws in the tonnage-based principle. For example, 9-ton and 11-ton containers belong to different grades, but the stowage requirements of many large ships are relatively low. Containers with a difference of fewer than 2 tons do not need to be stowed separately, while the tonnage principle requires separate stowage of such tonnage-edge containers, resulting in higher costs.

The fixed container collection point in the automatic container terminal yard significantly reduces the connection between different containers. It is usually only necessary to consider the relationship between containers in the same row when loading and unloading containers instead of observing the principle of light pressure of containers in the same row. The plan of the automated container terminal yard is based on the classification of ports. By introducing the index of poor quality in the same row, the scientific rationality of the plan is effectively improved.

Thanks to the "buffer-relay" mode based on the dual-machine configuration in the automated container terminal yard, the fluency of the yard system is improved, the waiting time of yard operation is reduced and the work efficiency is improved. More importantly, the dual-machine configuration makes it more convenient and quicker to arrange the box area. For example, workers can use idle ARMG to carry out operations such as turning over boxes and sorting boxes.

The dual-machine configuration makes it unnecessary to classify yard operations according to the classification methods of import containers, transit containers and export containers. The business process has been significantly optimized, the operation instructions are in an independent state, and the completion time and cost of a single operation instruction have been accurately evaluated, thus evaluating the completion time and cost of the whole operation. At the same time, it can provide data support for automatic stowage and operation quality evaluation of automated container terminal yards.

Different from the traditional truck collection process project, thanks to the fact that the AGV operation gets rid of the dependence on the operation at both ends of the quay bridge and the field bridge, the influence of the AGV transportation process on the system can be effectively controlled, and the information such as box number, box location, estimated cost, estimated time and operation route instruction order will be automatically generated by the system, which brings a lot of convenience for judging the conflict points of operation plan, preventing in advance, adjusting during the process and optimizing afterward.

The efficiency of the yard bridge is lower than or equal to that of a bridge crane, which is the basic principle that should be adhered to in the formulation of a yard plan. In such a situation, the ARMG can cooperate with a bridge crane at the front of the wharf to carry out container receiving and dispatching operations, while the operation instructions of each container area remain independent, and export containers will be stacked randomly according to ships and ports. The automated container terminal yard plan only needs to randomly disperse containers in the corresponding yards of port ship berths according to the same row and similar containers, and most of the transit containers are concentrated in the two-way ship container area, which is one of the core advantages of the automated container terminal yard plan.

As a matter of fact, the reason why the traditional container terminal yard adopts the centralized stacking mode is to reduce the driving distance of tire crane, while in the automated container terminal yard, the instructions are independent of each other and the scattered stacking of containers brings many conveniences to the delivery of containers.

Of course, the automated container terminal yard system also puts forward higher requirements for related software and hardware configurations. For example, export containers located in the same row should use the same type. According to the principle of random dispersion, similar export containers in the same row should be grouped (a row of one type of export container as a group) and evenly distributed in each container area.

In order to avoid job conflicts in the process of stowage and solve the pain point that the input and input of the yard system are difficult to predict accurately, it is necessary to use not only the buffer and relay provided by the dual-machine configuration but also the job list information provided by the system.

Comparison of typical automated container terminals in the world

Introduction of typical automated container terminals in the world

London Gateway Wharf of the United Kingdom

The developer of the London Gateway Wharf is DP World, located in the London Port, moving about 50 km, with a planned shoreline of 2.7 km and a water depth of 17 m at the front end of the wharf, equipped with six berths. The annual container throughput can reach 3.6 million TEU. The operation process of "double 40-foot quayside bridge + straddle carrier + automatic track crane" is adopted, and the shore ship operation is carried out by a double 40-foot quayside bridge with a lifting capacity of 80 tons, lifting height of 49 m and outward extension distance of 70 m.

The construction of the wharf consists of five phases, in which the first phase of the project includes three berths with a coastline of 1.2 km long, equipped with 12 quayside bridges, 28 straddle trucks and 40 automatic track cranes. At the same time, 40 yards and two refrigerated container areas (564 refrigerated container spaces in total) will be established in the first phase. The basic situation of container business in the first phase of the project is as follows. Empty containers account for 50% and heavy containers account for 50%; 20-foot containers account for 25%, and 40-foot containers account for 75%. Transit containers account for 10%, railway containers account for 35%, and land containers account for 55%.

Euromax Wharf, Rotterdam Port, Netherlands

The Euromax Wharf is one of the three major terminals owned by the European Container Terminal Company. It belongs to the Hutchison Whampoa Port Group and was put into production in 2010. It is located about 30 km west of the Rotterdam Port. The wharf coastline is 1.5 km long and the total area is about 84 square meters. In 2015, the container throughput of the wharf reached about 2.28 million TEU, with 16 quayside bridges including 4 barge quayside bridges, 58 automatic track cranes and 96 automatic guided vehicles. In May 2016, COSCO Pacific acquired a 35% stake in the wharf.

The operation process mode of Euromax Wharf is "double-trolley quay bridge + automatic guided vehicle + automatic track crane." The double-track quay bridge has a lifting capacity of 61 tons, a lifting height of 43 meters and an outreach of 70 meters and is responsible for shoreside vessel operations. There are four automatic guided vehicle operation lanes under the rear outward arm. Automatic guided vehicles are responsible for horizontal transportation on the seaside and can transport two 20-foot containers or one 40-foot container on a single vehicle. All yards are perpendicular to the shoreline and are equipped with two automatic track cranes (lifting about 49 tons), which realize the whole automatic operation. At present, a double-box operation is not supported and the truck reversing process is introduced outside the yard.

In terms of container business, Euromax Wharf transit containers account for a large proportion (accounting for 65% of the total container volume), and 15–25% of transit containers are transported to inland river terminals by barges. Statistics show that the average operation efficiency of the Euromax quay bridge is 30 natural boxes per hour and can reach a maximum of 33 natural containers per hour; the average ship hour efficiency is 150–170 natural tanks per hour, and the maximum is 221 natural tanks per hour.

Barcelona port, Spain, Barcelona Southern Europe Wharf

Like the Euromax Wharf, the Barcelona Southern Europe Wharf belongs to the Hutchison Whampoa Port Group, which is separated from the Catalonia Wharf of the latter. The wharf covers a total area of 1.32 million square meters and the planned coastline is 2.1 kilometers. The water depth at the front of the wharf is 16–18 m and the designed annual container throughput is 4.45 million TEU. The project includes two stages phases.

The first phase of the wharf project has a shoreline length of 1.5 km, five berths with an area of 100 square meters, a design annual container throughput of 3.15 million TEU, and a quay front water depth of 16.5 meters and is equipped with 18 quay bridges, 80 yard bridges and 42 straddle trucks. The second phase of the wharf has a 0.6 km long shoreline, two berths with an area of 32 square meters, a design annual container throughput of 1.3 million TEU, and a water depth of 8 m at the quay front and is equipped with 6 quay bridges, 32 yard bridges and 15 straddle trucks.

The operation process mode of the Barcelona South Europe Wharf is "single 40-foot quayside bridge + straddle carrier + automatic track crane," in which the 40-foot quayside bridge has a lifting capacity of 61 tons, a lifting height of 41 m and an extension distance of 66 m and is responsible for the operation of shore ships, and the intersection area between quayside bridge tracks is the operation of straddle carrier and quayside bridge. The distance between the roadside track and the edge of the container yard is 93 meters, with a hatch cover stacking area behind and two straddle high-speed lanes.

The straddle truck can lift up to 50 tons and adopts the operation mode of "stacking one over two." Each yard is equipped with two automatic track cranes with a lifting capacity of 40 tons, which adopts the fully automatic operation mode and does not support double-box operation yet. The effective length of the yard is about 325 m, which is more suitable for stacking containers in a straight line and single layer. Nine rows of containers will be stacked within the span of the automatic track crane, and the stacking height is "stacking five over one." The roadside yard will adopt the process mode of a truck reversing with a distance between it and the automatic track crane block is required to be greater than or equal to the length of two trucks.

In terms of container business, the transit containers at the Barcelona Southern Europe Wharf account for about 70% of the total containers. At present, the average operation efficiency of the quay bridge of the wharf is 34 natural containers per hour.

Busan New Container Terminal, South Korea

The Busan New Container Terminal is the first automated container terminal in Asia with a yard perpendicular to the shoreline. It is located in the Xingang Port Area of Busan Port, South Korea, and adopts the industrial operation mode of "single trolley quay bridge + straddle carrier + automatic track crane." Shanghai ZPMC is the manufacturer of quayside cranes and automatic track cranes of the wharf. The quayside crane can lift up to 66 tons, with an outward extension distance of 70 m, a rear depth distance of 25 m, a lifting height of 45 m and a door leg spacing of 18.3 m; the automatic rail crane can lift 40 tons, the rail spacing is 31 m, and it can stack 10 rows of containers. The stacking capacity is "stacking five over six," and the cart travels 210 m per minute, so it does not support double-box operation for the time being.

The Terex Group of the United States is the manufacturer of the straddle truck at the wharf, which adopts the stacking mode of "stacking one over two" and costs US$700,000. The United States Navy developed the operating system for the terminal, while ABB of Switzerland developed the equipment control system for it, which endowed the terminal with strong flexibility and higher production efficiency. Statistics show that the average operation efficiency of Quay Crane of the Busan New Container Terminal is between 32 natural containers and 38 natural containers per hour.

Virginia Container Terminal, USA

The Maersk Group developed and operated the Virginia Container Terminal, which was completed and put into operation in 2007. The terminal also adopted the design mode of yard perpendicular to the shoreline, and the operation process mode is "single trolley quay bridge + straddle carrier + automatic track crane." The ZPMC Group manufactured quayside bridges and yard bridges for it, of which the quay bridge has a lifting capacity of 66 tons, an extension distance of 70 meters, a back depth distance of 25 meters, a lifting height of 45 meters and a door leg distance of 18.3 meters; the automatic track crane can lift up to 40 t with a gauge of 31 m, which is suitable for the operation of "stacking five over six." Eight rows of containers can be stacked in the span and the driving speed is 300 meters per minute, so it does not support double-box operation for the time being.

Kalmar Company makes straddle trucks for Virginia container terminals, and the manufacturing cost of each straddle truck is about US$500,000. Statistics show that the average operating efficiency of quayside cranes in the Virginia Container Terminal is 32–36 natural containers per hour. In the terminal container business, transit containers only account for a small proportion; export containers account for about 52% of the total container business at the terminal, and the rest is imported containers.

In terms of operation process mode, the Virginia Container Terminal is quite similar to the Busan New Container Terminal. However, there is also a certain gap between them. The Virginia Container Terminal centrally arranges the refrigerated container area behind the automated yard, which can accommodate 7 rows of containers and is equipped with 424 refrigerated containers, which can be expanded to 960 refrigerated containers at the highest. The horizontal transportation of refrigerated containers is carried out by chassis truck technology.

There are 75 truck parking spaces on the land side of the Virginia Container Terminal, and the truck loading and unloading operation has been remotely controlled. Operators can interact with drivers in real time on the three display pages of keyhole and surveillance video through the terminal operating system, which can effectively improve the safety and standardization of loading and unloading operations.

After getting off the bus, the driver can confirm the relevant information in the parking booth, and the system can confirm whether he has reached the safe area through the pressure sensor installed on the carpet in the booth. The driver can further confirm the relevant operation information by swiping the card. After the confirmation is passed, the automatic track crane will begin to execute its work instructions. Although the land side of the Virginia Container Terminal is already fully automated, a combination of manual and machine operation is still used for safety purposes in a semi-automated mode.

TCB Terminal, Nagoya Port, Japan

Japan is a country with frequent earthquakes. Seismic performance must be considered in the process of container terminal design and equipment manufacturing in order to cope with earthquake disasters. The TCB Terminal is the first fully automated container terminal in Japan, and its automation level is at the forefront of the world.

The yard of the TCB Terminal is designed parallel to the shoreline, and its operation process mode is "single trolley quay bridge + automatic guided vehicle + automatic tire crane." Mitsubishi Corporation of Japan manufactured quayside cranes and automatic tire cranes for the wharf, while Toyota Corporation of Japan manufactured automatic guided vehicles for the wharf. At present, in terms of wharf operation efficiency, the average operation efficiency of TCB wharf quay bridge is 33 natural containers per hour, and the average waiting time for each container truck to lift and unload containers at the wharf is less than 10 minutes.

Comparison of typical automated container terminals in the world

As of December 2017, more than 40 automated container terminals had been built or were under construction around the world, mainly in Asia,

Europe and North America. Dependence and individualized demand of wharves to natural environment determine that there are obvious differences in software and hardware equipment and loading and unloading technology of automated container terminals in different regions. The following is an in-depth analysis of the six representative automated container terminals in the world, and a summary of the construction experience of automated container terminals, so as to provide valuable reference experience for the construction of automated container terminals in China.

There are obvious differences in terminal design and operation technology among the several automated container terminals mentioned in the previous chapters, especially the TCB Terminal in the Nagoya Port, Japan, which is the first automated container terminal in the world with automated tire cranes in its yard operation equipment. The reason why TCB Terminal did not choose the automatic track crane process scheme is that the automatic tire crane process scheme has comparative advantages in earthquake resistance and investment cost reduction. At the same time, TCB Terminal is also the first automated container terminal in the world with horizontally arranged yards. In order to reduce the walking distance of automatic tire cranes in the container area, it is necessary to make full use of automatic guided vehicles to carry out yard operations, while other automated container terminals adopt longitudinal yard design with automatic track cranes as the yard operating equipment.

Straddle carriers and automatic guided vehicles are the mainstream horizontal transportation equipment on the shore of an automatic container terminal. In order to give full play to the advantages of coupling operation between automatic guided vehicles and quayside cranes, most automated container terminals are designed with highly efficient double-trolley quayside cranes. In many cases, matching operations between straddle trucks and single-trolley quayside cranes can already achieve the expected operational efficiency of the terminal.

The automatic guided vehicle system at the South European Terminal is world-leading in its ability to accurately control the automatic guided vehicles and design a scientifically sound driving path for them, fully guaranteeing the operational efficiency of the terminal. A notable feature of the Barcelona Southern Europe Wharf is that it uses manual straddle trucks, whose operation efficiency reaches 34 natural boxes per hour, significantly higher than that of automatic guided vehicles.

As the three representative automated container terminals in Europe, the London Gateway Terminal in England, the Euromax Terminal in

Rotterdam Port in the Netherlands and the Barcelona Port in Spain have certain commonalities. The terminals are surrounded by well-developed logistics parks and convenient and fast transportation methods such as railways, which bring a lot of convenience to the collection and distribution of containers. Of course, in order to further improve the efficiency of yard operation, different docks have formulated different strategies. For example, the London Gateway Terminal has customized and designed an advanced container pallet, which can lift and circulate the container truck, place the container in the pallet by crane, and then use the container truck to transport, which can make full use of the decoupling control between the container truck and the crane and reduce the cost of waiting time for the container truck; the Euromax Terminal has introduced a locomotive lane change device, which allows locomotives to change lanes between tracks efficiently and flexibly.

Enlightenment from the development of typical automated terminals in the world

(1) Manual straddle carriers do not emphasize stacking heights, have a relatively low working height, facilitate steering, have significantly higher vehicle travel speeds than automatic guided vehicles and are relatively low cost. If the wharf can control the labor cost in a certain range, the use of manual straddle truck technology is also a good option.

(2) In order to improve the efficiency of loading and unloading ships, the automatic container terminals are often not reserved for container ports at night so that the yard has enough time to carry out container sorting operations. However, the improvement of loading and unloading efficiency is often based on sacrificing the best location of containers. For example, if containers are placed randomly, the efficiency of subsequent operations can easily be compromised in the absence of container management. Therefore, the continuous optimization of the loading and unloading process, with an emphasis on efficiency and taking into account container management operations, is an important issue that needs to be addressed by automated container terminals in the future.

With the support of the control platform, decoupling control of equipment handover and reducing the waiting time of equipment is an important principle to be adhered to in the design of an automatic wharf. For example, the container pallet rack of customized toner at the London Gateway Wharf can reduce the waiting time for trucks and cranes; the roadside track of the quayside bridge of the Busan New Container Terminal is equipped with a draggable ground-unlocking bracket, which can effectively control the waiting time for unlocking the quay bridge by decoupling control from the crane. In addition, the automatic container terminal can also realize decoupling control between the automatic guided vehicle and the automatic track crane by setting a bracket in the shore junction area of the yard, thus reducing the waiting time for both operations.

(3) The energy consumption of automatic rail cranes is an important issue in the industry. To solve this problem, the TCB Wharf takes automatic guided vehicles as yard equipment to effectively control the driving distance of automatic tire cranes, which can not only ensure production efficiency but also significantly reduce energy consumption.

(4) As infrastructure of an automated container terminal, most automated container terminals are equipped with two to three intelligent gates, and the automation degree of gates is not fixed, so semi-automatic gates or fully automated gates can be adopted. Among the above-mentioned automated container terminals, only the Busan New Container Terminal has applied semi-automatic gates, and all other terminals have adopted fully automated gates.

(5) At present, the above-mentioned terminal yard equipment and systems cannot carry out a double 20-foot container operation. In the future, those terminals whose 20-foot container volume accounts for a relatively high proportion of the total business volume should try to solve this problem by optimizing the operation process scheme.

(6) The terminal operating system and equipment control system play a key role in the operation of an automated container terminal. The terminal operating system plays the role of the command center and can generate various instructions to guide the operation of equipment; the terminal equipment control system plays the role of executor, at the same time, it can also give real-time feedback to the equipment status and provide the necessary support for the scientific decision-making of the terminal operating system.

(7) When selecting suppliers, automated container terminals should cooperate with relatively mature suppliers as much as possible. For example, quayside cranes and automated track cranes produced by

ZPMC are at the leading level in the world, while Konecranes, Karma and Trex are better at designing and manufacturing mobile machinery such as straddle carriers.

With many advantages such as reducing labor costs, reducing energy consumption, improving port efficiency and brand awareness, the construction value of automated container terminals has been highly recognized by countries all over the world. The pace of development has been particularly rapid in Asia, Europe and North America. Specifically in the domestic sector, port cities such as Qingdao, Shanghai and Xiamen have invested significant resources in automated container terminals. On December 10, 2017, the Shanghai Yangshan Deepwater Port Phase IV Automated Terminal opened for trial production, establishing China as the builder of the largest intelligent container terminal in the world. Although the construction of automated container terminals in China is still in the primary stage, with the participation of government, enterprises and capital, the transformation process of traditional container terminals will be further accelerated, which will bring great thrust to the comprehensive popularization of automated container terminals in China.

Postscript: Policy suggestions on promoting the development of the intelligent transportation industry in China

As a typical representative of high-tech integrated industry, the intelligent transportation industry has an extremely complex technical system and management objects. The Chinese government has issued a series of relevant policies to promote the stable development of the high-tech industry. However, it is obviously different from ordinary high-tech industries when considering the characteristics of the intelligent transportation industry, so it is necessary to issue more targeted industrial policies for it.

Differences between the intelligent transportation industry and other high-tech industries

(1) **It involves a wide range and has a strong driving force:** The intelligent transportation industry is a highly comprehensive crosscutting industry involving a wide range, which can bring strong thrust to the development of many related industries. First, the development of the

electromechanical industry will benefit greatly. Massive hardware equipment, such as traffic information collection, information communication and information release, are required for the realization of intelligent transportation, which will drive the electromechanical industry to enter the fast lane of rapid development; second, for the purpose of promoting further development of communication technology and information industry, the important foundations for the sustainable and stable operation of the intelligent transportation system are information generation, collection, processing and transmission, which inevitably requires strong support from communication technologies such as the Internet, Internet of Things and satellite communication and information industry.

In the end, the computer, microelectronics and software industries will be promoted to develop further. A perfect data and information-processing center is a key component of the intelligent transportation system, and the construction and maintenance of data- and information-processing centers requires the iteration of research and development and updating of relevant technologies and products in the computer, microelectronics and software industries. In other words, promoting the development of the intelligent transportation industry will not only improve the level of transportation development but also drive the development of a series of related industries, thus creating huge economic and social benefits.

(2) **Continuity in the long term and scale of capital demand:** Infrastructure investment and service investment are the two mainstream directions of intelligent transportation industry investment. As China's intelligent transportation industry is still in the primary stage of development, the investment will be mainly in infrastructure investment, which includes the electronic toll collection system, traffic management system, public transportation information platform system, emergency management system and other sub-sectors.

From the practical cases of pioneers in intelligent transportation construction such as the United States and Japan, the demand for investment funds in intelligent transportation infrastructure construction is characterized by continuity, long-term and scale. For example, from 1991 to 2010, the US government invested US$40 billion for promoting the construction of the intelligent transportation industry; from 1996 to 2015, the Japanese government invested 780 trillion yen in the development of intelligent transportation systems.

Different from ordinary transportation building facilities, intelligent transportation building facilities have a long construction period, which needs to be constantly updated and iterated according to technological innovation. It is normal to build while using, and a lot of manpower and material resources must be invested over a long period of time.

(3) **The integration of technology and the complexity of intellectual property:** Intelligent transportation products integrate various technologies and functional modules. However, different technologies and functional modules belong to different intellectual property subjects. Taking GPS navigation products as an example, this product should apply global systems for mobile communications technology (GSM), geographic information system (GIS), global position system technology (GPS), computer network communication, data processing technology, etc. The intellectual property subjects of these technologies are located in many countries, so a single manufacturer cannot provide services independently and multiple manufacturers need to participate together.

(4) **Uniqueness of operation mode:** The transaction between intelligent transportation product manufacturers and customers is not a one-time transaction. After the first transaction is completed, customers need a series of value-added services from manufacturers, such as information services, software upgrades, as well as system updates, etc. Manufacturers will continue to develop new value-added services, which leads to the uniqueness of the operation mode of the intelligent transportation industry. In the case of dynamic information service, the information service provided by intelligent transportation dynamic information service providers in the United States is free of charge, and the sale of advertising space is profitable.

Policy defects in the development of intelligent transportation industrialization

Promoting the development of the intelligent transportation industry has been highly valued by governments at all levels, but there are still obvious policy defects in its management practice.

(1) **The role of government is not clear:** Based on the practical cases of intelligent transportation in the United States, Japan, Germany and

other transportation powers, we can see that it is particularly critical for the government to clarify its role in the intelligent transportation industry. Generally speaking, the government should undertake four responsibilities: making development plans, solving funding problems, perfecting relevant systems and providing policy support.

- In terms of formulating development plans, the US Department of Transportation issued the "National ITS Project Plan" in March 1995, which clarified the 7 major areas covered by ITS and 29 user service functions; in 1995, Japan's Ministry of Construction and other 5 provincial offices jointly issued the "Implementation Policy of Informationization in the Fields of Roads, Transportation and Vehicles," which identified 9 major development areas and 11 promotion measures. In July of the following year, the five provincial offices jointly issued the "Overall Concept on Promoting ITS," which clarified the target functions and development and promotion ideas of ITS, laying a solid foundation for ITS construction in the next 20 years; in 1985, the European Union established the European Road Transport Information Technology Implementation Organization (TRICO), which was especially responsible for ITS construction, and launched the "Research and Development Plan for Intelligent Roads and Vehicle Equipment."

    In solving the funding problem, the US government issued a bill requiring governments at all levels to include the investment in the intelligent transportation industry in the basic investment plan, and the federal, state and local governments at all levels are the main force of investment; the Japanese government has adopted the mode of a government–enterprise alliance, and the government and enterprises jointly provide financial support for the development of intelligent transportation industry.

    In terms of improving relevant systems, the Japanese government has established a communication and coordination mechanism of real-time interaction and efficient coordination among government, non-governmental and academic institutions, which is an important foundation for Japan to build a perfect intelligent transportation management system.

    In terms of providing policy support, the United States and Japan have issued a number of laws and regulations. Taking the United States as an example, the United States Congress promulgated the "Land Comprehensive Transportation Efficiency Act" in

1991 and further improved the Act in 1997, promulgating the "Comprehensive Transportation Act." The new Act provides effective technical solutions to improve the efficiency of transportation networks.

China has adopted the idea that the Ministry of Communications, the Ministry of Science and Technology and other departments jointly promote the development of the intelligent transportation industry from top to bottom. However, a considerable number of local governments have not clarified their rights and responsibilities in the construction of intelligent transportation systems, and there is no competent construction unit and comprehensive coordination organization. Because some local governments fail to clarify their role in the development of the intelligent transportation industry, they cannot plan and guide the industrial development from a medium- to long-term strategic perspective, which brings many obstacles to the long-term stable development of the industry.

(2) **Investment and financing policies are not specific:** The development funds of high-tech enterprises in China are mainly self-raised. Although intelligent transportation belongs to the high-tech industry, its long-term and continuous capital needs determine that it is impossible to solve the problem only by self-raised funds of related enterprises. The way to solve the financial problem in the United States is government-led and enterprise participation, while in Japan, it is the combination of government and enterprises. At present, the main source of funds for the development of China's intelligent transportation industry is government investment, but there is no specific investment and financing policy to solve the funding problem in the future, which brings great uncertainty to the investment in the intelligent transportation industry.

In addition, some intelligent transportation construction projects are not all business-oriented in nature, and social welfare projects also occupy a large proportion. Investment strategies and schemes of different projects should be different, but the Chinese government has not classified related projects, resulting in a lack of pertinence of investment strategies and schemes.

(3) **Support for product research and development are insufficient:** The high-end market of intelligent domestic transportation is monopolized by overseas brands, and key core technologies need to be

imported from abroad. For example, in recent years, China's intelligent navigation industry has developed rapidly, and a large number of new intelligent navigation products have emerged, which have been widely used in smartphones, automobiles and other terminals. However, key core technologies and components are heavily dependent on imports, and similar problems exist in the field of intelligent traffic management. Although there are many factors leading to this unfavorable situation, the lack of government support for product research and development is undoubtedly an important factor.

(4) **There is a lack of corresponding policies to encourage and protect ITS construction and the establishment of market order:** Technology research and development and application are the top priority in the development of the intelligent transportation industry. However, there are many problems in China's intelligent transportation product market, such as inadequate protection of intellectual property rights, vicious competition resulting in the expulsion of good money from bad money, which has seriously hindered the research and development and application of related technologies. How to standardize the market order of the intelligent transportation industry is a key problem that needs to be addressed by the Chinese government in the future.

Policy choice of intelligent transportation industrialization development

(1) **Clarify the leading position of the government and make up for the lack of government management:** The government should be the leader in promoting the development of the intelligent transportation industry. National and local governments should set up a leading group responsible for coordinating and promoting intelligent transportation construction projects as a government-level project to improve the level of transportation development and help the national economy grow steadily, and accelerate the research and development of intelligent transportation industry development planning; incorporate intelligent transportation investment into the government's basic investment plan and give it necessary financial support; the government should guide enterprises to set up intelligent transportation industry alliances and associations, and introduce relevant policies to support its rapid development.

(2) **Improve the investment and financing system of the intelligent transportation industry:** Enriching and perfecting the investment and financing system of the intelligent transportation industry can provide financial support for related enterprises, especially start-ups. It has a key impact on accelerating the industrialization of intelligent transportation. Our government needs to speed up the establishment of an investment and financing system for the industrialization of intelligent transportation led by the government, with the participation of enterprises and a combination of direct integration and indirect financing.

First and foremost, it is necessary to clarify the nature of intelligent transportation construction projects and divide them into social welfare projects and business projects. For example, transportation management systems such as the traffic management system, bus management system and emergency management system are social welfare projects; the service information providing system and commercial vehicle management system are business-oriented projects.

Different projects have different investment schemes, and personalized investment strategic planning should be designed according to investment subjects, investment objects and investment returns. Government investment should be reserved for social welfare projects, while business projects can introduce social capital so that enterprises and investment institutions can fully participate in the construction of intelligent transportation.

Second, governments at all levels should optimize and improve the investment structure, tilt more resources to the field of intelligent transportation, focus on supporting public welfare projects and strategic projects with good demonstration results, and solve the financing difficulties of dynamic and innovative start-ups. At the same time, it is necessary to guide the flow of social capital, speed up the improvement of the investment and financing return mechanism of the intelligent transportation industry, improve the investment enthusiasm of capital institutions at home and abroad, encourage enterprises to research and innovate by means of subsidies and tax reductions, and improve the premium capacity of intelligent transportation products in China.

(3) **Establish a market order conducive to the development of the intelligent transportation industry:** What needs to be made clear is that the current intelligent transportation industry policy should not

only undertake the mission of guiding and supporting the long-term stable development of the intelligent transportation industry but also solve problems caused by imperfect market mechanisms. In the future, in order to establish a fair, just and orderly market order for the intelligent transportation industry, we must carry out the following work.

- Strengthen supervision, formulate a sound system of industry laws and regulations, and severely punish individuals and organizations that infringe intellectual property rights and engage in vicious competition.

- Establish a market access system for the intelligent transportation industry and raise the threshold of entry.

- Accelerate the improvement of intellectual property protection system and improve the transformation of scientific research achievements.

- Give full play to the role of industry organizations such as industry alliances and associations, strengthen industry self-discipline and, at the same time, provide convenient and quick communication channels for the public and enhancing public supervision.

Postscript

Artificial intelligence transportation has brought revolutionary changes to the development of transportation.

Historically, all previous industrial revolutions and transportation are closely linked. From the steam engine to internal combustion engine to electrification, it has not only brought about the innovation and progress of transportation but also promoted facilitated the transformation of transportation development mode and profoundly changed people's consumption concept, travel mode and even the connotation of social life. At present, a new round of scientific and technological revolution and industrial transformation is emerging in the world. The rapid development of cloud computing, big data, the Internet of Things, artificial intelligence, etc., has triggered mass technological changes and promoted a new qualitative leap in social productivity. The most important characteristic of transportation is the randomness of movement and the universality of geographical distribution. The new generation of information technology conforms to this characteristic. In particular, the vigorous development of mobile Internet, big data and cloud computing has promoted the profound integration of transportation and informationization. The formation of artificial intelligence transportation provides a systematic and integrated method for better travel, improves the efficiency of transportation, enhances the safety and reliability of transportation, makes transportation services more personalized and humanized, and the transportation mode, management mode and even social governance mode of transportation will undergo tremendous changes. The three revolutions of transportation in the future are the electrification and automation of automobiles and the sharing of travel modes.

The information of the Internet of Things and Internet of Vehicles bypasses human beings and becomes an information space outside independent physical space and social space. Transportation has entered the era of ternary space. Sharing, such as the emergence of new Internet formats, including online car and ride, has solved the first mile and the last mile of travel economically and effectively. In the next step, with the emergence of NTOCC, the three weaknesses in the freight industry can be changed, and the development of artificial intelligence can facilitate automatic driving and the application of intelligent vehicle-road systems, which will greatly improve the efficiency, quality and management efficiency of transportation services.

The central government attaches great importance to the information revolution, including artificial intelligence transportation. The report of the 19th National Congress of the Communist Party of China proposes to build a network power, a digital power, a transportation power and a digital society, etc. In his congratulatory letter to the first Digital China Construction Summit on April 22, 2018, General Secretary Xi Jinping pointed out that to accelerate the construction of digital China is to adapt to the new historical orientation of China's development, comprehensively implement the new development concept, cultivate new dynamic energy with information technology, promote new development with new dynamic energy and create new brilliance with new development. With the deep integration of information technology represented by the Internet and transportation field, transportation development has entered a new round of replacement stage, and intelligent transportation infrastructure, such as super railways, highways, automatic driving and unmanned aerial vehicles, has become a hot spot in various countries. New modes and new business models are emerging and taking on a strong vitality. Therefore, it is of great significance to upgrade our traditional transportation industry, promote the high-quality development of the whole industry, meet people's demand for better travel and accelerate the building of a strong transportation country.

Significant achievements have been made in the development of artificial intelligence transportation in China.

In recent years, China's artificial intelligence transportation has developed vigorously, the intelligent level of infrastructure and equipment has been improved significantly, new formats and products of transportation services have emerged constantly, the governance system and governance methods have been continuously optimized and the people's sense of gain has been continuously enhanced.

The intelligentization of infrastructure has continuously improved operational efficiency. Intelligent railway signal systems have been put into use widely. More than 40% of key sections, extra-large bridges and extra-long tunnels of trunk highway network have realized information dynamic monitoring, and the running status has basically achieved effective monitoring and full coverage. As much as 70% of key ministries and commissions in passenger stations and major ports have basically realized dynamic monitoring, and automated container terminals have been put into use in Qingdao Port, Xiamen Port and Shanghai Yangshan Port in China. There are more than 10,000 ETC lanes and more than 60 million cardholders.

The intelligent technical level of transportation equipment accelerates innovation, and technological innovation is promoted. The first batch of three closed test sites for autonomous driving has been recognized, the national intelligent networked vehicles and Shanghai pilot demonstration closed test areas have been built, and unmanned driving port areas, containers, trucks and logistics parks have been put into large-scale application. Unmanned aerial vehicle inspection and monitoring in highways have been applied in some areas, unmanned aerial vehicle logistics distribution is being piloted, distribution centers have basically realized automatic sorting, and automatic sorting robots have caused a sensation in international exhibitions. The Jingdong distribution robot has realized distribution operation in Haidian, Beijing, and the first fully automatic subway line in China was put into operation in Beijing at the end of 2017.

The innovative application of transportation services has achieved remarkable results. Artificial intelligence transportation projects and systems, such as network cars, bike sharing, 12,306 online railway ticketing, as well as logistics information platforms, are at the forefront of the world in terms of service scale and development level. In particular, we have contributed Chinese wisdom and Chinese solutions to the world governance issues such as network cars and bike sharing, which have enabled the public to obtain tangible benefits.

The governance application of industry collaboration is advancing rapidly. National networking systems, such as safe and smooth transportation and emergency wisdom, credit information service in the transportation and construction market, road transportation management, highway overload control, as well as statistical analysis, play an increasingly important role in industry management. The national connection was realized, and the networked joint control system of key operating vehicles in China was built, accounting for more than 95% of key operating vehicles. Significant achievements have been made in traffic construction. It has played an obvious role in strengthening post-event supervision and promoting market integrity governance.

An open and shared data resource system has been basically established. Through the cooperation between government and enterprises, a big data open cloud platform for comprehensive transportation has been established. At present, it has been connected to the transportation authorities of 25 provinces and cities across the country, including 43 enterprises such as Tencent, Baidu, AutoNavi, with 141 information service interfaces.

Compared with traditional expressway management, smart highway and information collection, processing, publishing and analysis are the main lines, and information technology, data communication and electronic integration technology are applied to build and manage expressways and strengthen the connection between vehicle roads and users, thereby forming a safe and efficient transportation system. Smart highways can realize many functions, such as collecting and transmitting traffic information, guiding traffic flow in time and space, and improve the environment of highway facilities. The highway can perceive safety status and issue early warning by itself, which can greatly reduce traffic accidents and ensure people's travel safety. Smart highways can also monitor everything on the road by using big data platforms and networks, realize IoT perception and provide support for future automatic driving. From the perspective of the transportation industry, the construction of smart roads and the landing of autonomous driving will apply key common technologies in a systematic and integrated manner. Frontier leading technology, modern engineering technology and disruptive technological innovation will not only lead to major changes in the intelligent transformation of road infrastructure and operation and maintenance management mode but also will change our current road travel mode and transportation organization mode subversively based on the traditional environment of people, vehicles and roads. From the perspective of the manufacturing industry, the construction of smart roads and the landing of autonomous driving will also become new kinetic energy for upgrading traffic engineering facilities and transportation equipment and become a new growth point for accelerating the development of the advanced manufacturing industry.

The Ministry of Transport is very concerned about the practical application of automatic driving through a collaborative approach to vehicle infrastructure. We attach great importance to the construction of smart roads. We believe that the construction of smart roads and the intelligent upgrading of highway infrastructure are necessary for the development of roads and an important symbol of moving towards a powerful transportation country. At present, a number of demonstration projects supporting autonomous driving have been carried out. In the construction of smart highways, especially in the future-oriented development of autonomous driving technology, we pay more attention to the synergy of vehicle infrastructure. The main reason is that the path of autonomous driving based on traditional car companies is to connect smart cars with smart cars, that is, to realize the path of autonomous driving intelligently by traditional car networking technology. However, in such a process, it is difficult to cope with the complex traffic environment because of the technology of automatic driving. However, China's traffic environment is particularly complex, and there are many mixed traffic and unruly phenomena. Therefore, if we want to rely on the complete intelligence of cars to realize our automatic driving, there would be a significant economic cost, so its prospect may not be so good in application. Therefore, we also attach great importance to the mode of vehicle infrastructure cooperative based on smart cars and smart roads, that is to say, through the standardization, normalization and digitalization of infrastructure, an effective vehicle infrastructure cooperative system can be established, and intelligent vehicles that can already meet the requirements can realize safe automatic driving by relying on smart road networks. Such a path may have more possibilities in the application prospect than a path that relies solely on smart cars. I believe there are three problems that need to be grasped well in the construction of smart highways.

First, we should focus on the two core characteristics of safety and high efficiency. Safety is the eternal theme and bottom-line requirement of highway construction. The construction of a smart expressway must vigorously promote efficiency on the premise of ensuring safety. Efficiency is not only manifested in terms of speed but also in terms of breakthroughs and reservations in design speed. For example, compared with similar expressways, if our smart expressway can increase our average running speed by more than 20%, its efficiency is very significant. Moreover, the emergency response efficiency of our operation department will also be improved so that our investment in smart highway construction will have practical significance. At the same time, it is important to show the equipment that has passed the road test and to equip the vehicle infrastructure to collaborate in the testing and application demonstration of autonomous driving so that it becomes a smart demonstration highway that supports the practical application of autonomous driving, which mainly requires the support of autonomous driving technology. Do not underestimate this point. The Chinese Premier met the US Secretary of Transportation in April 2018 and the Door to China's negotiations was open (http://www.gov.cn/guowuyuan/2018-04/27/content_5286443.htm). When talking with the leaders of the Ministry, he was very concerned about the development of autonomous driving technology, what China's overall design now is, and what the next step is. He was very concerned about this area because in the eyes of Americans, it is also a leading area, that is, a high-tech field, and the United States will face competition from China. For the Secretary of Transportation of the United States, the issue of autonomous driving is very professional. Of course, it is very cautious to talk to us about cooperation, but for us, as a future leader, it could be disruptive and we should attach great importance to breakthrough technologies and actively create better conditions for the development of high technology in the process of digital transformation of our infrastructure.

The second is to achieve systematic and integrated application of different innovative technologies. Pilot demonstrations of smart highway construction are being carried out all over the country, but they are basically piloted on one or two innovative technologies, which means fragmentation. We hope that the construction of smart highways can systematically and integratively apply common key technologies, leading cutting-edge technologies, modern engineering technologies and disruptive technologies. For example, we can combine the further development of the BeiDou system in China and make full use of the key common technologies of BeiDou, which is considered from the national security strategy. BeiDou is our own global positioning system. Of course, it may not be as good as a GPS in some functions as of now, but it is particularly important for our country's high-tech security. We promote the perfection of the BeiDou system and the improvement of technology through large-scale application in the civil industry. This is also a requirement of the national security strategy. For example, intelligent anti-collision signs can automatically alert passing vehicles when to issue a warning and pilot the application of disruptive technologies such as V2S-supporting devices. At the same time, it is necessary to form relevant standards and specifications through pilot demonstration, explore and form experiences that can be replicated and popularized, and finally form a standard system for smart highway construction in China.

Third, we should pay attention not only to technological innovation but also to mechanism innovation and give full play to the practical efficiency of safety, green, high efficiency and economy. We must attach great importance to the optimization and perfection of the management system, such as the management mechanism of the smart highway cloud platform and the control intelligence mechanism. It is necessary to carry out special research on the highway management system and economy in the construction stage to support the optimization and perfection of the highway operation management system. At present, we are focusing on the work of toll stations on the mainline of expressways, which may bring about great changes in the current toll system, which raises the bar not only for our technological innovation but also for the mode of management and operation. At present, the promotion of this work must be based on the wide coverage and full popularization mode of ETC system so as to achieve safe and reliable operation.

However, for the purpose of achieving full coverage of ETC and installing ETC on all vehicles, there may be a new breakthrough in the policies and regulations of ETC installation, for example, whether vehicles using expressways should compulsorily have ETC installed, which means that they should be improved at the national system level. At the same time, how to make people willing to install, that is, people should have a sense of gain, and it should not make them feel that it will increase trouble. This requires policy, for example, whether we can consider giving large-scale preferential tolls to vehicles installed with ETC so as to realize the requirement of reducing the toll mentioned by the General Secretary and the Prime Minister at the National Economic Work Conference and the two sessions. At the same time, it is necessary to greatly improve the ability of ETC installation and service operation, which can make users install quickly and conveniently and makes it very convenient to recharge. It cannot be that there aren't enough recharge points in some provinces right now. It also needs to be very convenient. Now the development of information technology can realize the direct recharge of the mobile phone network; this should be technically fruitful; however, in terms of management mechanism, it should break the current state of provincial division and unify management policies, systems, technical standards and supervision modes. Of course, this also involves a series of policy issues.

For example, in Shanghai and Beijing, the charges for trucks are based on models, while in many provinces, they are based on machine weight. To sum up, it is the only way to promote the high-quality development of transportation by informationization.

Key tasks of developing artificial intelligence transportation

Informationization is the most powerful new kinetic energy to promote the transformation and upgrading of transportation. To give full play to the leading role of artificial intelligence transportation in promoting high-quality development, insist on taking artificial intelligence transportation as the main direction of industry development; focus on infrastructure, production organization, transportation services and decision-making supervision in accordance with goal-oriented, module-driven, demonstration-led and market-driven principles; and promote the digitalization of transportation, networking of transmission and intelligent supervision. Promote the high-quality development of transportation and provide favorable support for the construction of a powerful transportation country.

First, we should promote the digitalization of all factors and the whole cycle of transportation infrastructure, promote the application of building information model and high-resolution earth observation technology in project planning, design, construction, operation and maintenance, and establish a three-dimensional traffic geographic information system to realize the digital presentation and dynamic tracking of infrastructure, equipment, signs and markings, operation dynamics and surrounding environments such as railways, highways, waterways, civil aviation and postal services. For major transport infrastructure projects, whole life cycle health testing can be achieved to control health in real time, detect and accurately dispose of hidden problems in time and extend the life cycle of the structure.

The second is to promote the intelligentization and automation of production organizations. Vigorously develop the new mode and format of logistics organization in Internet plus, build a service system covering all links of the logistics chain, and provide one-stop and one-order services for domestic and international logistics. Relying on various logistics information platforms, promote the integration and innovation of online and offline resources, realize the open sharing of logistics resources, value-added and win-win, establish a logistics service system integrating trunk and branch connection, urban–rural connection and warehouse distribution, promote the automation and intelligent development of tools and equipment, realize the transformation of the front end of intelligent terminal society from manual operation to intelligent control, realize advanced functions such as intelligent decision-making and collaborative control, and comprehensively improve the efficiency and management level of transportation operations.

The third is to promote the integration and convenience of transportation services, promote cross-border integration in the field of travel; encourage all kinds of platform-based enterprises to provide passengers with personalization of the whole process from departure to destination, door-to-door integrated travel solutions that make travel simpler and advocate the concept of sharing; obtain by demand; provide customized travel services that change randomly; greatly reduce the number of private transport vehicles; promote the seamless interconnection between travel and various production and life scenes such as office, shopping, entertainment and social interaction; and create an intelligent mobile space.

The fourth is to promote the precision and synergy of industry governance; deepen the safety and emergency wisdom of industry macro decision-making, supervision and law enforcement, and the operation level of big data in government services and other fields; realize the integration of comprehensive transportation operation states such as railways, highways, waterways, civil aviation, postal services and urban public transportation, comprehensive evaluation, forecast and early warning, and emergency linkage; enhance the ability of comprehensive transportation coordination and emergency linkage; improve the modernization level of industry governance and decision-making planning; promote the digitalization of transportation licenses and law enforcement cases; provide integrated online government services; promote the cross-regional and cross-departmental sharing of traffic credit and comprehensive law enforcement information; and achieve the effect that dishonesty in one place will lead to restrictions everywhere.

Promote the advanced development of artificial intelligence traffic

First, we should strengthen the top-level design and plan for medium- and long-term development. It is necessary to plan ahead strategically and to build consensus, and moreover, we should base ourselves on the national conditions, focus on supporting the construction of a powerful transportation country, study the transformation and upgrading of new technologies such as mobile Internet, big data and artificial intelligence on the transportation industry, analyze new travel modes, logistics organizations and governance models, and clarify the medium- and long-term development goals and realization paths of artificial intelligence transportation.

Second, adhere to key breakthroughs, pragmatically promote development, promote pilot projects such as a new generation of traffic control networks and smart highways, accelerate the integration and application of advanced information technology and transportation, and by taking high-precision application as the core and information as the support, deepen the industrial application of BeiDou system, carry out the pilot application of big data in transportation and tourism services, explore the application of cross-industry and cross-regional data fusion, and use big data to enhance the collaborative management and public service capabilities of the industry.

Third, we should strengthen cross-border coordination and form a working synergy. It is necessary to clarify the positioning of government and enterprises, encourage the innovation of technical services and business models with enterprises as the main body, focus on the innovation of strategic planning, policy standards and governance models, strengthen the linkage of transportation development departments, deepen the coordinated development mechanism of departments, coordinate the resources of various industries, and jointly promote the formation of leadership forces at the national level.

Fourth, we must be wary of disorganization, isolated islands and two-sidedness. From 2014 to 2017, the investment in the shared market increased from US$2 billion to US$21 billion. However, the boom was followed by a wave of bankruptcies. You can see that not only did our bike sharing transition from a small blue car to a small yellow car produce a large amount of urban garbage, but the refund of the deposit also caused social events, resulting in a huge waste of social resources. Therefore, the development of artificial intelligence transportation should guard against economic and social problems. On the other hand, it is difficult to share wisdom. We must break down this information barrier, eliminate information islands and promote the sharing and opening of information resources. In addition, we should make full use of the new business model of technological innovation, optimize the service process in the field of transportation services, standardize the management behavior and avoid the problem of two-sidedness in the management improvement of information technology and transportation business.

The great cause of developing artificial intelligence in transportation requires the collective contribution of wisdom and strength from all sectors of society. It has a broad stage, but it also has huge risks and challenges. We should work together, overcome difficulties and continue to create a new environment for the innovative development of artificial intelligence transportation so as to make a new and greater contribution to building a strong transportation country and achieving high-quality transportation development.

Bibliography

Cable, V. and Perry, C. Unmanned driving cars are expected to hit the road in Britain within three years. *Automobiles and Accessories*, 2017, (33): 12–15.

Carlo, Ryan, Frankin, Michael and Kerr, Ian. *Dialogue between Artificial Intelligence and Law*. Shanghai: Shanghai People's Publishing House, 2018: 145–149.

Chai Zhanxiang. *Autopilot Changes the Future*. Beijing: Machinery Industry Press, 2017: 235–238.

Chen Huiyan. *Introduction to Unmanned Driving Cars*. Beijing: Beijing Institute of Technology Press, 2014: 134–138.

Chen Huiyan, Xiong Guangming and Gong Jianwei. *Theory and Design of Unmanned Vehicles*. Beijing: Beijing Institute of Technology Press, 2018: 58–62.

China Artificial Intelligence Industry Development Alliance. *Artificial Intelligence Wave: 100 Frontier AI Applications for Science and Technology to Change Life*. Beijing: People's Post and Telecommunications Publishing House, 2018: 55–59.

China Intelligent Transportation Association. *Compilation of Intelligent Transportation Products and Technologies*. Beijing: Electronic Industry Press, 2017: 69–73.

Diao Shengfu and Wang Yin. Focus of unmanned driving cars and analysis of social governance. *China Statistics*, 2017, (09): 2.

Gao Yanjie and Yu Ziye. *Deep Learning: Core Technologies, Tools and Case Analysis*. Beijing: Machinery Industry Press, 2018: 46–52.

Gong Jianwei, Jiang Yan and Xu Wei. *Model Predictive Control of Unmanned Vehicles*. Beijing: Beijing Institute of Technology Press, 2014: 79–83.

Goodfellow, Ian, Bengio, Yoshua and Couvell, Aaron. *Deep Learning: Artificial Intelligence Algorithm*. Beijing: People's Post and Telecommunications Press, 2017: 79–86.

Guo Ge and Yue Wei. *Vehicle Cooperative Control in Intelligent Transportation System*. Beijing: Machinery Industry Press, 2016: 37–45.

Hu Yuanjiao. Research on the development of unmanned driving automobile industry from the perspective of philosophy of science and technology—A case of Hefei. *Innovation and Technology*, 2018, (07): 2.

Huang Zhijian. *Intelligent Transportation and Unmanned Driving*. Beijing: Chemical Industry Press, 2018: 26–32.

Jones, Handel and Zhang Chenxiong. *Artificial Intelligence+: How AI and IA Reshape the Future*. Beijing: Machinery Industry Press, 2018: 163–167.

Kurzweil, Ray. *The Future of Artificial Intelligence*. Hangzhou: Zhejiang People's Publishing House, 2016: 88–95.

Li Deyi and Yu Jian. *Introduction to Artificial Intelligence*. Beijing: China Science and Technology Press, 2018: 58–72.

Li Hongfei. Research on key technologies of unmanned driving vehicles based on urban environment. *Communication World*, 2018, (08): 2–3.

Li Kaifu and Wang Yonggang. *Artificial Intelligence*. Beijing: Cultural Development Press, 2017: 69–74.

Li Ruimin and Qiu Hongtong. *Intelligent Transportation System Planning, Design and Case*. Beijing: China Building Industry Press, 2016: 43–47.

Liu Shaoshan. *The First Unmanned Driving Technical Book*. Beijing: Electronic Industry Press, 2017: 28–32.

Lucci, Stephen and Kopek, Danny. *Artificial Intelligence* (2nd edition). Beijing: People's Post and Telecommunications Press, 2018: 83–86.

Meng Tian. *Theoretical System and Application of Intelligent Transportation System*. Shanghai: Shanghai University Press, 2018: 231–240.

Nick. *A Brief History of Artificial Intelligence*. Beijing: People's Post and Telecommunications Press, 2017: 73–78.

Pei Baochun and Wang Yaoyu. *Driving Diagram of Automatic Car*. Beijing: Chemical Industry Press, 2016: 105–110.

Qu Dayi, Chen Xiufeng, Wei Jinli and Bing Qichun. *Intelligent Transportation System and Its Technology Application* (2nd edition). Beijing: Machinery Industry Press, 2017: 134–140.

Quantian Liangfu. *Intelligent Future: How Unmanned Driving Will Change Our Lives*. Hangzhou: Zhejiang University Press, 2015: 48–54.

Russell, Novig. *Artificial Intelligence: A Modern Method* (3rd edition). Beijing: Tsinghua University Press, 2013: 168–174.

Tang Xiaoou and Chen Yukun. *Fundamentals of Artificial Intelligence*. Shanghai: East China Normal University Press, 2018: 36–38.

Tencent Research Institute, Internet Law Research Center of China Information and Communication Research Institute, Tencent AI Lab, Tencent Open Platform. Artificial intelligence: The starting point of national artificial intelligence strategic action. Beijing: Renmin University of China Press, 2017: 158–164.

Vander Waerden, P., Aloys, B. and Harry, T. Travelers micro-behavior. *Proceedings of the 82nd Annual Meeting of the Transportation Research Board.* Washington D. C., 2003: 1–12.

Wang Fuwen. Development status and challenges of unmanned driving cars. *Journal of Cangzhou Normal University,* 2017, (04): 24–25.

Wang Haopeng. Development and prospect of unmanned driving cars. *Technology Wind,* 2018, (03): 34–37.

Wang Nan, Li Lili, Chen Pengdong and Wang Yuanshao. On the development and challenges of unmanned driving cars in urban environment. *Internal Combustion Engines and Accessories,* 2018, (17): 2–3.

Wang Quan. *From Internet of Vehicles to Automatic Driving—The Road of Networking and Intelligentization of Automobile Traffic.* Beijing: People's Posts and Telecommunications Publishing House, 2018: 146–152.

Wang Shifeng. *Road Recognition Technology of Unmanned Vehicles Based on Artificial Intelligence.* Beijing: Machinery Industry Press, 2018: 156–158.

Wang Shujun. *Illustration of the Whole Driving Process: With Animated Video Version.* Beijing: Chemical Industry Press, 2017: 78–82.

Wang Xiaoyuan and Sun Feng. *Intelligent Transportation System.* Chengdu: Southwest Jiaotong University Press, 2018: 36–45.

Woody Lipson and Melba Kuman. *Unmanned Driving.* Beijing: Wenhui Publishing House, 2017: 36–39.

Xiong Guangming, Gao Li, Wu Shaobin, Zhao Yanan and Li Dajie. *Intelligent Behavior of Unmanned Driving Vehicles and Its Test and Evaluation.* Beijing: Beijing Institute of Technology Press, 2015: 47–52.

Xu Jianmin. *Intelligent Transportation System.* Beijing: People's Communications Publishing House, 2014: 48–52.

Young, W. and Thompson R. MPARKSIM/1(2): A computer graphics approaches for parking — Lot layouts. *Traffic Engineering and Control,* 1987, 28(3): 120–123.

Yu Dexin, Zhang Wei, Lin Ciyun and Wang Shuxing. *Top-level Design and Key Technologies of Expressway Intelligent Transportation Information Platform.* Beijing: Chemical Industry Press, 2016: 23–27.

Yu Quan. *Intelligent Transportation System of Expressway.* Beijing: People's Communications Publishing House, 2018: 69–72.

Zhang Junyou. *Intelligent Transportation System and Its Application.* Harbin: Harbin Institute of Technology Press, 2017: 59–63.

Zhao Guanghui. Analysis of talent training in comprehensive transportation system. *Talent Development*, 2010, (11): 1–2.

Zhao Guanghui. Enlightenment of implementing the principle of the Party managing talents in transportation system. *Development of Human Resources*, 2010, (05): 3.

Zhao Guanghui. Game research on the subject of talent development in transportation industry. *Contemporary Economic Management*, 2009, (01): 3–4.

Zhao Guanghui. Prospect of China's transportation service strategy during the 13th Five-Year Plan period. *Reform and Strategy*, 2015, (5): 2.

Zhao Guanghui. *Research on the Development of Transportation Talents*. Wuhan: Hubei People's Publishing House, 2008: 132–136.

Zhao Guanghui. Research on the evolution and policy of China's "Internet plus" integrated transportation service. *China Circulation Economy*, 2016, (3): 3–5.

Zhao Guanghui. *Research on the Interaction Mechanism between Talent Structure and Industrial Structure and Related Policies*. Wuhan: Hubei People's Publishing House, 2007: 174–178.

Zhao Guanghui. Talent development in transportation industry faces three major challenges. *Chinese Talents*, 2010, (07): 2–4.

Zhao Guanghui and Chen Lihua. *Course of Highway Traffic Emergency Management*. Beijing People's Communications Publishing House, 2013: 37–42.

Zhao Guanghui, Li Lianlian and Shan Lihui. Integrated transportation service: evaluation of Internet and big data application. *Integrated Transportation*, 2015, (9): 1–2.

Zhao Guanghui and Tian Yishun. A summary of the development of modern transportation industry. *Journal of Management Cadre College of Ministry of Transport*, 2010, (01): 1–2.

Zhao Guanghui and Tian Yishun. Progress and direction of research on integration of industrial human resources. *Science, Science & Technology and Economy*, 2010, (03): 2–3.

Zhao Guanghui and Tian Yishun. *Transportation Social Service Capacity*. Beijing: People's Communications Publishing House, 2013: 56–59.

Zhao Guanghui and Zhu Gusheng. *Internet+ Transportation: The New Revolution Era of Intelligent Transportation Is Coming*. Beijing: People's Post and Telecommunications Press, 2016: 126–133.

Index

Printed in the United States
by Baker & Taylor Publisher Services

Printed in the United States
by Baker & Taylor Publisher Services